Mary Jones, Diane Fellowes-Freeman

Sang

Cambridge Science

Coursebook

8

CAMBRIDGE
UNIVERSITY PRESS

CAMBRIDGE
UNIVERSITY PRESS

University Printing House, Cambridge CB2 8BS, United Kingdom

One Liberty Plaza, 20th Floor, New York, NY 10006, USA

477 Williamstown Road, Port Melbourne, VIC 3207, Australia

314–321, 3rd Floor, Plot 3, Splendor Forum, Jasola District Centre, New Delhi – 110025, India

79 Anson Road, #06–04/06, Singapore 079906

Cambridge University Press is part of the University of Cambridge.

It furthers the University's mission by disseminating knowledge in the pursuit of education, learning and research at the highest international levels of excellence.

Information on this title: education.cambridge.org

First published 2019
20 19 18 17 16 15 14 13 12 11 10 9 8 7 6 5 4 3 2

Printed in Malaysia by Vivar Printing

A catalogue record for this publication is available from the British Library

ISBN 978-1-108-72047-2 Paperback

NOTICE TO TEACHERS
References to Activities contained in these resources are provided 'as is' and information provided is on the understanding that teachers and technicians shall undertake a thorough and appropriate risk of assessment before undertaking any of the Activities listed. Cambridge University Press makes no warranties, representations or claims of any kind concerning the Activities. To the extent permitted by law, Cambridge University Press will not be liable for any loss, injury, claim, liability or damage of any kind resulting from the use of tha Activities.

Introduction

Welcome to your Cambridge Secondary 1 Science course!

The main areas of science

The book is divided into three main sections, each one dealing with one of three main areas of science.

There are no sharp dividing lines between these three branches of science. You will find many overlaps between them.

Biology – the study of living organisms

Chemistry – the study of the substances from which the Earth and the rest of the Universe are made

Physics – the study of the nature and properties of matter, energy and forces.

Learning to be a scientist

During your course, you will learn a lot of facts and information. You will also begin to learn to think like a scientist.

Scientists collect information and do experiments to try to find out how things work. You will learn how to plan an experiment to try to find out the answer to a question. You will learn how to record your results, and how to use them to make a conclusion.

When you see this symbol SE, it means that the task will help you to develop your scientific enquiry skills.

Using your knowledge

It's important to learn facts and scientific ideas as you go through your science course. But it is just as important to be able tc **use** these facts and ideas.

When you see this symbol A+I, it means that you are being asked to use your knowledge to work out an answer. You will have to think hard to find the answer for yourself, using the science that you have learnt. (A+I stands for Applications and Implications.)

Contents

Physics

Unit 9 Measuring motion

Unit 10 Sound

Unit 11 Light

Unit 12 Magnetism

Reference

1.1 Photosynthesis

Where do you get your energy from?

Your energy comes from the food that you eat. Energy is passed from one organism to another along a food chain.

Every food chain begins with a plant. Plants capture energy from light, and transfer some of the energy into the food that they make. When we eat food, we get some of that energy.

In this unit, we will look at how plants use energy from light to make food.

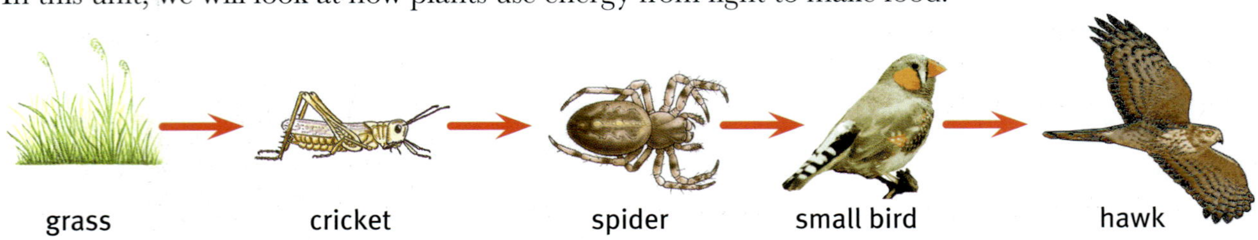

The arrows in a food chain show the energy passing from one organism to another.

Making with light

'Photo' means to do with light. 'Synthesis' means 'making'. So 'photosynthesis' means 'making with light'. Photosynthesis is the way that plants make food, using energy from light.

This forest in New Zealand is a giant food factory.

Questions

1. Think of **two** more words that begin with 'photo'. What does each of your words mean? Photography and Photo copy.
2. In the food chain above, at which point does photosynthesis take place? grass.

What else do plants need for photosynthesis?

- Plants use **water** in photosynthesis. They get the water from the soil.
- Plants use **carbon dioxide** in photosynthesis. They get the carbon dioxide from the air.

You already know that plants make food by photosynthesis. But they also make a very important gas – **oxygen**.

We can summarise photosynthesis like this:

Water and carbon dioxide are changed into food and oxygen, using energy from light.

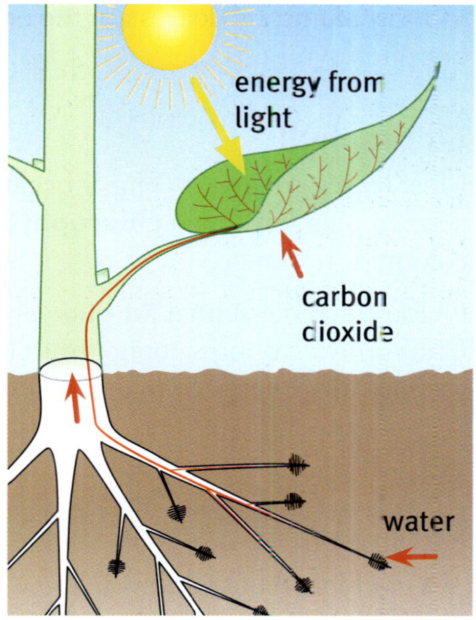

Biomass

Plants use the food that they make in photosynthesis to make new cells and tissues. Material that is made of living cells and tissues is called **biomass**.

Activity 1.1
Plants and light

SE

You are going to find out what happens to plants that do not get light.

1. Sow some small seeds on damp filter paper, in two identical dishes. Leave them in a warm place to germinate. Make sure that they do not dry out.
2. When the seeds have germinated, put one set into a dark cupboard, or into a closed cardboard box. Leave the other set in a light place. Keep giving them both a little water. Try to make sure that the temperature is the same for both sets of seedlings.
3. After two days, compare the appearance of the two sets of seedlings. You could also make labelled drawings of a seedling from each set.

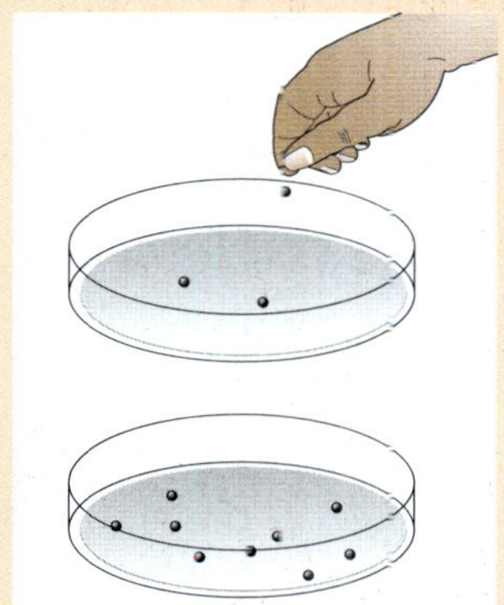

Questions

A1 Explain why it was important to keep one set of seedlings in the light. to verify that the leave use light to grow.

A2 Explain why it was important that the temperature was the same for both sets of seedlings. for a fair test.

Summary

- Photosynthesis is the way that plants make food, using energy from light.
- Some of the food that is made becomes new biomass in the plant.
- Plants use water and carbon dioxide in photosynthesis.
- Plants make food and oxygen by photosynthesis.

1.2 Leaves

Leaves capture energy from light.

In most plants, the leaves are the organs that carry out photosynthesis.

Chlorophyll

Most leaves are green. This is because they contain a green pigment called **chlorophyll**. (A pigment is a coloured substance.)

Chlorophyll is essential for photosynthesis. Chlorophyll captures energy from light. The leaf can then use this energy to make food.

Questions

1. Think about what you know about the structure of cells. What is the name of the part of a plant cell – also beginning with 'chloro' – that contains chlorophyll?
2. A+I Suggest why leaves are green, but roots are not.
3. A+I Think back to Activity **1.1,** where you grew some seedlings in the dark. What happened to the chlorophyll in them?

The structure of a leaf

The picture shows the different parts of a leaf.

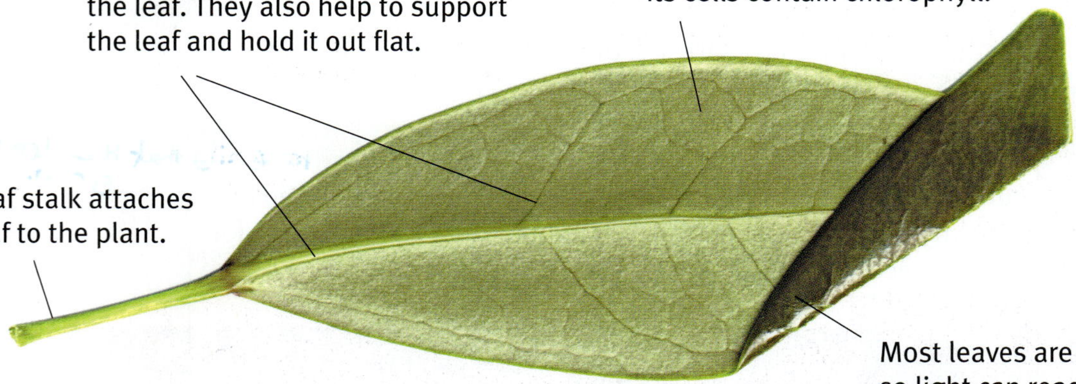

How a leaf is adapted for photosynthesis.

Inside a leaf

The diagram on the right shows what a leaf looks like if you cut it across, and then look at the cut edge.

Leaves are so thin that it is difficult to imagine they contain several layers of cells. It is the cells in the middle of the leaf that carry out photosynthesis.

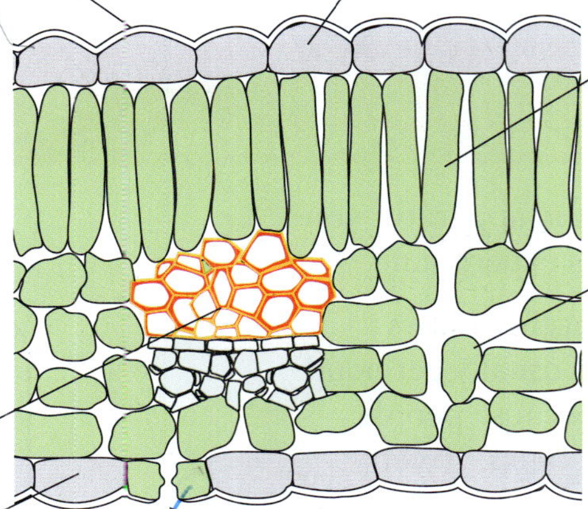

Activity 1.2

Which surface has the most stomata?

SE

Take a fresh, green leaf. Push the leaf into some warm water. Watch carefully to see where air bubbles appear on the leaf surface.

Questions

A1 On which surface of the leaf did most bubbles appear?

A2 The bubbles contained gas that came out from inside the leaf. Which part of the leaf do you think the gas came from? (Look at the diagram of the inside of the leaf above.)

A3 Suggest how the gas got out of the leaf.

A4 Use what you know about the effect of heat on gases to explain why the gases came out of the leaf when it was put into warm water.

Summary

- Leaves are adapted to carry out photosynthesis.
- Leaves are green because they contain the green pigment chlorophyll, which absorbs energy from light.
- Leaves have tiny holes in their lower surfaces, called stomata, which allow carbon dioxide to get into the leaf from the air.

1.3 Investigating photosynthesis

How can we tell if a leaf is photosynthesising? One of the simplest ways is to check if it is giving off (releasing) oxygen gas. This is easiest to do if the leaf is under water, because the oxygen gas makes bubbles.

Activity 1.3A

Collecting the gas produced in photosynthesis

SE

The diagram shows the apparatus you need to set up for this experiment.

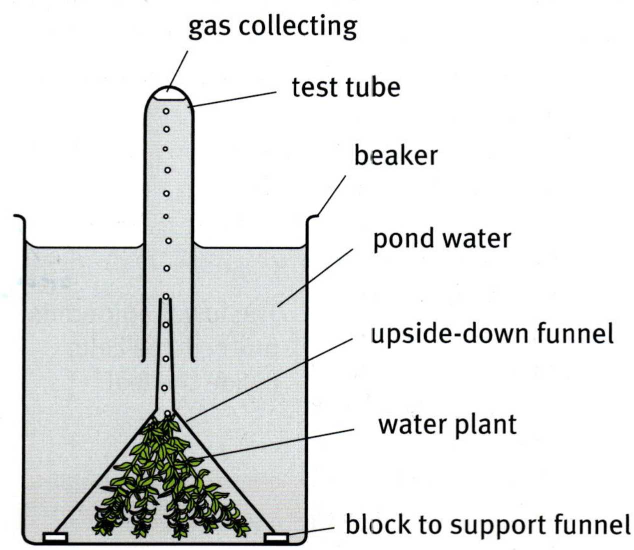

You can use any plant that grows under water. You can usually get pond weed at a pet shop, because people buy it to put into fish tanks. If you live near the sea, you can use seaweed instead.

Leave the apparatus in a place where the plant will get plenty of light. If it is very warm and sunny, you may see the gas collecting quickly. If it is colder and not so bright, you may need to leave it for a day to give time for the gas to collect.

When you have collected about half a test tube of gas, you can test it to see if it is oxygen, like this:

1. Put your hand into the water in the beaker, and hold the test tube near its opening. Put your thumb over the opening, taking care to keep the test tube under water.
2. Keeping the tube open end downwards, take it out of the water.
3. Get a partner to light a wooden splint, then blow it out so that it is just glowing.
4. Now gently take off your thumb, to let the water fall out of the tube.
5. When all the water has fallen out, quickly but carefully put the glowing splint into the tube. Try not to touch the wet sides, or you will put it out!
6. If the gas is oxygen, it will make the glowing splint burst into flame.

Questions

A1 Explain why you needed to use a water plant for this experiment.

A2 Explain why you needed to leave the apparatus in a light place.

Activity 1.3B
Investigating the rate of photosynthesis

SE

You are going to plan and carry out an experiment to investigate this question:

Is there a correlation between light intensity and the rate of photosynthesis?

A **correlation** is a relationship. If there is a correlation between light intensity and photosynthesis, then we would expect that changing the light intensity will result in a change in the rate of photosynthesis.

1. Write out your plan for your experiment. Here are some ideas you can use.
    - You can use a water plant like the one that you used for Activity **1.3A**.
    - To measure the rate of photosynthesis, you can measure how much gas the plant gives off in a certain length of time. For example, you can measure the depth of gas that collects in the test tube in one hour. For a quicker experiment, you can count how many bubbles the weed gives off in one minute. If you do that, then you don't need a funnel or test tube to collect the gas.
    - To give the plant a high light intensity, you can place a lamp close to the plant. For a lower light intensity, place the lamp further away.
    - Think carefully about all the variables that you must keep the same in your experiment.
    - Decide whether you should do several repeats for each light intensity, so you can calculate a mean for each one.
2. Predict the results you expect to get, and explain why.
3. Check your plan with your teacher before you begin.
4. Now carry out your experiment. Make changes to your plan if you think you can improve it.
5. Record and display your results so someone else can easily understand them.
6. Write down a short conclusion to your experiment, and compare your results with your predictions.

Summary
- A good way to find out if a water plant is photosynthesising is to see if it gives off bubbles of oxygen.
- If photosynthesis is happening at a faster rate, then more oxygen is given off per minute.

1.4 Roots

Roots are usually underground, so we often do not notice them. But, for many plants, the roots take up just as much space as the above-ground parts of the plant.

For a plant, its roots are just as important as its leaves.

Functions of roots

The roots of a plant have several functions.

- Roots absorb water and minerals from the soil. These are then transported to all the other parts of the plant.
- Roots anchor the plant firmly in the ground, so it is not pulled out when the wind blows strongly, or when an animal pulls on the leaves.
- Some plants store food in their roots.
- When conditions are difficult – for example, in a cold winter, or a dry summer – some plants allow their above-ground parts to die. Only the underground roots continue to live. New shoots (above-ground parts) grow from the roots when conditions become better.

Activity 1.4A
Roots for food

We make use of many roots that store food. The plant stores the food for its own use, but we can also eat this food.

Choose **two** different roots that humans eat as food.

For each root, find out what the complete plant looks like.

Make a labelled drawing of the plant. Describe how we use the root for food.

Roots are good sources of food for humans.

How roots absorb water and minerals

Soil is made up of tiny rock particles. There is usually water in the spaces between the particles. There are minerals dissolved in the water.

You may remember that special cells called **root hairs** grow out of the surface of roots. Root hair cells provide a really big surface through which water and minerals can be absorbed.

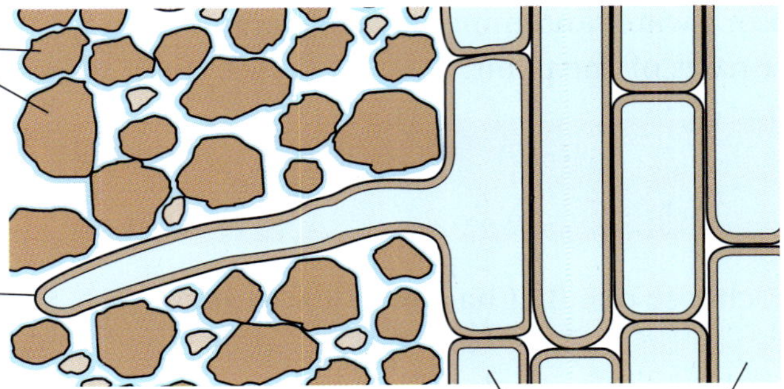

A root hair cell.

This photograph of a root was taken using a microscope. You can see that it is covered with thousands of tiny root hairs.

Questions

A+I 1 Explain how the absorption of water by roots helps photosynthesis to take place.

A+I 2 Suggest why most plants die very quickly if their roots are cut off.

3 Explain how root hairs help plants to absorb a lot of water in a short time.

Activity 1.4B

Which way up?

SE

1 Take a tall glass jar. Roll up a piece of strong absorbent paper so that it fits inside the jar. Add a little water and allow it to soak into the paper.

2 Take three soaked bean seeds. Carefully put them between the paper and the side of the jar. Place each one a different way up.

3 Put the jar in a warm place. Check it each day to see if it needs more water – it is important to keep the seeds moist but not too wet.

4 When all of the seeds have grown roots, make drawings of them.

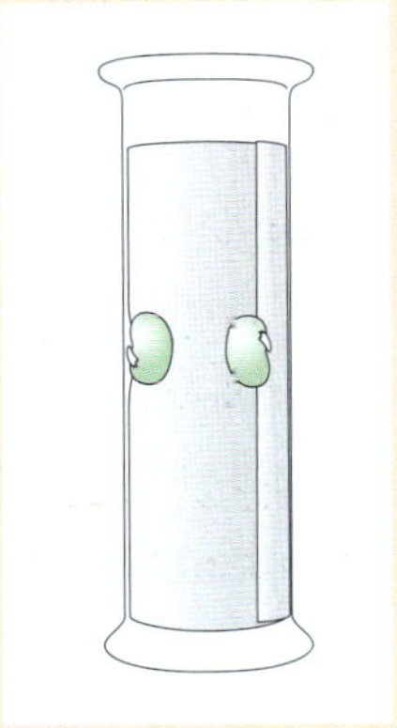

Questions

A1 What do you notice about the directions the roots have grown in?

A2 Suggest how this would help a bean plant to survive.

Summary

- Roots absorb water and minerals from the spaces between soil particles.
- Roots anchor a plant in the ground.
- Roots can store food for the plant.
- Roots can sometimes survive harsh conditions that kill the above-ground parts of the plant.

1.5 Transporting water and minerals

We have seen that the roots of a plant absorb water and minerals. How are these transported from the roots to all the other parts of the plant?

Activity 1.5A

Transport in a celery stalk

SE

1 Collect a stalk of celery. If possible, choose one that has some leaves at the top.
2 Put some water containing a coloured dye into a beaker. Stand the celery stalk in the dye. Make sure you stand the stalk the right way up.
3 Every now and then, look at the stalk. You should be able to see the coloured dye moving up inside it. (This can sometimes happen very quickly and sometimes very slowly, so be prepared!)
4 When the dye has reached the top of the stalk, take the stalk out of the dye and wash it in clean water.
5 Carefully cut across the stalk. Look at the cut end using a hand lens. Make a drawing of what you can see.

Questions

A1 Suggest why it is important to wash the celery stalk before cutting across it.

A2 Flowering plants, such as celery plants, contain long tubes called xylem vessels. (You pronounce the 'x' in xylem as though it is a 'z'.) These vessels transport water and substances dissolved in the water. Use your results to describe where the xylem vessels are in a celery stalk.

Activity 1.5B

How does temperature affect the rate at which water is transported in a celery stalk?

SE

You are going to plan and carry out an experiment to try to answer the question in the title.

Think about the following questions.

- What variable will I change? How will I change it?
- What will I measure? How will I measure it? When will I measure it?
- What variables will I try to keep the same? How will I keep them the same?
- Are there any safety risks in my experiment? If so, how can I keep safe?
- How will I record my results? Can I draw a graph? If so, what will I put on the graph axes?
- What do I think the results will be? Why?

When you have written your plan, check it with your teacher.

After you have done your experiment, identify the trends and patterns you can see. Compare your results with your predictions.

Xylem vessels

When you did Activity **1.5A**, you saw that the coloured dye did not soak into all of the celery stalk. It stayed inside the **xylem** vessels.

Xylem vessels are long, hollow tubes that carry water and minerals from the roots of the plant to its leaves. In a tree, the xylem vessels reach all the way up the trunk and to the very tips of the branches. The xylem vessels continue inside the leaves.

Xylem vessels are very tiny. The spots that you saw in the celery stalk each contain several xylem vessels.

The diagrams show where the xylem vessels are in a root, a stem and a leaf. The dark blue areas show where xylem vessels are found.

Xylem vessels have very strong, hard walls. This means that they help to support the plant, as well as transporting water and minerals.

The wood in a tree trunk is made up of xylem vessels. If you are working at a wooden desk, you may be able to see the xylem vessels that make up the wood.

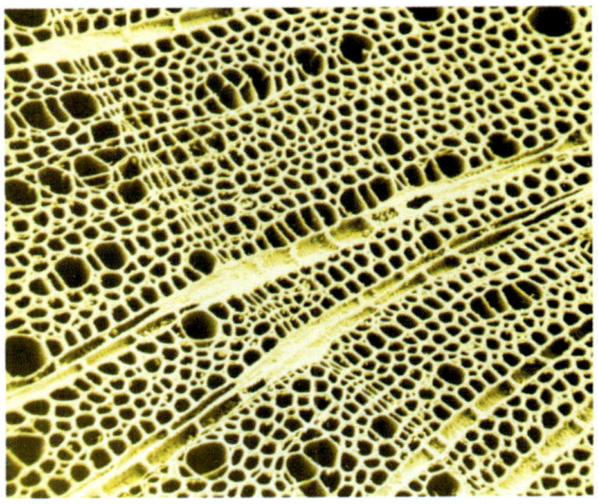

This is a piece of wood seen with a powerful microscope. Each hole is the cut end of a xylem vessel.

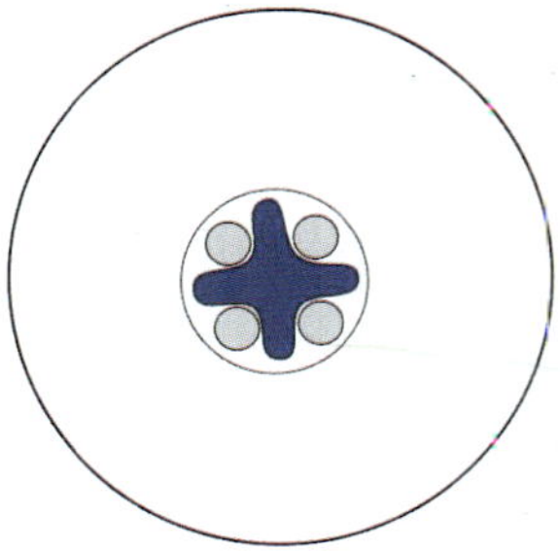

The position of xylem vessels in a root.

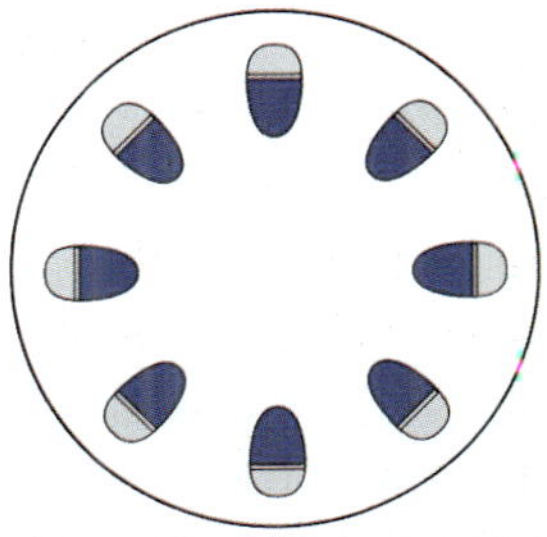

The positions of xylem vessels in a stem.

The positions of xylem vessels in a leaf. In a leaf, the xylem vessels are inside the veins.

Summary

- Water and minerals are transported from a plant's roots to its leaves inside long, hollow tubes called xylem vessels.
- The veins in a leaf contain xylem vessels.
- Wood is made up of xylem vessels.

Unit 1 End of unit questions

1.1 The words below all have something to do with photosynthesis. Choose the correct word to match each description.
You may use each word once, more than once or not at all.

air **carbon dioxide** **chlorophyll** **chloroplast** **epidermis**
oxygen **palisade layer** **soil** **stomata** **veins**

- **a** This gas is used by plants in photosynthesis.
- **b** This gas is made by plants in photosynthesis.
- **c** Plants get their water for photosynthesis from here.
- **d** This green pigment absorbs energy from sunlight.
- **e** This tissue in a leaf is where most photosynthesis takes place.
- **f** These tiny holes in a leaf allow gases to move in and out. [6]

1.2 The photograph shows the upper surfaces of leaves from two different plants.
The leaves are both shown life-size.

Construct a table that you can use to compare the structure of the two leaves.
Then complete your table to show at least **five** differences between the leaves. [6]

1.3 Anurag did an experiment to compare the rate of photosynthesis of two types of seaweed.
The diagram shows the apparatus he used.

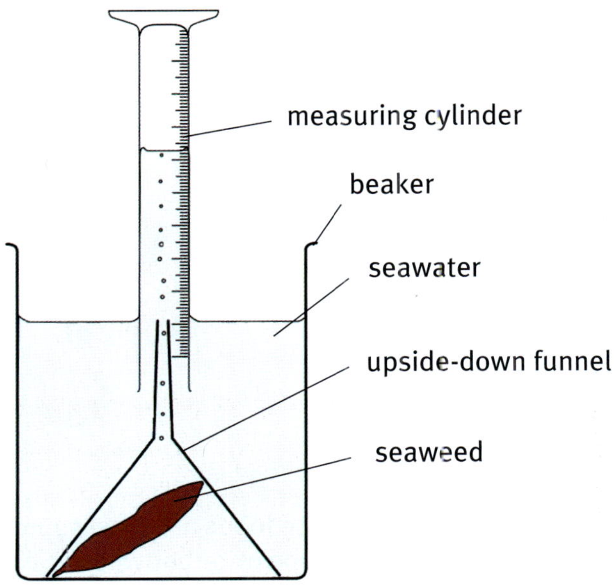

a What variable should Anurag change in his experiment? [1]

b List **three** variables that Anurag should keep the same. [3]

c What should Anurag measure in his experiment? [2]

1.4 **a** Describe how a plant obtains water. [2]

b Describe how water is transported to the leaves of the plant. [2]

2.1 Nutrients

Everyone enjoys eating tasty food. Food gives us pleasure. It also gives us the **nutrients** that we need to stay healthy.

Nutrients are substances in food that the body uses:

- to provide energy
- to provide materials for making the chemicals that are needed to make cells and other parts of the body.

Different kinds of food contain different nutrients.

These foods are good sources of protein.

Protein, carbohydrate and fat

The nutrients that we need to eat in the largest quantity are protein, carbohydrate and fat.

Protein is used for making new cells. Protein is also used for making many important chemicals in the body, such as enzymes (see pages **28–29**) and antibodies (see page **37**). Cells can use protein to supply energy.

Carbohydrate is used to provide energy. **Starch** and **sugar** are two kinds of carbohydrate.

These foods are good sources of starch (a type of carbohydrate).

Fat also provides energy. Fat can be stored in the body. Fat stores underneath the skin provide insulation. Fat is needed to make new cell membranes.

These foods contain a lot of fat.

Vitamins and minerals

Vitamins and **minerals** are nutrients that we need in only very small quantities. They do not provide energy. There are many different kinds of vitamins and minerals that we need to eat. Fruit and vegetables are a good source of some of them. There is more information about two vitamins and two minerals on page **20**.

Fibre and water

Fibre (roughage) helps to keep food moving easily through the digestive system. We get fibre from fresh fruit and vegetables, and also from foods made from whole seeds such as brown rice or wholemeal bread.

Water is sometimes considered to be a nutrient. Between 60% and 70% of the body is made up of water.

These foods contain a lot of fibre.

Questions

1 Explain the difference between food and nutrients.
2 The headings on the previous page contain the names of the seven kinds of nutrients. List them all.
3 Which **three** nutrients provide the body with energy?

Activity 2.1
Testing foods for carbohydrates

SE

Starch and sugar are two types of carbohydrate.

You can find out if a food contains starch using iodine sc
You can find out if a food contains sugar using Benedict

Macronutrients are those nutrients that are required by the body in large quantities such as protiens, carbohydrates and fats. micronutrients are those that are required by the body in smaller quaintities such as vitamins and minerals.
Proteins is on pg 18 the first pic.

1 First, test each food for starch.
   - Put a small amount of the food onto a white tile.
   - Add a drop or two of iodine solution. If the iodine blue-black, there is starch in the food.
2 Next, test each food for sugar.
   - Chop or crush a small amount of the food, and put it into a boiling tube. Add a little water and stir or shake it well.
   - Add enough Benedict's solution to make the mixture look blue.
   - Put the boiling tube into a water bath at about 80 °C. Leave it for about 5 minutes.
   - If there is sugar in the food, the colour will change as shown on the right.
3 Record your results in a results table like the one below. Add as many more rows as you need.

no sugar | a small amount of sugar | a lot of sugar

Food	Colour with iodine solution	Did it contain starch?	Colour with Benedict's solution	Did it contain sugar?

Summary
- We need to eat seven different types of nutrients – protein, carbohydrate, fat, vitamins, minerals, fibre and water.
- Different kinds of foods contain different combinations of nutrients.

2.2 A balanced diet

Your **diet** is the food that you eat each day. Your diet should provide you with enough of each kind of nutrient. It should also give you the right amount of energy.

A diet that provides all the different kinds of nutrients, and the right amount of energy, is called a **balanced diet**.

Nutritional deficiencies

If a person does not eat enough of a particular nutrient, their body may not be able to work properly. They may have a nutritional **deficiency disease**.

For example, a child who does not have enough protein in her body may not be able to make enough new cells. She will not grow properly.

The table shows information about two vitamins and two minerals, and the deficiency diseases that develop if they are lacking in the diet.

This photograph shows approximately how much of your diet should be made up of each of the five food groups.

Nutrient	Example	Good sources	Function in the body	Deficiency disease
vitamins	vitamin C	citrus fruits	helps to make strong skin	scurvy – the skin becomes weak, so sores develop
	vitamin D	dairy products	needed to make bones and teeth	rickets – the bones are weak, so the legs may become bent
minerals	iron	red meat, dark green vegetables	needed to make haemoglobin, which carries oxygen in the blood	anaemia – the blood cannot carry enough oxygen, and the person feels very tired
	calcium	dairy products, fish	needed to make bones and teeth	the bones and teeth become weak

Scury lack of vitmin C. Kwashiorkar lack of Protien. Marasmus lack of over all nutrients. Rickets lack of vitamin D.

Not too much

There are some nutrients that you should avoid eating too much of. Too much sugar can make your teeth decay. Too much fat in the diet can increase the risk of developing heart disease when you are older.

Eating too much fat and carbohydrate may mean that you take in more energy each day than you use. The body stores these extra nutrients as fat. Everyone needs some fat stores, but it is not good to have too much. Being seriously overweight can cause damage to joints, and increase the risk of developing heart disease and diabetes.

What should I eat?

These students are giving some good guidelines for eating a balanced diet.

Question

1 The sentences below are reasons for the pieces of advice the students are giving. Match each reason with the piece of advice.

- **a** This means you will get some of each kind of nutrient, including the different vitamins and minerals.
- **b** These contain fibre and lots of vitamins.
- **c** This often contains a lot of fat, and very few vitamins or minerals. It is fine to eat some of it, as long as you eat plenty of other kinds of foods as well.
- **d** Not eating enough food will prevent the cells, tissues and organs in your body having enough energy to keep healthy.
- **e** When you get older, it can increase your risk of getting heart disease or diabetes.

Summary

- A balanced diet contains some of all the types of nutrients, and about the same amount of energy that your body uses each day.
- A diet that is missing a particular nutrient can cause a nutritional deficiency disease.
- A good diet has plenty of foods containing protein, vitamins and minerals, but not too much fat or sugar.

2.3 Digestion and absorption

The alimentary canal

Your mouth is the entrance to a long tube called the **alimentary canal**. The other end of the tube is called the **anus**.

The diagram summarises what happens to the food that an animal eats, as it travels through this tube.

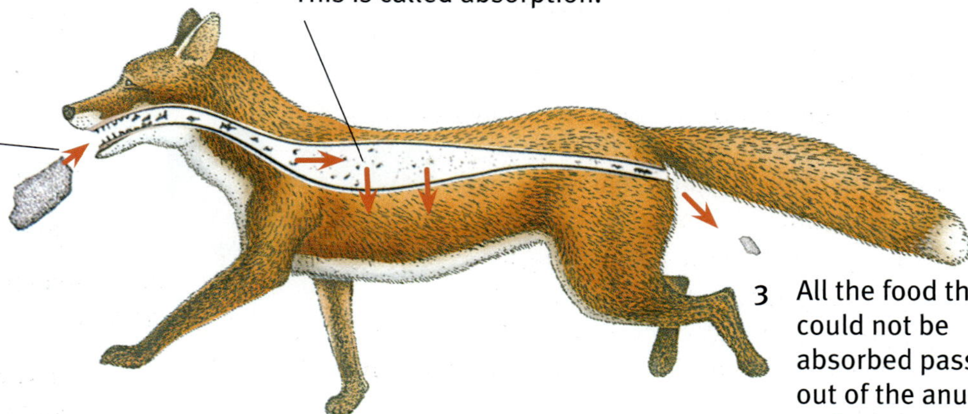

What happens inside the alimentary canal.

Absorption and digestion

The food inside the alimentary canal can only reach your body cells if it can get out through the walls of the tube. This process is called **absorption**.

Protein, starch and fat are important nutrients. Each of these nutrients is made up of large **molecules**. A molecule is the tiniest particle of a substance that can exist.

Molecules of protein, starch and fat are so big that they cannot get through the walls of the alimentary canal. So, in order to get these nutrients to your cells, the big molecules have to be broken down into much smaller ones. Then the small molecules can be absorbed.

This is what digestion is. **Digestion** is the breakdown of large molecules into small ones, so that they can be absorbed.

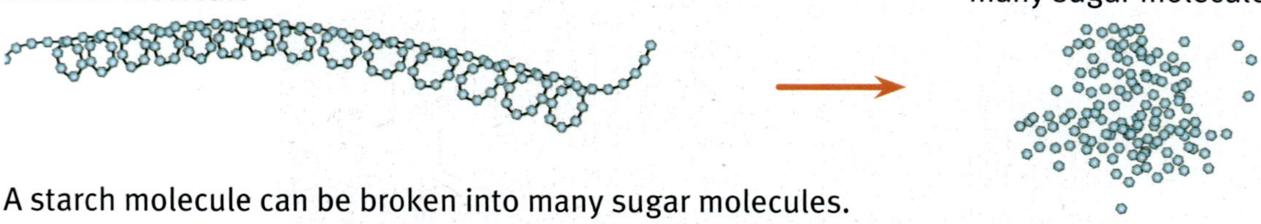

A starch molecule can be broken into many sugar molecules.

Activity 2.3
A model of absorption

SE

Visking tubing is similar to the walls of the alimentary canal. It has tiny holes in it – much too small for you to see – that will let small molecules go through, but not big molecules.

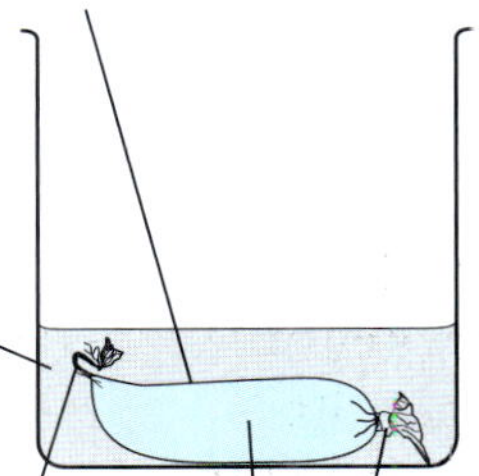

1. Collect a piece of Visking tubing. Moisten it with water. Rub it between your fingers until it opens up into a tube.
2. Tie a knot in one end of the tube.
3. Very carefully, using a dropper pipette, fill your Visking tubing with a 'meal' of starch solution and sugar solution. When it is nearly full, use cotton to tie it very tightly around the top.
4. Rinse your tubing in water, to wash off any starch or sugar that got onto the outside of it.
5. Put your tubing into a beaker. Add enough water to the beaker to cover the tubing. Leave it for about 15 or 20 minutes.
6. Now take a sample of water from the beaker and test it for starch. Record your results.
7. Take a second sample of water from the beaker and test it for sugar. Record your results.

Questions

A1 Explain why it was important to tie both ends of the tubing very tightly.
A2 Explain why it was important to wash the outside of the tubing.
A3 Which nutrients – starch or sugar – were able to get out of the tubing?
A4 Use what you know about starch molecules and sugar molecules to suggest an explanation for your results.
A5 Imagine you have eaten a meal containing starch and sugar. Do both of these nutrients need to be digested inside your alimentary canal? Explain your answer.

Summary

- Nutrients cannot be used by body cells until they have been absorbed through the walls of the alimentary canal.
- Only small molecules can pass through the wall of the alimentary canal.
- Digestion is the breakdown of large molecules of nutrients to small molecules, so that they can be absorbed.

2.4 The human digestive system

The diagram shows the human digestive system. The digestive system is made up of the alimentary canal, plus the salivary glands, liver and pancreas.

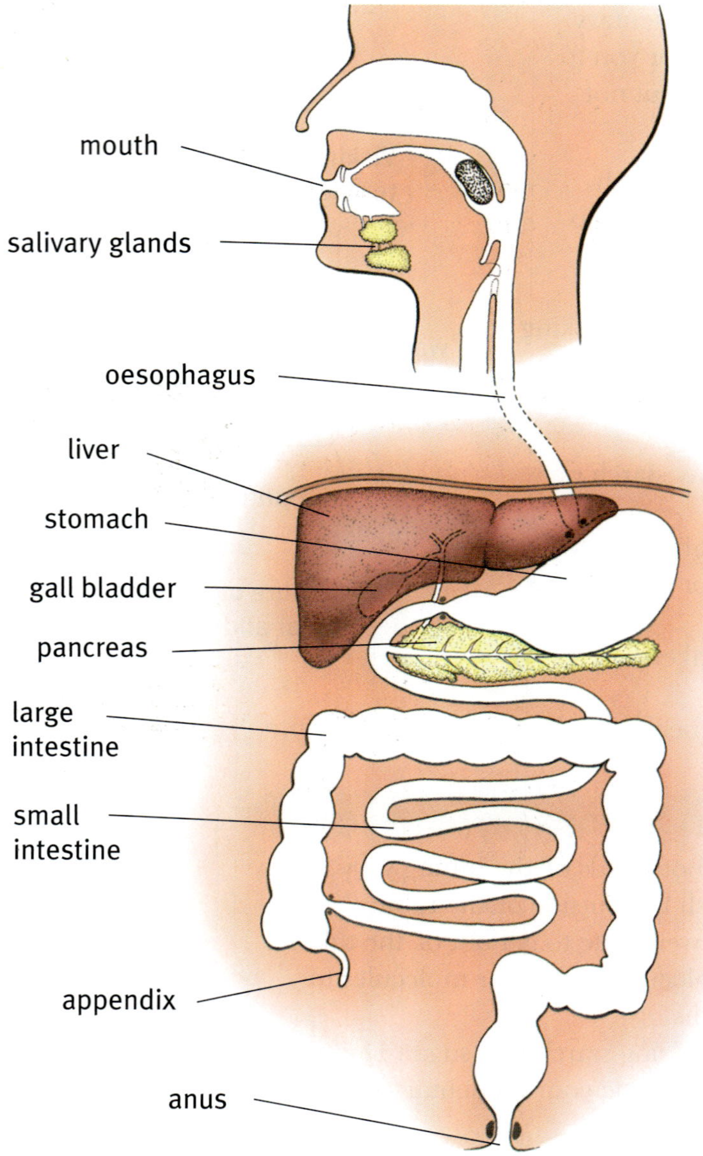

The human digestive system.

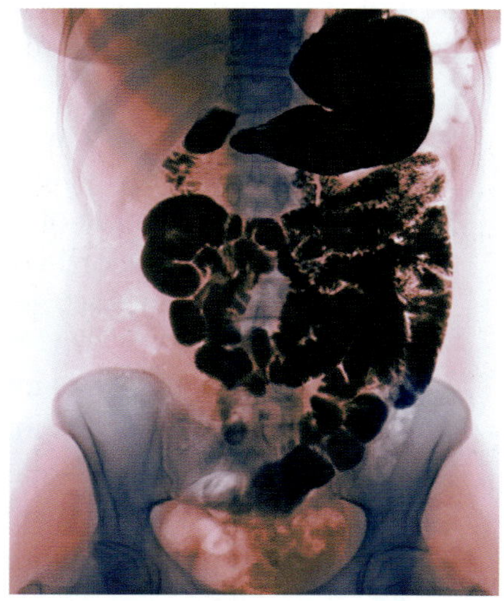

An X-ray image of part of the alimentary canal. Can you work out which parts are shown?

The food goes to mouth, then oesophagus, stomach, small intestine, large intestine, Rectum and anus.

Questions

1 After it has been swallowed, food moves along through the space inside the alimentary canal. Write down, in order, the name of each part of the alimentary canal that food passes through as it travels from the mouth to the anus.

2 Name **three** organs, shown in the diagram, that food does **not** pass through.

Gall bladder, liver, pancreas.

Functions of organs in the digestive system

Mouth Teeth chew food into smaller pieces. Saliva starts to break down starch to sugar.

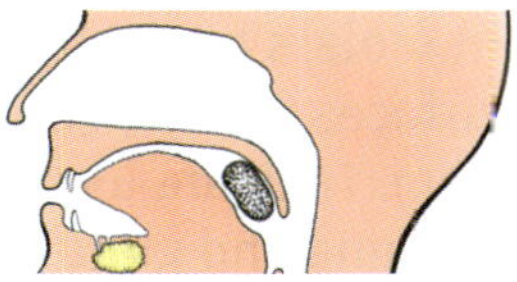

Oesophagus Food just passes through here without changing.

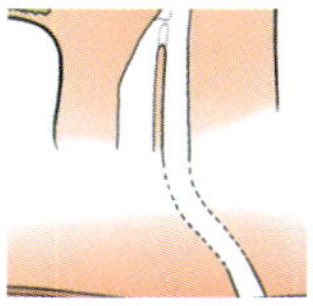

Stomach Hydrochloric acid kills micro-organisms in the food. Stomach juices begin to break down protein to amino acids.

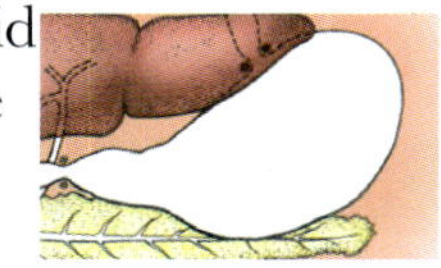

Small intestine Juices from the pancreas finish breaking down starch, protein and fat to small molecules. These small molecules are then absorbed through the walls of the small intestine. Water, vitamins and minerals (which are already made of very small particles) are also absorbed.

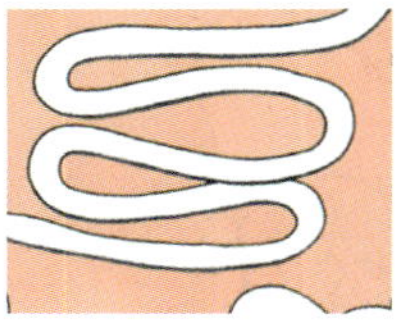

Large intestine All the food that could not be digested and absorbed passes through here. A little more of the water in it is absorbed. The undigested food collects up and forms faeces.

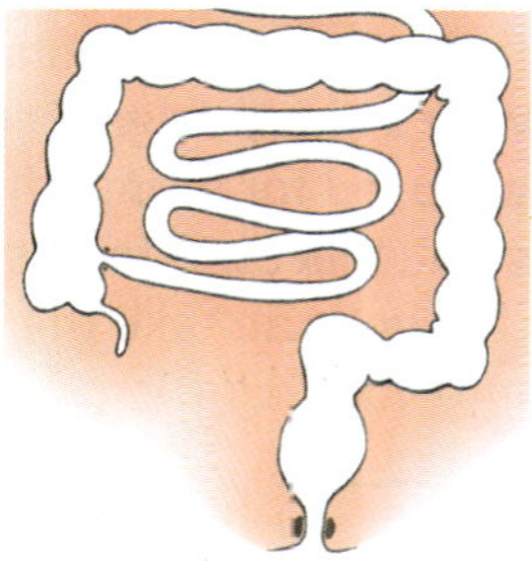

Liver The liver makes bile. The bile is stored in the gall bladder. Bile flows into the small intestine, where it helps with fat digestion.

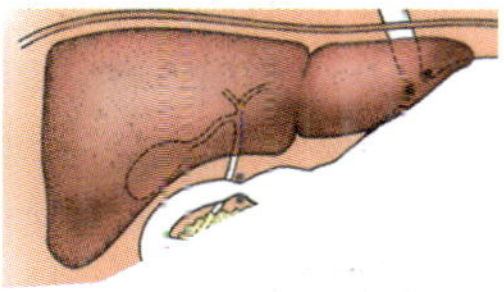

Pancreas The pancreas makes pancreatic juice. Pancreatic juice flows into the small intestine, where it helps to digest protein, starch and fat.

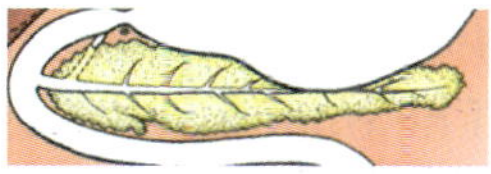

Summary

- The alimentary canal is a long tube that runs from the mouth to the anus.
- Inside the alimentary canal, nutrients are first digested and then absorbed.
- Digestion happens inside the mouth, stomach and small intestine. Absorption happens inside the small intestine and large intestine.

2.5 Teeth

The mouth is the first part of the alimentary canal. Inside your mouth there are four different kinds of teeth – incisors, canines, premolars and molars.

Incisors are chisel-shaped, with a sharp edge. They are used for biting off small pieces of food so that you can take the food into your mouth.

Canines are more pointed than incisors. In humans, they are used in the same way as incisors.

Premolars have broad surfaces with ridges on them. They are used for crushing and grinding food when you chew.

Molars are like premolars, but sometimes a bit bigger. They are also used for crushing and grinding food.

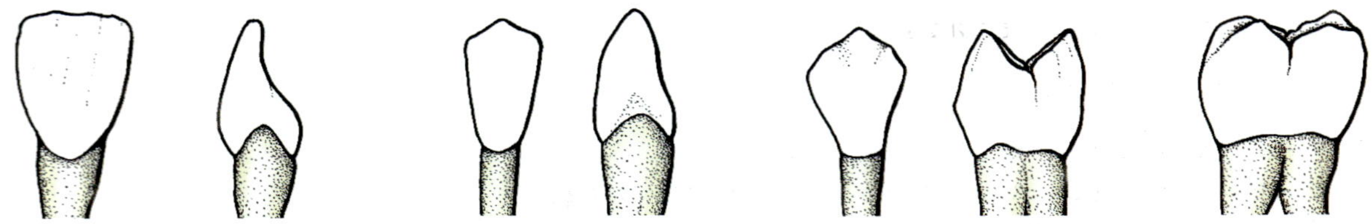

The four kinds of human teeth.

Questions

A+I

1. 'Canine' means 'dog tooth'. What do dogs use their canine teeth for?
2. Explain how the shape of incisors helps them to carry out their function.
3. Explain how the shape of molars helps them to carry out their function.

The structure of a tooth

The diagram shows what an incisor tooth looks like if it is cut in half. The diagram also shows the gum and jawbone. Teeth are held in the jawbone by strong fibres.

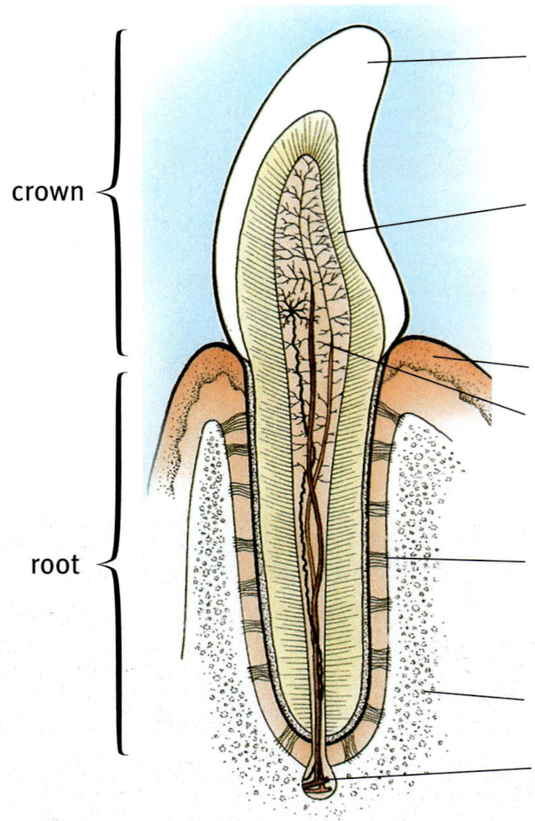

The structure of an incisor tooth.

Caring for your teeth

The enamel on your teeth is very strong. However, it can be dissolved by acids. If that happens, you may get a hole in your tooth. This can be painful when the hole reaches the pulp cavity, where there are nerve endings.

This means that drinking lots of acidic fizzy drinks (like cola or lemonade) can harm your teeth. Even if you don't eat or drink acidic things, you may still get acid in your mouth. This is because bacteria in your mouth break down food remains left on and between your teeth – especially sugary things. The bacteria make acid when they break down the food remains.

To avoid getting holes in your teeth:

- Don't drink fizzy drinks, or eat sugary food, all day long.
- Clean your teeth thoroughly after breakfast and before you go to bed.
- Use a toothpaste containing fluoride. Fluoride helps to strengthen the enamel on your teeth.

Activity 2.5
How do fizzy drinks affect teeth?

SE

You'll only be able to do this activity if you can find two teeth. Your teacher may be able to provide these.

1 Tie a piece of strong cotton around each tooth, long enough to hang over the edge of a beaker. Tie the other end around a small stone or weight.
2 Pour some fizzy drink (for example, cola) into one beaker. Pour the same depth of tap water into the other beaker.
3 Hang one tooth in the fizzy drink, and the other tooth in the water.
4 Observe the teeth at least once a week for several weeks. Write down your observations and conclusions.

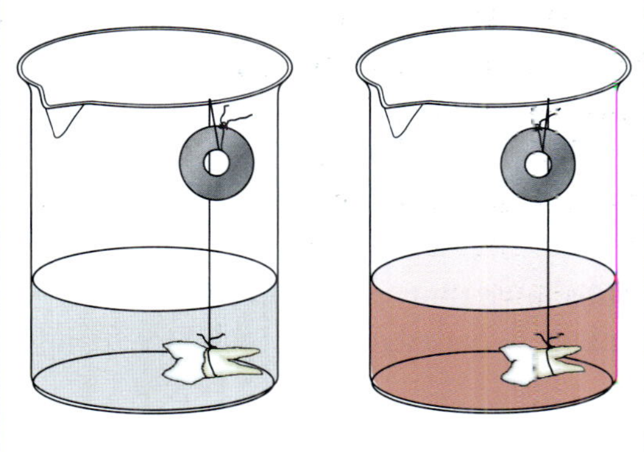

Summary

- Teeth break down large pieces of food into small pieces.
- Humans have four types of teeth – incisors, canines, premolars and molars.
- Teeth have an outer covering of very hard enamel, which contains calcium. Inside the tooth are the dentine and the pulp cavity, which contain living cells.
- Enamel can be dissolved by acids.

2.6 Enzymes

We have seen that large molecules of nutrients must be broken down into small molecules, so that they can be absorbed.

Teeth break down big pieces of food into small pieces. But they don't have any effect on the molecules of the different nutrients that make up the food.

The large nutrient molecules are broken down into small molecules by chemicals called **enzymes**.

Digestion as a chemical reaction

Digestion changes a substance made up of large molecules into a new substance made up of small molecules.

When one substance is changed into a different substance, we say that a **chemical reaction** has taken place. The diagram shows a chemical reaction that happens during digestion.

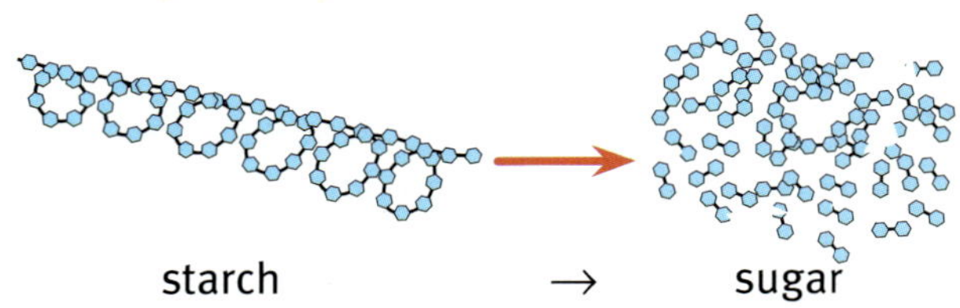

Starch is changed to sugar by a chemical reaction.

Questions

1 Explain why digestion by enzymes is a chemical reaction.

A+I 2 Do teeth cause a chemical reaction to take place? Explain your answer.

Catalysts

The enzymes inside the alimentary canal make these chemical reactions happen. The enzymes are not changed themselves. They just help to speed up the reactions.

A substance that speeds up a chemical reaction, but is not changed itself, is called a **catalyst**. So enzymes are biological catalysts.

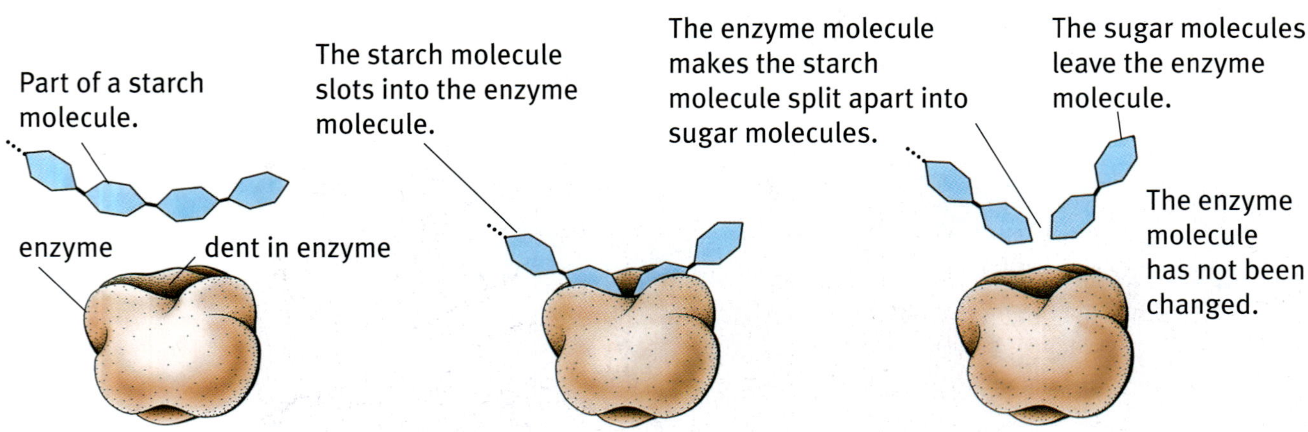

How an enzyme makes starch molecules break down to sugar molecules.

Questions

3 Teeth help to break down large pieces of food into lots of smaller pieces. Suggest how this can help enzymes to digest the food faster.

4 A protein molecule is made up of a long chain of smaller molecules called amino acids. Draw a series of diagrams showing how an enzyme digests protein molecules to amino acid molecules. Use the diagram at the bottom of the previous page as a starting point.

Activity 2.6

Using an enzyme to digest starch

SE

The enzyme that digests starch is called amylase.

1 Label two test tubes **A** and **B**.
2 Put 5 cm^3 of starch solution into each of tubes **A** and **B**.
3 Add 5 cm^3 of amylase solution to tube **A**. Add 5 cm^3 of water to tube **B**. Leave both tubes in a warm place for about 20 minutes.
4 Using a clean dropper pipette, take a small sample of liquid from tube **A**. Put it onto a white tile, and add some iodine solution. Write down the result.
5 Repeat step **4** with a sample from tube **B**.
6 Using a clean dropper pipette, take another sample from tube **A**. Put it into a boiling tube, and add some Benedict's solution. Place the boiling tube into a water bath at about 80 °C. Leave it for two or three minutes, then write down the result.
7 Repeat step **6** with a sample from tube **B**.
8 Record all of your results clearly, and try to explain them.

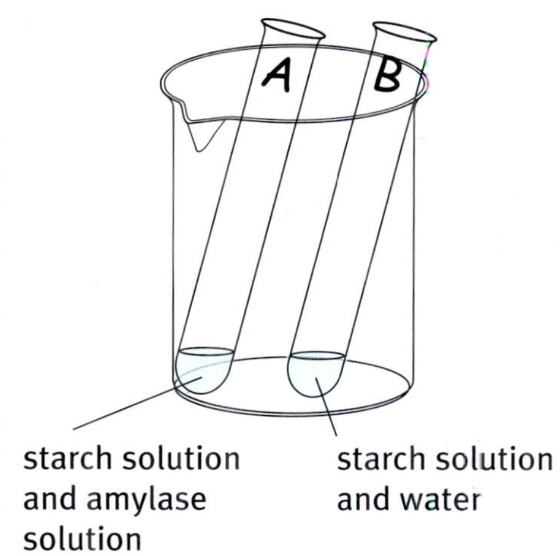

Summary

- When one substance is changed into a different substance, a chemical reaction has taken place.
- Digestion is a chemical reaction in which a substance made of large molecules is changed into a substance made of small molecules.
- Enzymes are molecules that act as biological catalysts. Enzymes help reactions to take place quickly. The enzymes are not changed themselves.

Unit 2 End of unit questions

2.1 Copy and complete these sentences, using words from the list.
You may use each word once, more than once or not at all.

atoms **large** **molecules** **pieces** **small**

Teeth break down large lumps of food into smaller .... Then, enzymes break down the large .... of the nutrients in the food into small .... This allows the nutrients to pass out of the alimentary canal through the wall of the .... intestine. [4]

2.2 The table shows the carbohydrate content of ten foods.

Food	Carbohydrate content / g in 100 g of food
apple	9
banana	20
beans	17
biscuits	66
bread	45
grilled chicken	0
coconut	4
egg	0
fish	0
mutton	0
rice	30

a Which food contains the most carbohydrate? [1]
b Bolormaa ate 50 g of biscuits. How much carbohydrate did she eat? [1]
c Rice does not contain sugar. What kind of carbohydrate does rice contain? [1]
d What do the four foods that do **not** contain carbohydrate have in common? [1]

2.3 The diagram shows part of the human alimentary canal.

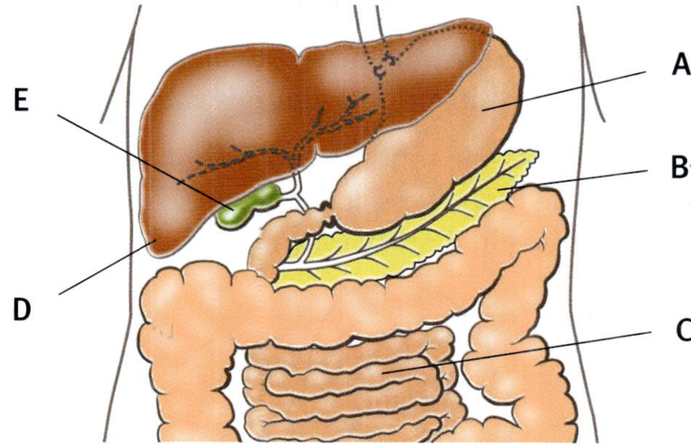

a Name parts **A** and **D**. [2]

b Give the letters of **two** labelled parts where protein digestion takes place. [2]

c Give the letter of **one** labelled part where digested nutrients are absorbed. [1]

2.4 Rhianna tested two different foods using iodine solution and Benedict's solution. These were her results.

> spaghetti – went blue-black with iodine solution, went blue with Benedict's solution
>
> honey – went orange-brown with iodine solution, turned brick red with Benedict's solution

a Describe how Rhianna tested the foods with Benedict's solution. [2]

b Construct a results table and fill it in to show Rhianna's results clearly. [3]

c What conclusions can Rhianna make from her results? [4]

2.5 Nakula investigated the effect of heat on amylase. Amylase is an enzyme that makes starch molecules break down into sugar molecules.

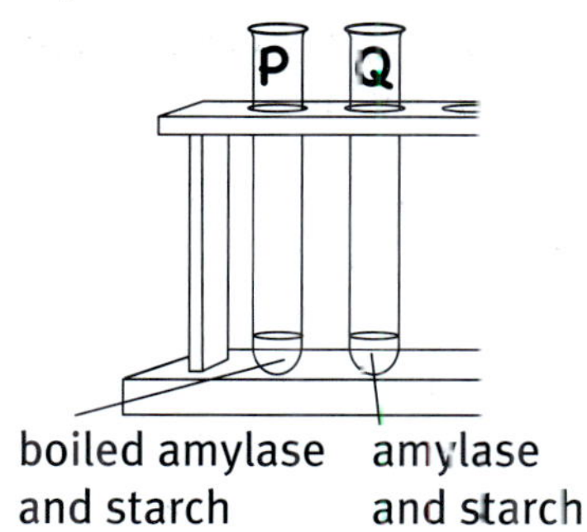

- Nakula put some amylase solution into two boiling tubes, **P** and **Q**
- He boiled the solution in tube **P**. He did not heat tube **Q**.
- He waited until the solution in tube **P** had cooled down to room temperature.
- He added equal volumes of starch solution to tube **P** and tube **Q**.
- After 10 minutes, he tested both tubes for sugar.
- Nakula found that there was sugar in tube **Q**, but not in tube **P**.

a What was the variable that Nakula changed in his experiment? [1]

b State **two** variables that Nakula kept constant in his experiment. [2]

c Nakula wrote this conclusion to his experiment:
'My results show that boiling destroys amylase'.
Explain how Nakula's results support his conclusion. [3]

3.1 The human circulatory system

Sit very still and quiet. Put your fingers on your neck, just underneath your chin. Can you feel your pulse?

Each pulse that you can feel is caused by one beat of your heart. All through your life, your heart keeps on beating, pushing blood around your body.

The blood travels round the body inside tubes called **blood vessels**. The diagram shows the basic plan on which the blood vessels are arranged. The heart and blood vessels together make up the circulatory system.

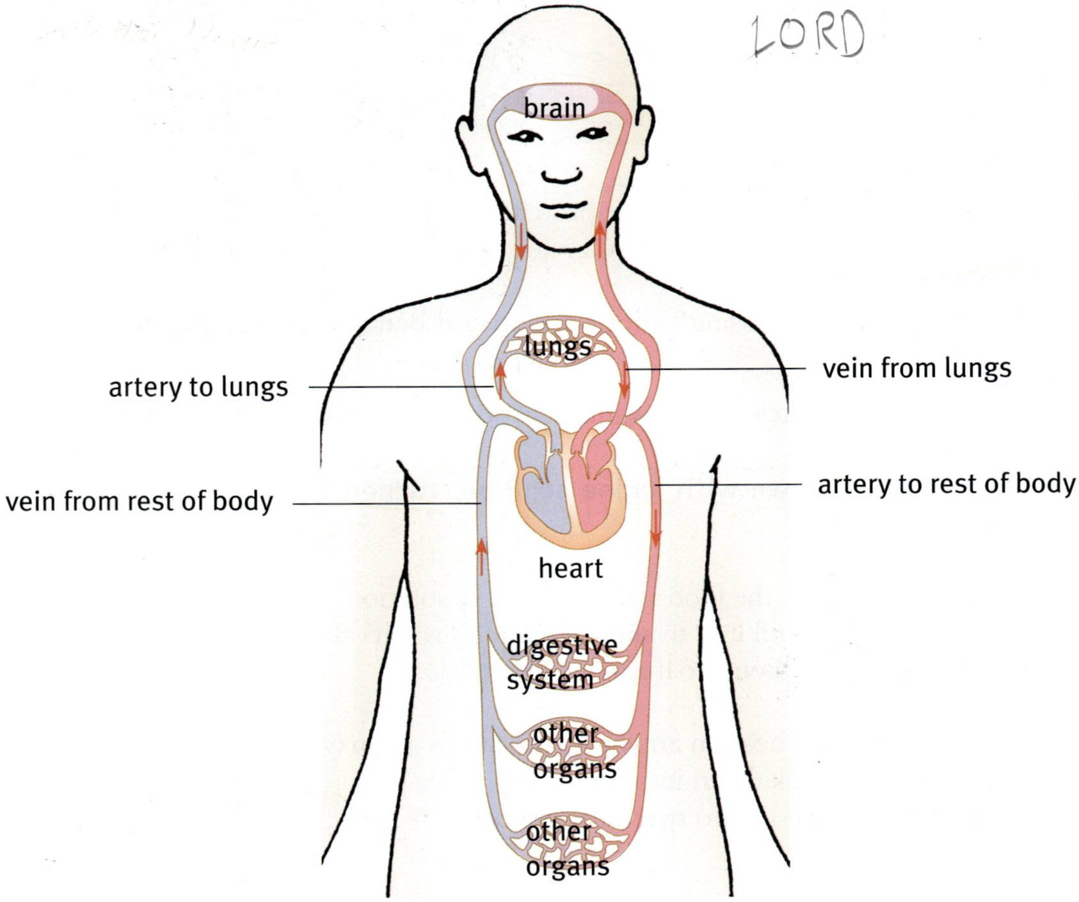

The human circulatory system.

Questions

Look at the diagram to answer these questions.

A+I **1** In which direction do arteries carry blood – away from the heart, or towards the heart?

A+I **2** In which direction do veins carry blood – away from the heart, or towards it?

A+I **3** The circulatory system is like a one-way traffic system. Describe **two** different routes by which blood in the left side of the heart can get to the right side of the heart. (Remember – the person in the diagram is facing you.)

Oxygenated and deoxygenated blood

One of the most important functions of the circulatory system is to supply oxygen to all the cells in the body.

Oxygen enters the blood as the blood passes through the lungs. The oxygen **diffuses** from the air inside the lungs, into the blood. When blood contains a lot of oxygen, it is bright red. We say that the blood is **oxygenated**.

Oxygen leaves the blood as the blood passes through tissues where the cells are using up oxygen. The oxygen diffuses from the blood, into the body cells. When blood has lost most of its oxygen, it becomes a more blueish-red. We say that the blood is **deoxygenated**.

You can see blood vessels inside the elephant's ear.

Question

4 Look at the diagram of the human circulatory system. Which side of the heart contains oxygenated blood?

Activity 3.1
Modelling the circulatory system

Design and make a model to show the human circulatory system.

Your model should include something to represent:

- the heart, with the two sides joined together but not allowing blood to move directly from one side to the other
- the blood vessels that run between the heart and the lungs
- the blood vessels that run between the heart and the tissues in the rest of the body.

You might be able to add something that moves to your model, such as red and blue beads to represent the blood.

Summary

- The heart and blood vessels make up the circulatory system.
- Blood flows out of the heart inside arteries, and back into the heart inside veins.
- Blood picks up oxygen as it passes through the lungs, and releases oxygen as it passes through the tissues in the rest of the body.

3.2 The heart

The diagram shows where your heart is. It is just under your ribs, slightly to left of centre of your body.

Your heart is about the same size as your clenched fist. It is made of very strong muscle. The muscle in the heart contracts and relaxes over and over again, all through your life. However tired you are, your heart still keeps beating.

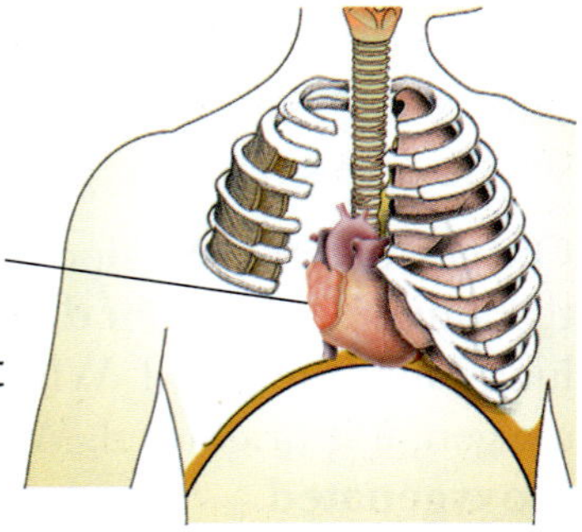

The position of the heart in the human body.

The structure of the heart

The diagram shows what the inside of the heart looks like.

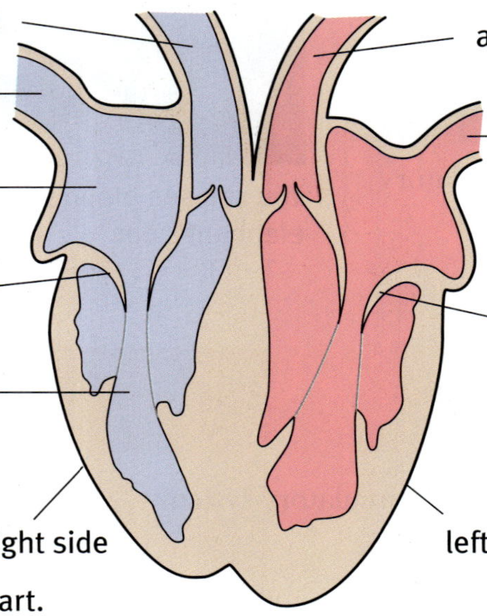

The structure of the heart.

Question

A+I

1 The heart has four chambers – an upper and lower chamber on the left, and an upper and lower chamber on the right.

- **a** Into which chamber does blood from the lungs flow?
- **b** Out of which chamber does blood flow, on its way to the rest of the body?
- **c** Which two chambers contain oxygenated blood?

How the heart works

The heart is made of muscle. This muscle contracts and then relaxes. When muscle contracts, it gets shorter. This makes the walls of the heart chambers squeeze inwards. This pushes blood out of the heart.

There are valves between the upper chambers and the lower chambers. The valves only let the blood flow from the upper chamber to the lower chamber. There are also valves in the big arteries coming out of the heart. These valves only let the blood flow out, not back into the heart.

This is what happens during one heart beat:

- The heart muscle contracts, pushing blood out into the arteries.
- The heart muscle relaxes, allowing blood to flow into the heart from the veins.

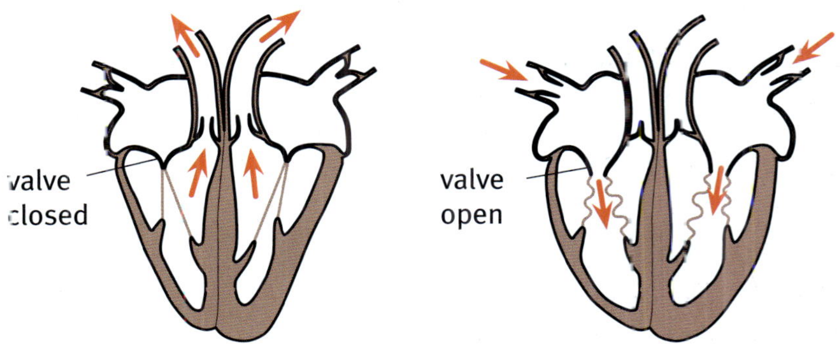

How the heart pumps blood.

Activity 3.2
Investigating the effect of exercise on pulse rate

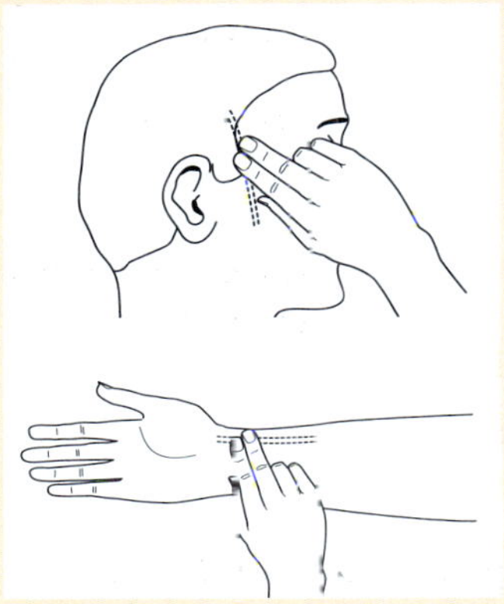

Each time your heart muscle contracts, it sends blood surging through your arteries. You can feel this surge of blood if you put your fingers on a place where there is an artery near the surface of the body. The diagrams show two good places to try.

Each surge of blood is called a **pulse**. Your pulse rate is the number of pulses in one minute.

1 Read through what you are going to do. Draw a results table, ready to write in your results as you collect them.
2 Work with a partner. Ask them to sit very still and relaxed for a few minutes. Then count their pulse rate.
3 Now ask your partner to do some exercise for two minutes. Your teacher will suggest a good exercise to do.
4 As soon as your partner has finished exercising, count their pulse rate again.
5 Continue to count their pulse rate every two minutes for ten minutes.
6 Draw a graph to display your results.
7 Use your results to write a short conclusion.

Summary

- The heart is made of muscle, which contracts and relaxes to pump blood around the body.
- The heart contains valves to make sure the blood always flows in the right direction.

3.3 Blood

Everyone knows that blood is a red liquid. But if you look at blood under a microscope, you may get a surprise. The liquid part of blood is not red at all – it is a very pale yellow colour. What makes blood red is the cells that float in this liquid.

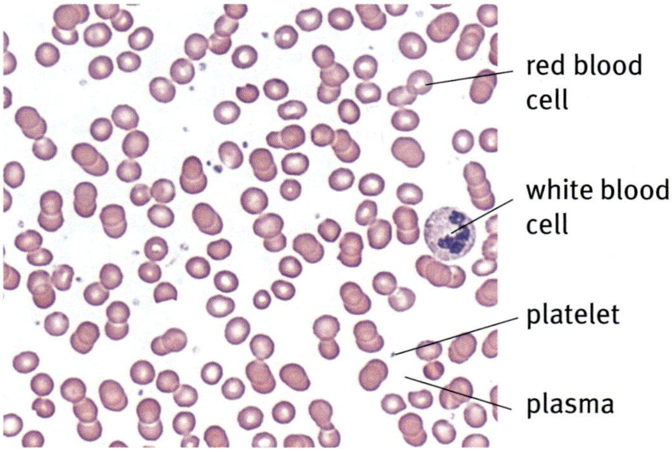

This is what human blood looks like under the microscope. The white blood cells have been stained with a dye, to make it easier to see them.

Question

A+I

1 Look at the photograph of blood.
   - **a** Approximately how many red blood cells are there for each white blood cell?
   - **b** Describe **two** ways in which white blood cells look different from red blood cells.

Plasma

Plasma is the liquid part of blood. It is mostly water. Plasma contains many different substances dissolved in it. For example, sugar is transported around the body dissolved in the blood plasma. The sugar is absorbed into the blood in the small intestine, and is carried all over the body to the cells that need to use it for energy.

Red blood cells

Most of the cells in the blood are red blood cells. Red blood cells are unusually small cells. They are red because they contain a red pigment called **haemoglobin**.

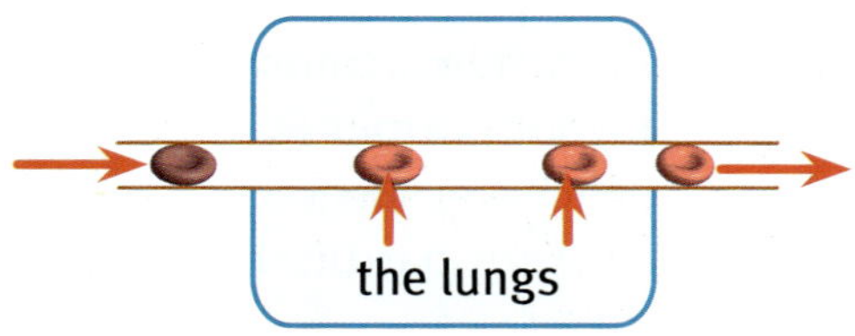

Oxygen diffuses into the blood from the lungs.

When blood flows through the lungs, oxygen diffuses into it. The oxygen combines with the haemoglobin inside the red blood cells. The haemoglobin becomes **oxyhaemoglobin**. This is a very bright red.

When the blood flows through the body tissues, the oxygen separates from the haemoglobin. The oxygen diffuses out of the red blood cells and into the tissues. The oxyhaemoglobin becomes just haemoglobin again. This is a dull blueish-red.

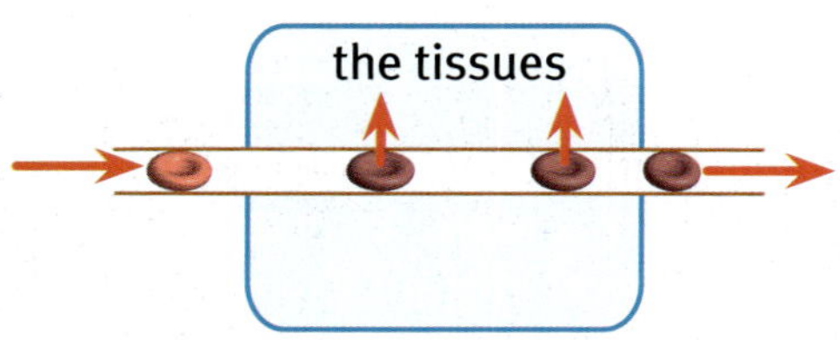

Oxygen diffuses out of the blood into the tissues.

White blood cells

White blood cells are larger than red blood cells, and they always have a nucleus. White blood cells help to defend us against bacteria and viruses that get into the body.

Some kinds of white blood cells put out 'fingers' that capture the bacterium. The white blood cell then produces enzymes that kill and digest the bacterium.

Other white blood cells produce special molecules that attach to the bacteria and kill them. These molecules are called **antibodies**.

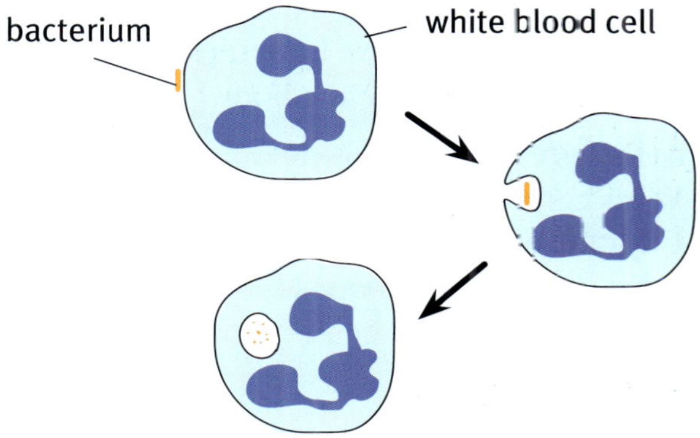

Some white blood cells take in bacteria and kill them.

Platelets

Platelets are little fragments of cells. If a blood vessel gets damaged, the platelets help the blood to clot and seal the wound.

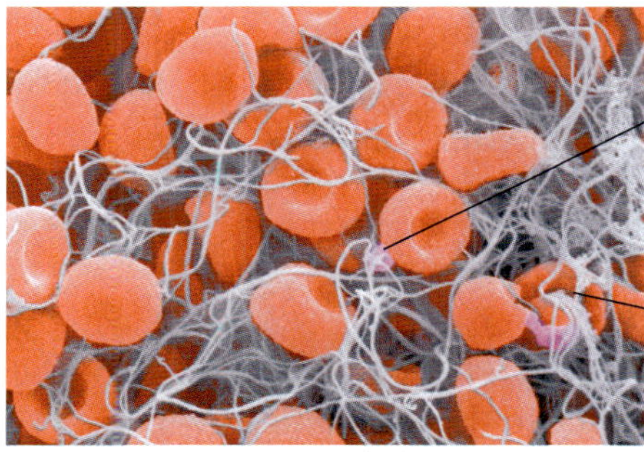

Platelets produce chemicals that cause fibres to form in the blood.

Red blood cells get trapped in the fibres.

A photograph of a blood clot, taken using an electron microscope.

Question

2 Copy and complete this table.

Component of blood	What it looks like	What it does
red blood cell		
white blood cell		
platelet		
plasma		

Summary

- Blood is made up of different kinds of blood cells floating in a liquid called plasma.
- Red blood cells transport oxygen.
- White blood cells destroy invading micro-organisms.
- Platelets help blood to clot.
- Plasma transports dissolved substances such as sugar.

3.4 Blood vessels

The tubes through which blood flows are called **blood vessels**. We have three main kinds of blood vessels in the body.

- **Arteries** carry blood away from the heart.
- **Veins** carry blood back to the heart.
- **Capillaries** connect the arteries to the veins. They carry blood close to every tissue in the body.

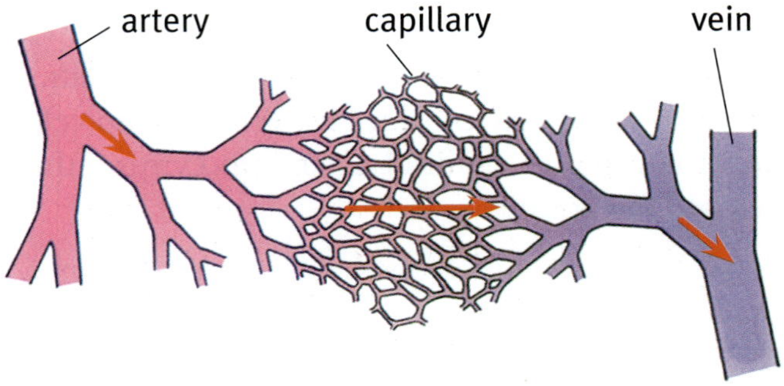

Capillaries carry blood from arteries into veins.

Questions

A+I **1** Kareena says, 'Arteries carry oxygenated blood, and veins carry deoxygenated blood.' Explain why she is wrong. (Page **32** will help you.)

A+I **2** Suggest why you can feel your pulse in an artery, but not in a vein.

Arteries

Arteries have very thick, strong, elastic walls. They need to be strong because they have to withstand the strong forces as the heart pumps blood through them. Their elastic walls are able to expand and spring back as the blood surges through. You can feel this happening when you feel your pulse.

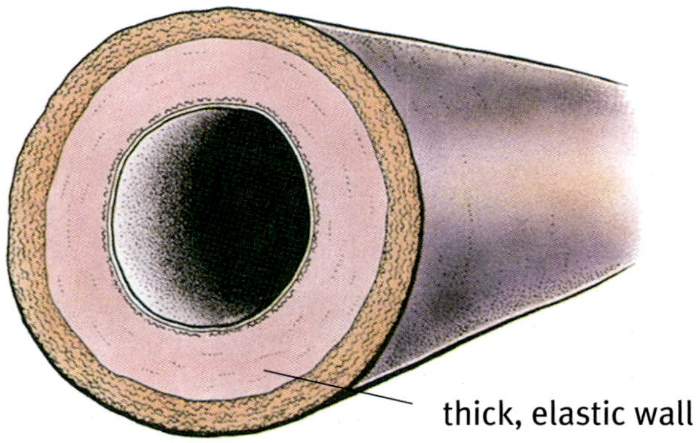

The structure of an artery.

Capillaries

Capillaries are very tiny. The smallest ones can only be seen with a microscope. They are just big enough to allow red blood cells to get through them.

Capillaries have thin walls, made up of only one layer of cells. This means that substances in the blood – such as oxygen and sugar – can easily get out. The function of capillaries is to supply cells with things that they need, and take away their waste products.

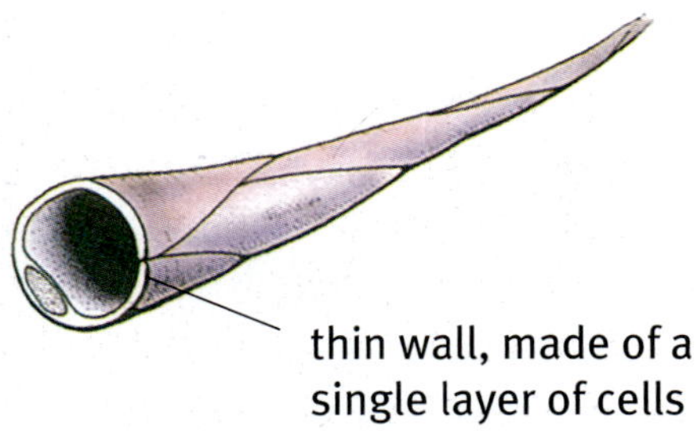

The structure of a capillary.

Veins

Veins are a similar size to arteries. However, their walls are much thinner, and the space inside them is larger. Veins do not need thick walls, because by the time blood flows into the veins it has lost most of the force that the heart gave it. They do not need very elastic walls either, because the blood is flowing smoothly rather than in surges.

Veins contain valves, which only let the blood flow one way – towards the heart.

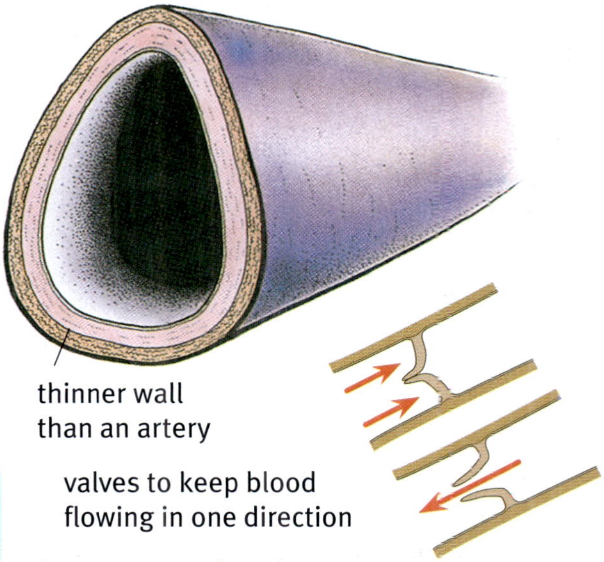

The structure of a vein.

Question

3 Construct a table to summarise the structures and functions of arteries, capillaries and veins.

Activity 3.4
Circulatory system poster

Design and make a poster to show information about the human circulatory system.

Begin by deciding what you will try to show. Include no more than one or two of the following:

- a plan of the circulatory system
- the heart and how it works
- blood – what it contains and what it does
- the different kinds of blood vessels.

You may be able to use books and the internet to find out extra information about the topics that you choose. For example:

- What makes blood flow upwards in the veins from your feet to your heart?
- How is the heart muscle supplied with oxygen and sugar?

Summary

- Blood vessels are tubes that carry blood around the body.
- Arteries carry blood away from the heart. Veins carry blood towards the heart. Capillaries carry blood between arteries and veins.
- Arteries have thick, elastic walls to withstand the strong surges of blood. Capillaries are tiny, with very thin walls. Veins have thinner walls than arteries. Veins contain valves.

Unit 3 End of unit questions

3.1 Copy and complete these sentences using words from the list. You may use each word once, more than once or not at all.

blood **contracts** **muscle** **stretches** **tubes** **valves**

The heart is made of .... This muscle .... and relaxes rhythmically, pumping blood around the body. There are .... inside the heart that make sure the blood keeps flowing in the correct direction. [3]

3.2 The diagram represents the circulatory system.

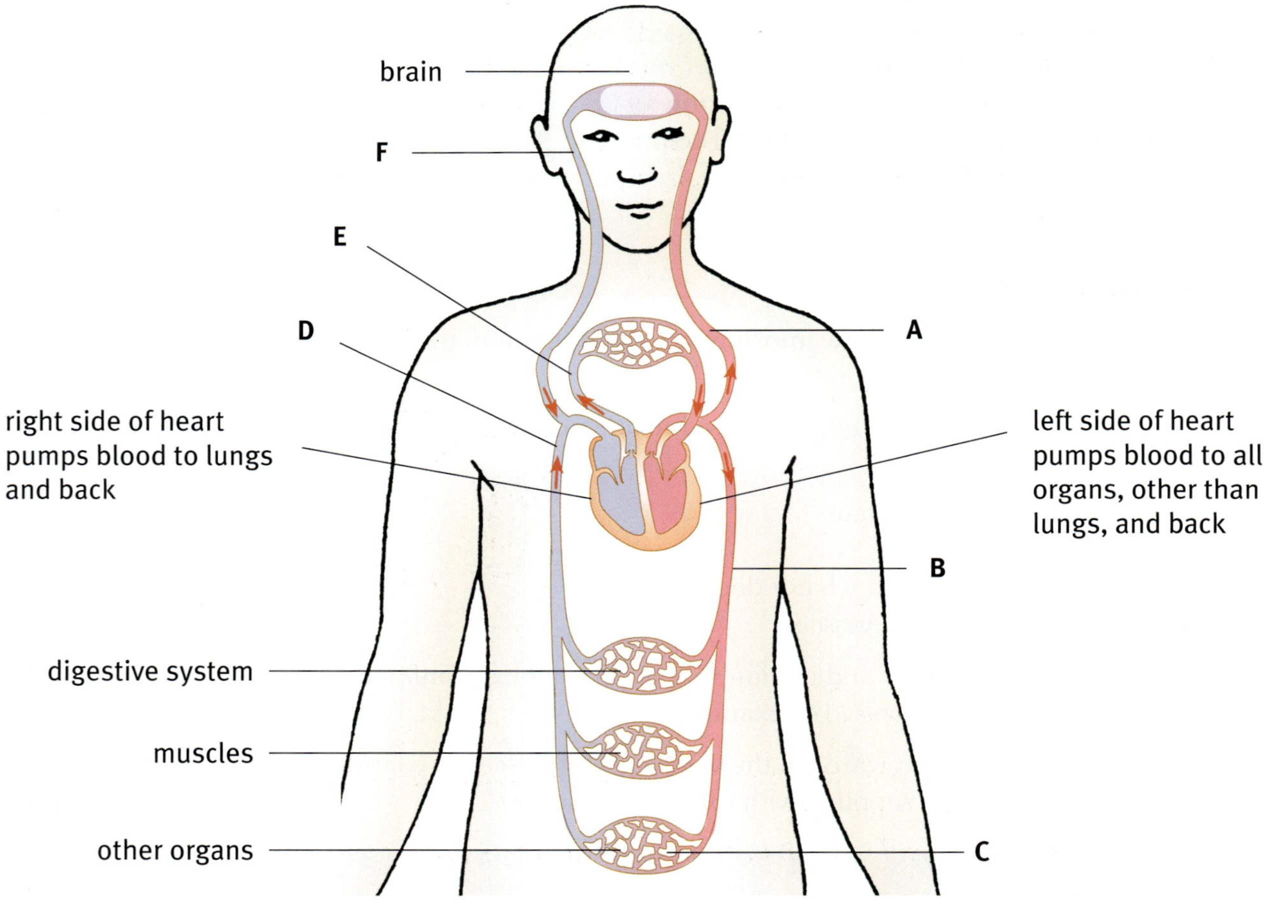

a Write down **three** letters that show arteries. [2]

b Write down **one** letter that shows capillaries. [1]

c Write down **two** letters that show veins. [1]

d Write down **three** letters that show vessels containing deoxygenated blood. [2]

3.3 Krystyna investigated how a person's pulse rate changes when they exercise. She tested four of her friends. Belinda and Jasmina do a lot of sport. Jade and Mara prefer to read books and play computer games.
Krystyna measured the four girls' pulse rates, in beats per minute, when they were relaxing. Then she asked them to run up two flights of stairs, and measured their pulse rates again. These are her results.

Belinda 65, 102
Jasmina 72, 105
Jade 70, 110
Mara 74, 120

a Draw a results table, and fill in Krystyna's results. Remember to label the rows and columns of your results table fully. [4]
b Display Krystyna's results in the way you think is best. [5]
c Write down **one** conclusion that Krystyna can make from her results. [1]
d Krystyna decided that she did not have enough evidence to decide whether being fit affects a person's pulse rate. Was she right? Explain your answer. [2]

3.4 The diagrams show two blood cells.

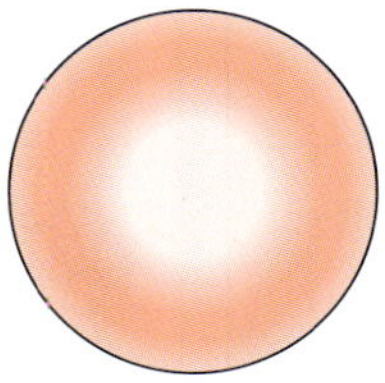

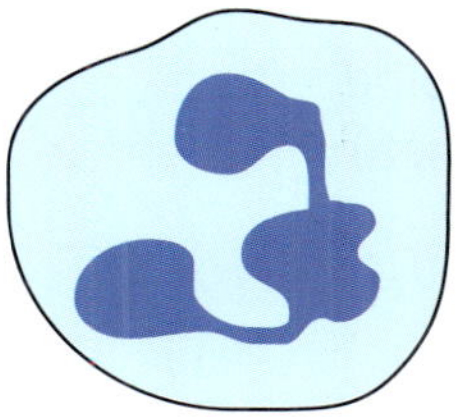

a Make a copy of the drawing of the red blood cell. Label the cell membrane and the cytoplasm. [2]
b Name **one** structure that most cells have, but that red blood cells do not have. [1]
c Describe **one** other way in which red blood cells differ from most other cells in the human body. [1]
d Explain how red blood cells are adapted to carry out their function. [2]
e Describe the function of white blood cells. [2]

4.1 The human respiratory system

Every cell in your body needs a supply of oxygen. The cells use the oxygen for **respiration**. They produce carbon dioxide as a waste product.

The oxygen comes from the air around you. About 20% of the air is oxygen. The carbon dioxide that your cells produce goes back into the air around you. About 0.04% of the air is carbon dioxide.

The organs that help to get oxygen from the air into your blood, and to get rid of carbon dioxide, make up the **respiratory system**.

When you breathe in, air flows through the trachea and then into the two bronchi, which carry it deep inside the lungs. When you breathe out, air flows back in the opposite direction.

Inside the lungs, oxygen passes from the air into the blood, and carbon dioxide passes out of the blood into the air. This is called **gas exchange**. You will find out more about this in the next topic.

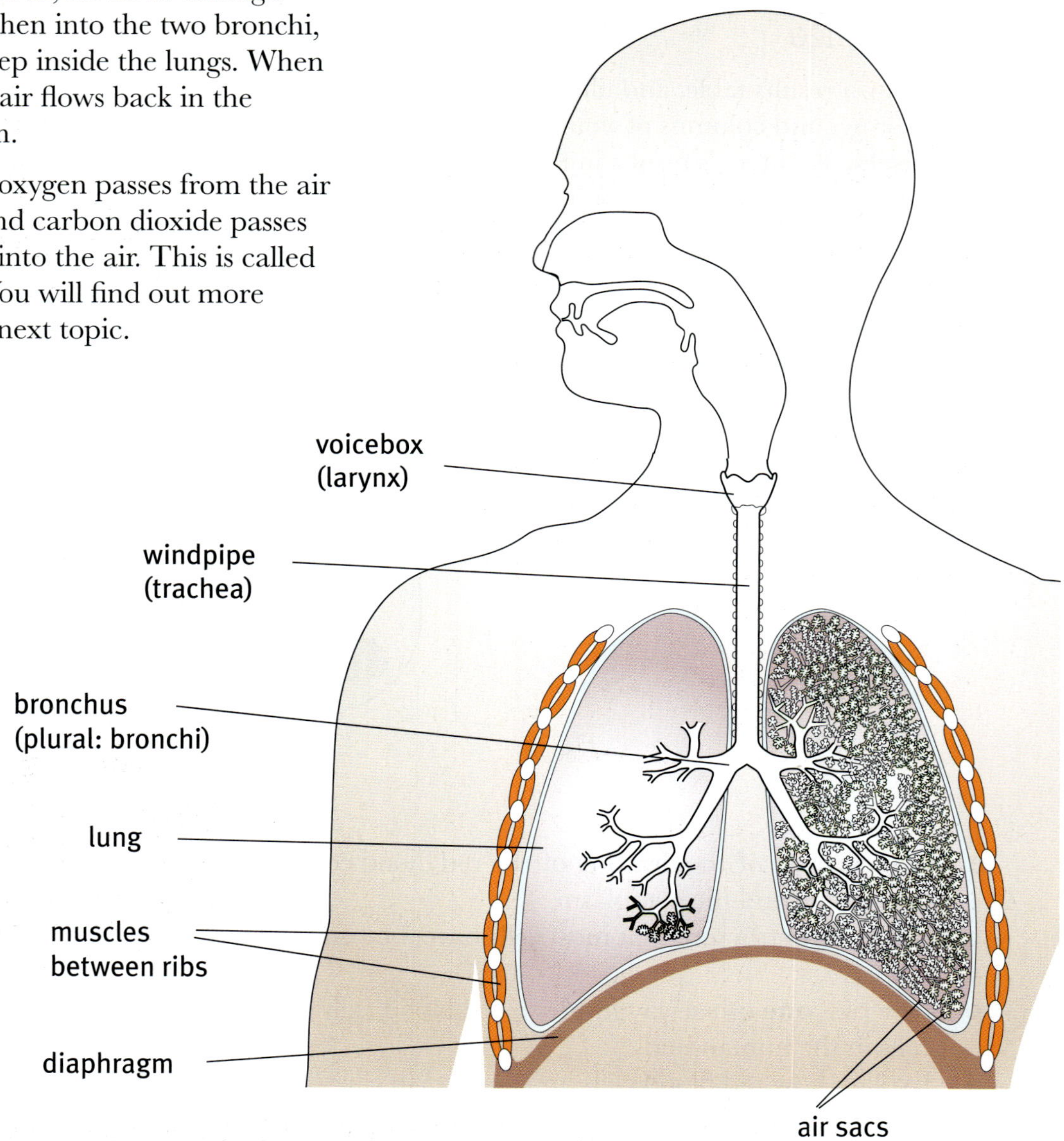

The structure of the human respiratory system.

Question

1 Write a sentence to describe the function of each of these parts of the human respiratory system.

a trachea **b** bronchus

Activity 4.1

Measuring the volume of air you can push out of your lungs

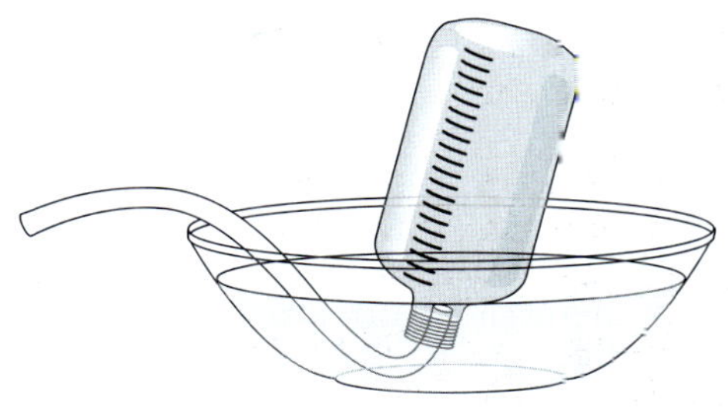

1 You need a large, plastic bottle – preferably one that can hold at least 3 dm^3 (3 litres) of water. First, you need to mark a scale on the bottle to show the water level when it holds different volumes. In your group, discuss how you can do this. Then mark the scale carefully on the bottle. Your scale should go all the way to the top of the bottle.

2 Fill the bottle right to the very top with water. Put the lid on.

3 Put water into a large bowl until it is about half full. Turn the bottle upside down, and stand it in the water in the bowl. Carefully remove the top. All the water that you put into the bottle should stay inside it. (If it doesn't, start again!)

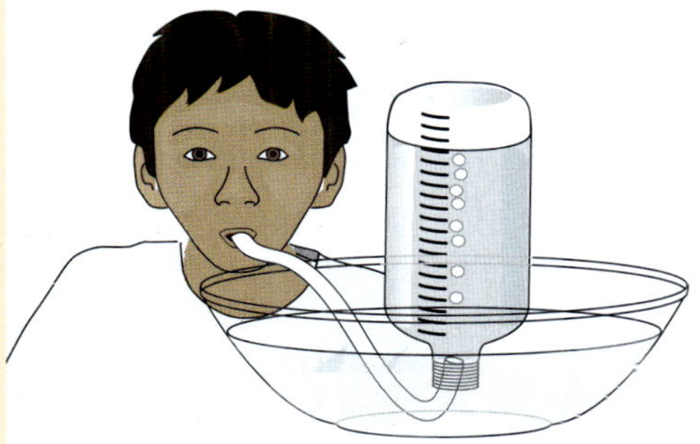

4 Slide a piece of tubing into the bottle. Take a deep breath in, then breathe out as much air as you can through the tubing. Your exhaled air will go into the bottle and push out some water.

5 Use the scale on the bottle to find the volume of air you breathed out.

6 If you have time, repeat steps **2** to **5** two more times. Use your three results to calculate a mean value for the volume of air you can push out of your lungs.

Summary

- The respiratory system includes the trachea, bronchi, lungs, diaphragm and the muscles between the ribs.

4.2 Gas exchange

Air sacs in the lungs

The photograph on the right shows what your lungs look like inside, magnified about 300 times. You can see that they are full of spaces. These spaces are called **air sacs** or **alveoli**, and they are full of air.

You cannot see them in the photograph, but there are lots of very tiny blood capillaries in the living tissue between the air sacs (which looks brown in the photograph).

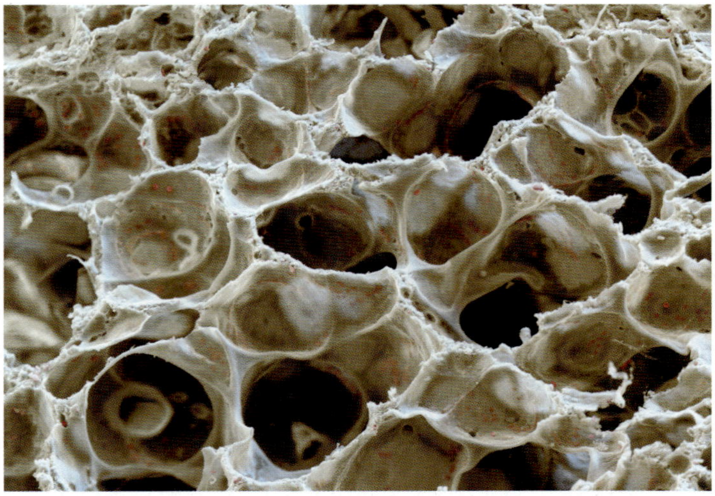

Part of a human lung, seen using a powerful microscope.

How gas exchange takes place

The diagram on the right shows one of these air sacs and a nearby blood capillary.

The blood inside the capillary has come from the heart. Before that, it came from the organs of the body. The cells in these organs used up oxygen and produced carbon dioxide. So this blood contains only a little oxygen, and a lot of carbon dioxide.

The air inside the air sac has come from outside the body. It contains a lot of oxygen and very little carbon dioxide.

Oxygen therefore **diffuses** from the air sac into the blood capillary. It diffuses into the red blood cells. (You can read about diffusion on page **70**).

Carbon dioxide diffuses from the blood inside the capillary into the air sac.

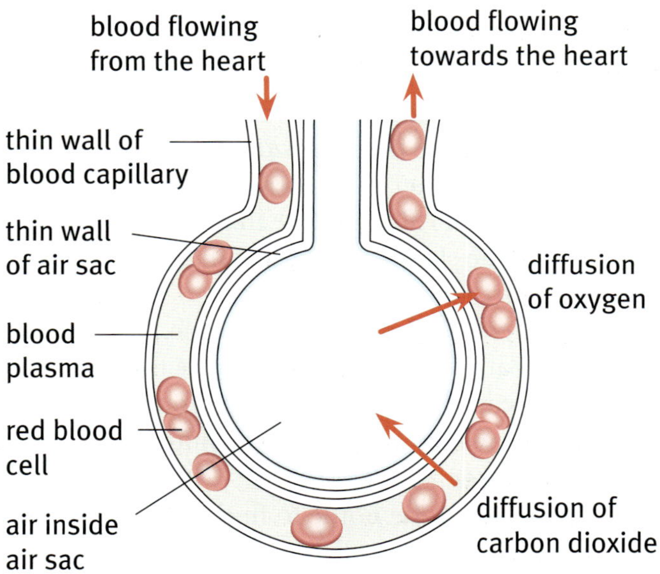

Gas exchange in an air sac.

Questions

1. Name the red pigment inside red blood cells that helps to carry oxygen.
2. Name the large blood vessel that carries blood from the heart to the lungs.
3. A+I Using what you know about particle theory, explain how oxygen diffuses from an air sac into the blood.
4. A+I The walls of the air sacs and the capillaries are both very thin. Suggest how this helps gas exchange to take place quickly.

Activity 4.2

Why are air sacs so small?

SE

Your teacher will give you two Petri dishes filled with agar jelly.

1. Use a cork borer with a diameter of 10 mm to make 8 holes in the jelly in one dish. Space the holes evenly over the dish.
2. Use a cork borer with a diameter of 5 mm to make 32 small holes in the jelly in the second dish. Try to space the holes evenly over the dish.
3. Using a dropper pipette, carefully fill each hole in both dishes with a solution of a coloured dye. Record what happens after five minutes and after half an hour.

Questions

A1 Describe your observations in each dish.

A2 The holes you made in the jelly represent the air sacs in the lungs. The coloured dye represents oxygen in the air sacs.
Explain how your observations help to show what happens to oxygen in the lungs.

A3 The total volume of the liquid in the 8 large holes is the same as the total volume in the 32 small holes. Use your results to explain why it is better to have a lot of very tiny air sacs in your lungs, rather than a few big ones.

Summary

- Gas exchange is the diffusion of gases into and out of the body. This happens inside the air sacs in the lungs.
- Oxygen diffuses from the air sacs into the blood. Carbon dioxide diffuses the other way.
- Air sacs are very tiny, have very thin walls, and have blood capillaries lying closely alongside them. This helps gas exchange to take place quickly.

4.3 Aerobic respiration

Living cells need energy to stay alive. They get their energy from nutrients, especially glucose.

Glucose contains chemical potential energy. Inside cells, glucose takes part in a **chemical reaction** called **respiration**. In this reaction, the glucose combines with oxygen. The chemical potential energy in the glucose is released, so that the cells can use it.

glucose + oxygen → carbon dioxide + water

The oxygen that combines with the glucose in this reaction comes from the air. So this is sometimes known as **aerobic respiration**. We can define aerobic respiration like this:

Aerobic respiration is the release of energy from glucose by reacting it with oxygen inside living cells.

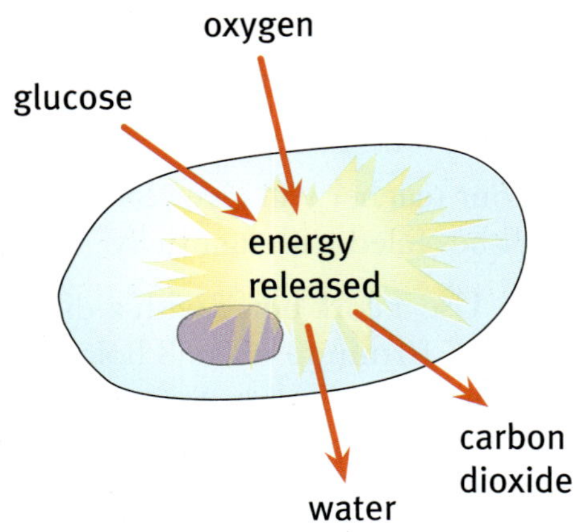

Aerobic respiration takes place inside cells.

Questions

1. Name the **two** new substances that are made when glucose reacts with oxygen inside a cell.
2. Use what you know about digestion and the human circulatory system to describe how glucose gets to a cell in a muscle.
3. Use what you know about gas exchange and the human circulatory system to describe how oxygen gets to a cell in a muscle.
4. Explain the difference between respiration and breathing.

Respiration and heat production

Some of the energy that is released from glucose during respiration is heat energy. Everything that respires releases heat energy.

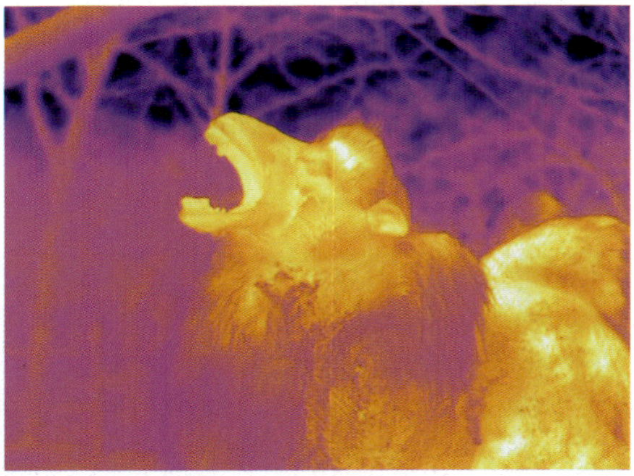

This photograph is called a thermogram. It shows objects with different temperatures in different colours. Black is coldest, then purple, red, orange, yellow and finally white.

Questions

5. Which are the hottest parts in the photograph? How can you tell?
6. Explain why these parts are hotter than their surroundings.

Activity 4.3
Respiring peas

SE

All living things respire, even seeds. Seeds respire especially quickly when they are germinating. You can make pea seeds start to germinate by soaking them in water for about an hour.

1. Set up your apparatus as in the diagram. Take care to make everything exactly the same for the two pieces of apparatus, except that one contains dead peas and the other contains live, germinating peas.
2. Take the temperature inside each flask, and record the two temperatures in a results table.
3. Continue to take the temperature inside both flasks at regular intervals. Your teacher will suggest when you can do this.
4. Draw line graphs to show how the temperature in each flask changes over time. Put time on the *x*-axis and temperature on the *y*-axis. Draw both lines on the same pair of axes. Remember to label the lines to say which is which.

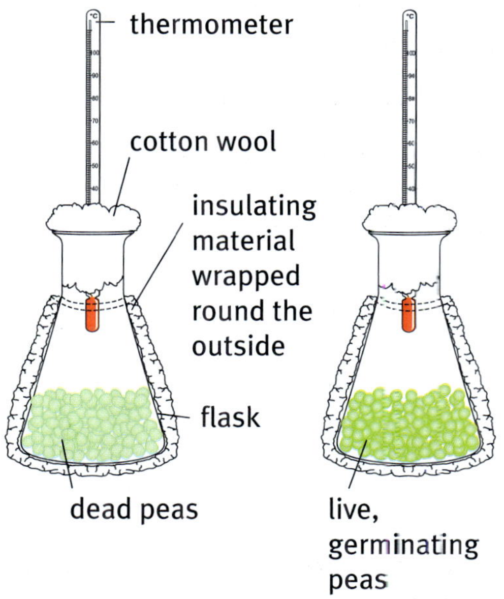

Questions

A1 What was the variable that you changed in this experiment?
A2 What was the variable that you measured in this experiment?
A3 State **two** variables that you kept the same in this experiment.
A4 Suggest an explanation for the results that you obtained.

Summary

- Cells need energy, which they obtain from nutrients such as glucose.
- Cells obtain energy from glucose by a chemical reaction called respiration.
- In aerobic respiration, oxygen combines with glucose. Carbon dioxide and water are produced.

4.4 Keeping fit

How fit are you? A fit person can do moderate exercise easily, without getting too tired too quickly.

For most of us, we just need to be able to run for a bus, to go for a cycle ride or to climb a few flights of stairs. A professional athlete – such as a footballer, tennis player or racing car driver – has to be fit enough to do really vigorous exercise for a long time.

A professional tennis player has to be very fit to be able to play a match that might last up to five hours.

Energy for muscles

When you are exercising, your muscles need energy. Inside the muscle cells, energy is released from glucose, by respiration. The energy is transferred to movement energy in the muscles.

The harder your muscles work, the faster they respire. So hard-working muscles need really good supplies of the two reactants in respiration – glucose and oxygen.

Glucose and oxygen are brought to the muscles in the blood. This is why your heart beats faster when you exercise. The heart pumps blood more quickly to the muscles.

You also breathe faster when you exercise. Faster breathing moves air in and out of the lungs more quickly. This means that more oxygen can get into the blood from the air sacs each minute.

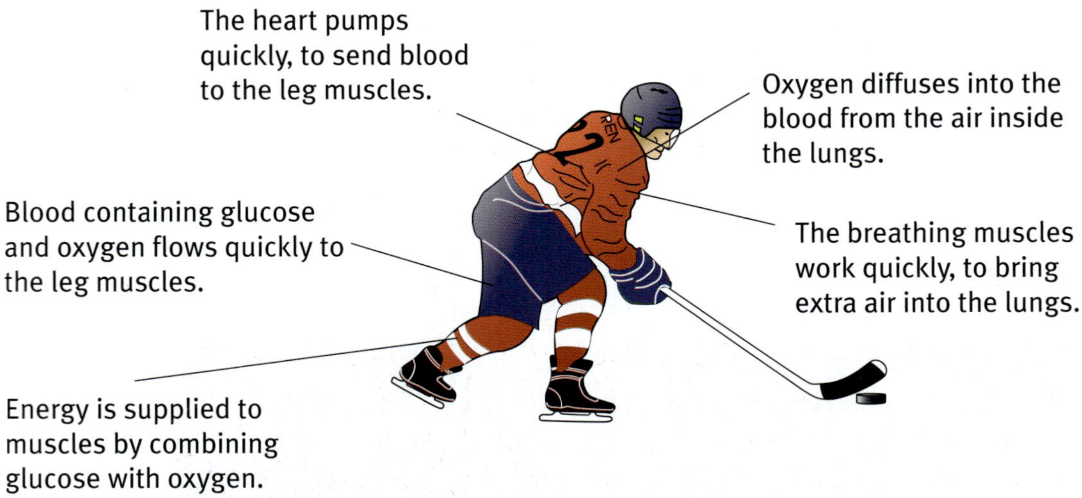

An ice hockey player's muscles use a lot of energy.

Activity 4.4
Investigating the effect of exercise on breathing rate

SE

Plan and carry out an experiment to find out how a person's breathing rate changes when they do exercise.

You could use Activity **3.2** on page **35** to give you some ideas.

Check your plan with your teacher before you do your experiment.

Record your results in a results table. Display your results as a graph.

Write a short conclusion for your experiment.

Diet and fitness

Doing regular exercise will help you to keep fit. Exercise helps your heart and breathing muscles to get strong, so they can work hard for you when you need them to. Exercise also strengthens your muscles.

What you eat also affects your fitness. If someone eats too much and gets very overweight, they will become unfit because:

- the extra mass of their body means that more energy is needed to move it around
- the heart has to work much harder to push blood around the larger body
- the space inside the arteries may get narrower, because fat deposits build up inside them.

A good diet can help you to feel fit and energetic.

Questions

1 Explain why each of the effects described in the bullet points above would make it more difficult to do energetic exercise.

2 Explain why a professional sportsperson often has a diet that contains:

a plenty of protein on most days

b carbohydrate (such as rice or pasta) just before a competition.

Summary

- Being fit means that you can do moderate exercise easily, without tiring too quickly.
- A fit person has a circulatory system that can get oxygen and glucose to the muscles quickly.
- Regular exercise and a good diet will help you to keep fit.

4.5 Cigarettes and health

One of the easiest ways to make yourself unfit, and to make your lungs and heart work less well, is to smoke cigarettes.

The World Health Organization estimates that, each year:

- 4.2 million people will die early as a result of smoking cigarettes
- cigarettes kill half of all the people who smoke them regularly
- smoking kills more people each year than all the deaths from HIV/AIDS, drugs and road accidents added together.

People who do not smoke cigarettes themselves may get ill if they breathe in other people's cigarette smoke. Children are especially at risk, if adults in their home regularly smoke cigarettes.

What is in cigarette smoke?

Nicotine

Nicotine is a **drug**. A drug is a substance that changes the way the body works. Some drugs – for example, aspirin and antibiotics – are useful. However, nicotine is a harmful drug.

Nicotine is **addictive**. This means that, once your body has got used to it, it is very difficult to stop taking it.

Nicotine makes blood vessels get narrower, so the heart has to work harder to push blood through them. Smokers are much more likely to develop heart disease than non-smokers.

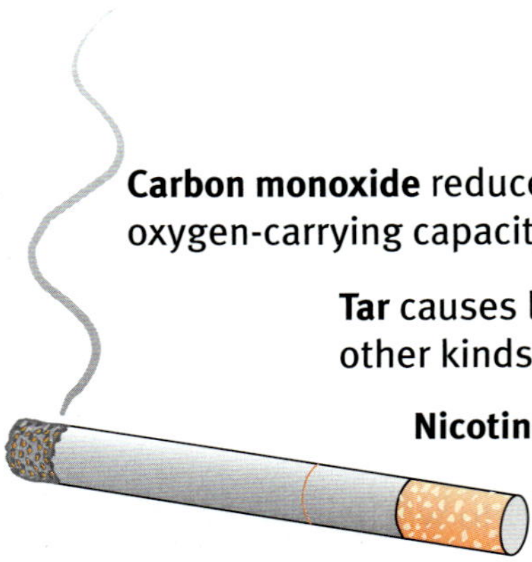

The components of cigarette smoke.

Tar

Tar in cigarette smoke causes **cancer**. Cancer is a disease in which some cells divide uncontrollably, forming a lump called a tumour. Many cancers can now be treated, but it is still very difficult to treat cancer in the lungs. Smoking cigarettes increases the risk of developing all types of cancer, but especially lung cancer.

Carbon monoxide

Carbon monoxide is an invisible gas. It combines with the haemoglobin inside red blood cells. This means that they cannot carry as much oxygen.

Particulates

Particulates are tiny particles of soot and other substances. They get into the lungs and damage the cells. The thin walls of the air sacs may break down. This makes it much more difficult for oxygen to get from the air sacs into the blood.

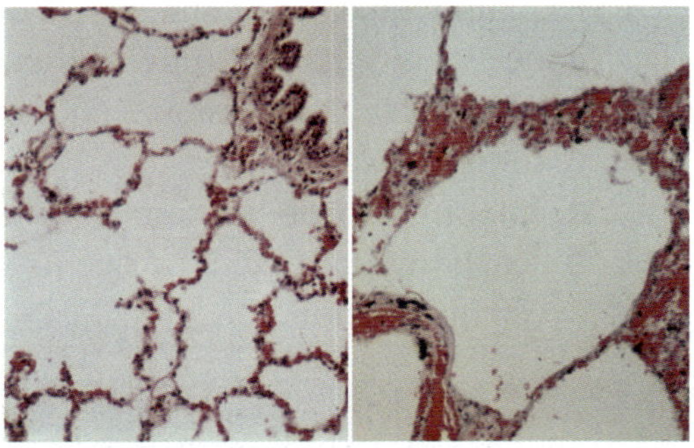

These photographs were taken using a microscope, both with the same magnification. They show lung tissue from two different people. The one on the left is from a healthy person. The one on the right is from a smoker.

Questions

A+I

1. Explain why smokers find it very hard to give up smoking.
2. Some people smoke low-tar cigarettes. Discuss whether or not this is a good idea.
3. Compare the appearance of the lung tissue in the two photographs on the previous page.
4. Most professional sportsmen and sportswomen do not smoke. Explain why.

A+I

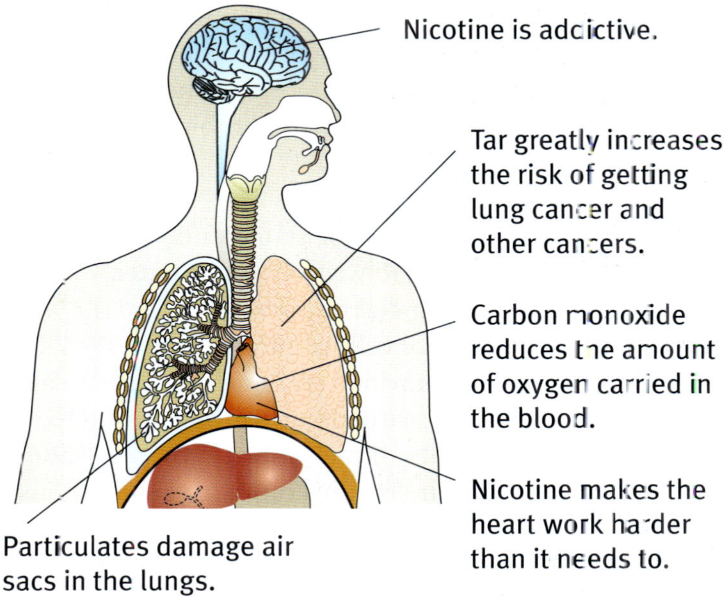

How cigarette smoke affects the body.

Activity 4.5
Smoking questionnaire

Construct a questionnaire to investigate one or more questions about smoking.

For example, you could try to find out:

- why people have chosen to smoke or not to smoke
- what people know about the ways in which cigarettes affect health.

People are more likely to answer your questionnaire if it is quite short and easy to complete.

Show your questionnaire to your teacher before you try it out. Your teacher will give you guidance about how you can use it.

Summary

- Nicotine is a drug in cigarette smoke. It is difficult for smokers to give up smoking because nicotine is addictive.
- Smoking increases the risk of getting heart disease and cancer.
- Smoking reduces the amount of oxygen transported in the blood.
- Smoking damages the air sacs so it is difficult to get enough oxygen into the body.

Unit 4 End of unit questions

4.1 Respiration is a chemical reaction that happens inside cells.

a Copy and complete the word equation for respiration.
glucose + ... → carbon dioxide + ... [2]

b This reaction is known as aerobic respiration. Explain why it is described as 'aerobic'. [2]

4.2 In each of these groups of statements, only one is correct. Choose the correct statement and write down its letter.

a **A** Every living cell respires.
B Only animal cells respire.
C The way in which plant cells respire is called photosynthesis. [1]

b **A** Expired (breathed out) air is carbon dioxide.
B Expired air contains more carbon dioxide than inspired (breathed in) air.
C Expired air contains more oxygen than inspired air. [1]

c **A** Respiration means moving your muscles to draw air into the lungs.
B Respiration means the diffusion of gases between the air sacs and the blood.
C Respiration means the release of energy from glucose, inside cells. [1]

4.3 The diagram shows an air sac and a blood capillary.

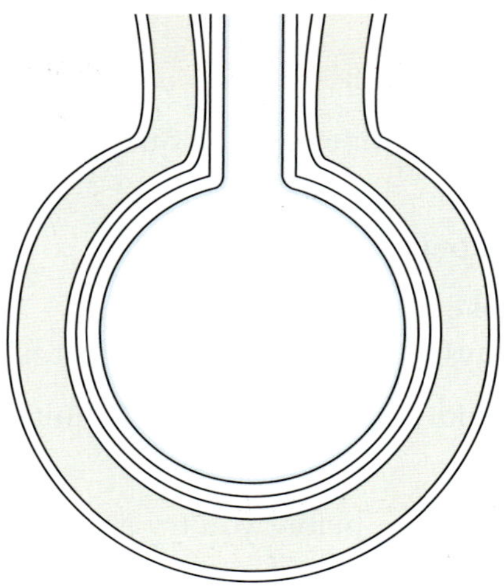

a Copy the diagram. Label:
- the blood capillary
- the wall of the air sac. [2]

b Draw two red blood cells in the correct place on your diagram. [1]

c Draw an arrow to show the direction in which oxygen diffuses. Label your arrow **O**. [1]

d Draw another arrow to show the direction in which carbon dioxide diffuses. Label your arrow **C**. [1]

e The blood leaving the lungs in the capillary travels to another blood vessel and then to the heart. What are the names of the blood vessel and the part of the heart it will first enter? [2]

4.4 Emile did an experiment to compare the rate of respiration in woodlice (small crustaceans) and maggots (the larvae of houseflies). The diagram shows how he set up his experiment.
Limewater is a clear liquid. It goes cloudy when carbon dioxide is present.

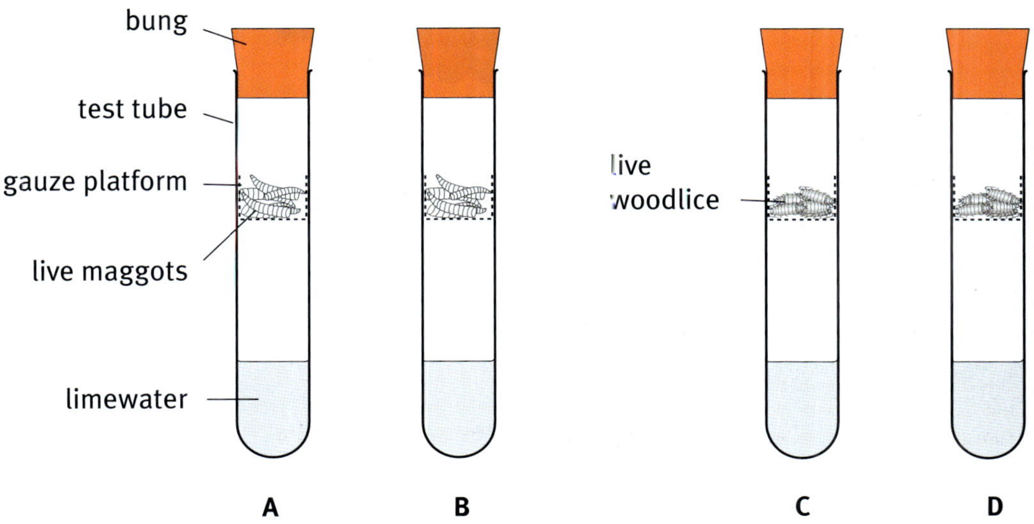

a Suggest why Emile used four tubes in his experiment, rather than two. [2]

b Describe **three** variables that Emile needed to keep the same in his experiment. [3]

c Emile timed how long it took for the limewater to go cloudy in each tube. These are his results.

A 6 minutes
B $6\frac{1}{2}$ minutes
C $8\frac{1}{2}$ minutes
D 9 minutes

Draw a results table, and write in Emile's results. [4]

d Write a conclusion that Emile can make from his results. [1]

5.1 Particle theory

Using particle theory

Scientists use the idea that all matter is made of particles to explain the properties of solids, liquids and gases. In Stage **7** you learnt about the arrangement of particles in these three states of matter.

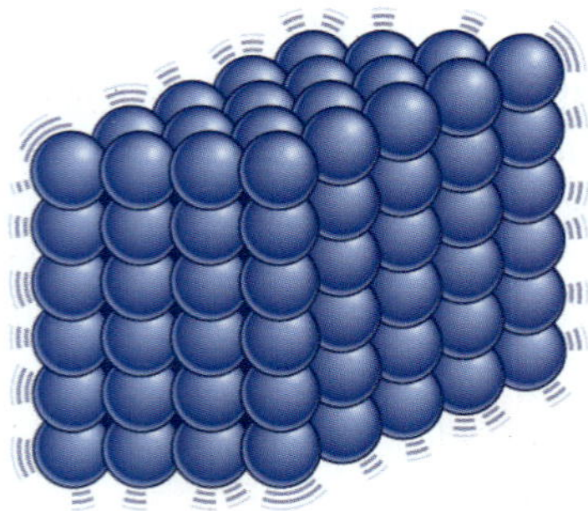

The particles in solids are arranged in regular rows with the particles touching each other.

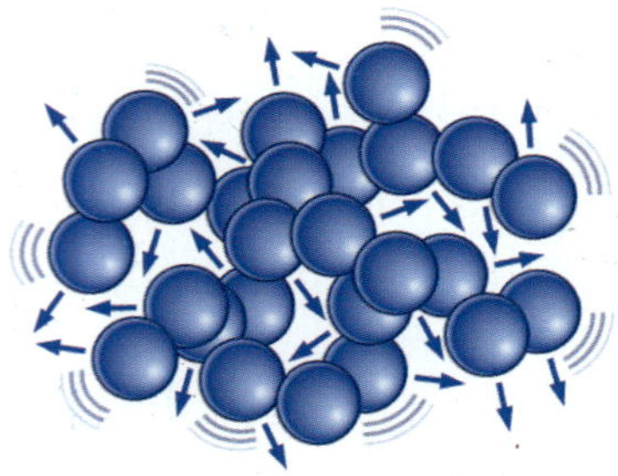

The particles in liquids are arranged with the particles touching each other but not in a pattern of rows.

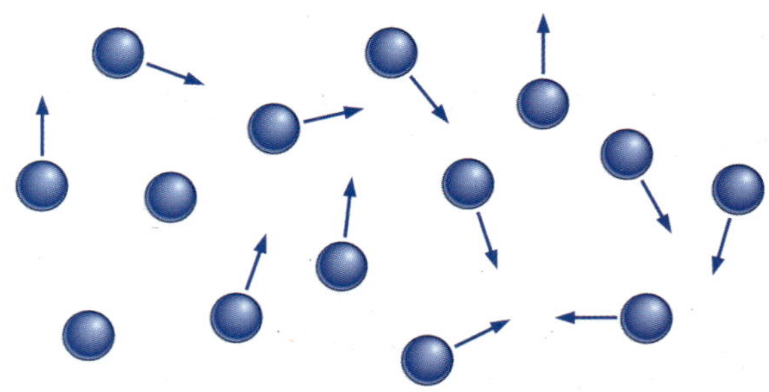

The particles in a gas do not touch each other.

The particles in solids are held firmly in place by forces of attraction. The particles can only vibrate – they cannot move or change places.

The particles in liquids are held together by weaker forces of attraction. The particles can move past each other.

The particles in a gas are not attracted to each other and they can move freely.

In order for particles to move or vibrate, they need energy. The more energy they have, the more they can move or vibrate.

Questions

A+I **1** Explain why a solid expands when it is heated.

A+I **2** Explain how the liquid in a thermometer changes so that it can be used to measure a temperature.

A+I **3** Use particle theory to explain why solids and liquids cannot be compressed (squashed into a smaller volume).

A+I **4** Use particle theory to explain why liquids and gases can flow.

Changing state

Matter exists as solid, liquid or gas. Particle theory can explain changes of state from solid to liquid, liquid to gas, liquid to solid or gas to liquid.

For example, when a solid is heated, the particles vibrate more, because some of the energy is transferred to the particles. The particles may have enough energy to escape the strong forces holding them together in their places. The particles can now move past each other. The solid has melted to form a liquid.

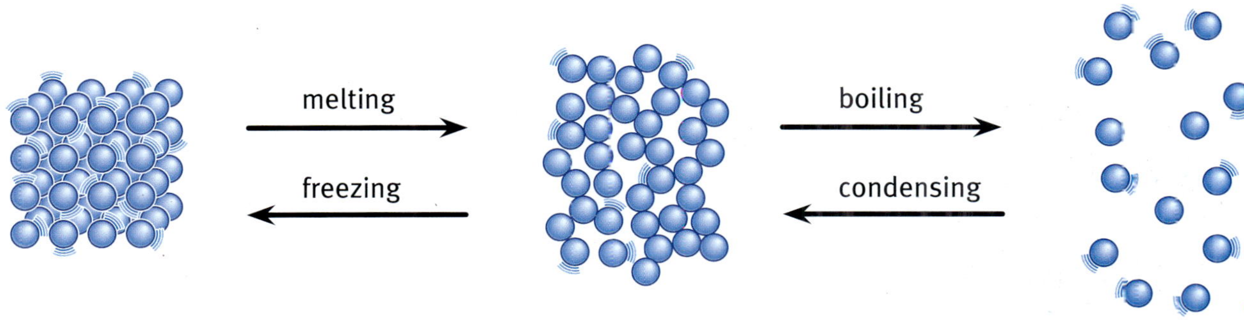

The diagrams show how the arrangement of the particles changes when there is a change of state.

Questions

A+I 5 Explain, using particle theory, how a liquid changes to a gas.

A+I 6 Explain, using particle theory, how a liquid changes to become a solid.

A+I 7 Explain, using particle theory, what happens when steam in the bathroom hits a cold surface, such as a mirror.

8 Copy the flow chart. The arrows represent the processes involved when matter changes state. Add the name for each process to your flow chart.

solid —A→ liquid —B→ gas

solid ←D— liquid ←C— gas

Summary

- All matter is made up of particles.
- Particle theory can be used to explain the properties of the three states of matter.
- Particle theory can be used to explain the changes between the states of matter.

5.2 Diffusion

Explaining diffusion

If you very carefully put a drop of food dye into a glass of water, you can see the dye very slowly spread out. Eventually the dye spreads throughout the water.

You can explain this using particle theory. The particles in the food dye and in the water are free to move. The particles of food dye and water move randomly, bumping into each other and changing direction. After some time, these random movements cause them to become evenly spread. This is called **diffusion**.

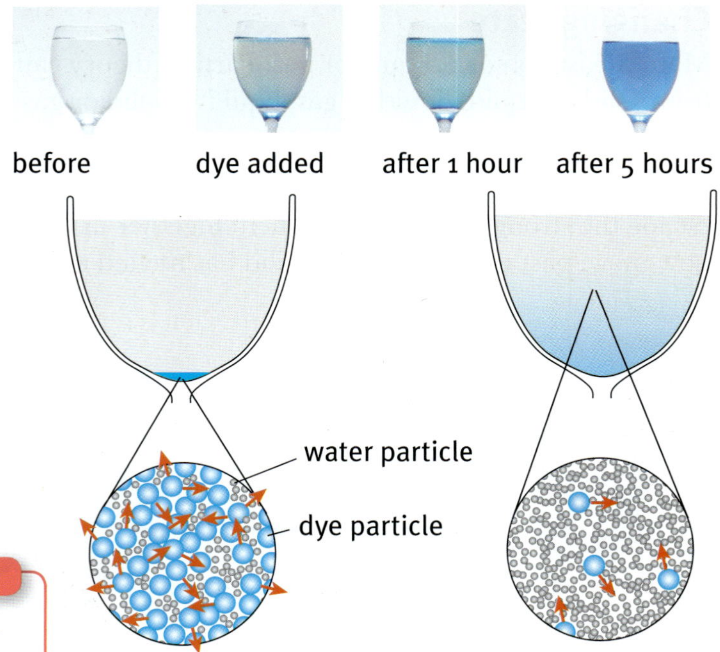

Diffusion happens because of the random movement of particles.

Question

A+I

1 Predict what would happen to the speed at which the food dye diffuses if you warm the liquid. Explain your prediction.

Diffusion in gases

Diffusion also happens in gases. Gas particles move more freely than the particles in liquids.

Bromine forms a yellow-brown coloured gas. Oxygen is a colourless gas. If they are placed together, you can watch as they diffuse into each other.

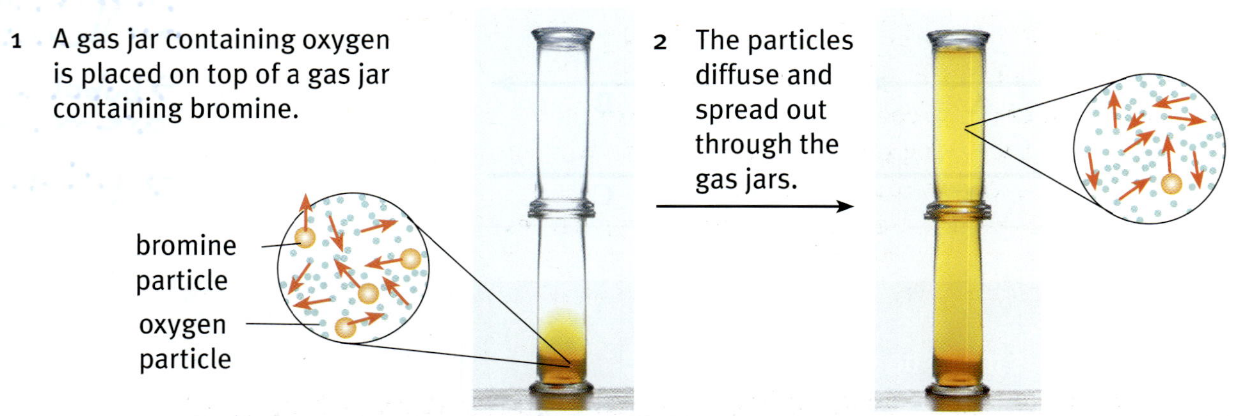

Particles of oxygen and bromine are moving about quickly.

The spaces between the particles allow the gases to mix together.

The particles are now evenly spread between the two gas jars.

Question

A+I

2 Why is diffusion faster in a gas than in a liquid?

Activity 5.2
Showing diffusion

In this experiment you can see diffusion taking place.

Your teacher will give you a dish containing a jelly called agar, which has been made using water and Universal Indicator solution.

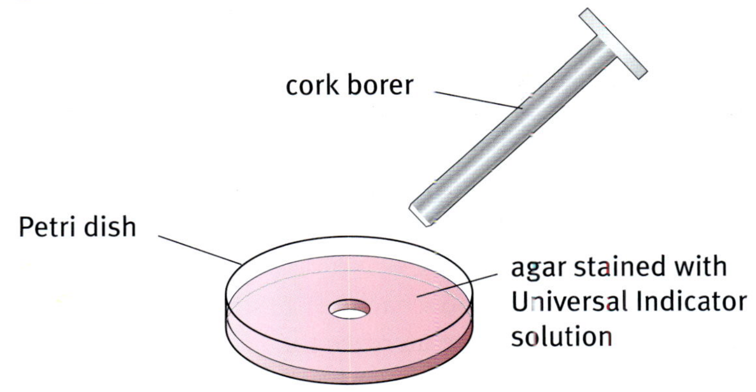

Carefully cut a circle from the jelly in the centre of the dish. Use a dropper pipette to place a small amount of sodium hydroxide solution in the hole you have made.

Questions

A1 What is Universal Indicator solution used for?
A2 What does the colour of the jelly tell you?
A3 Record what happens over a period of time. You may find it useful to draw diagrams.
A4 Explain what is happening in terms of particles.

Summary

- Diffusion happens because particles move about randomly.
- Diffusion happens more quickly in gases than in liquids.

5.3 Investigating diffusion

Using diffusion

To make tea in a teapot, you pour boiling water onto the tea leaves. Particles from the tea leaves diffuse into the hot water. You can make the tea stronger and darker by leaving the tea leaves in the pot for a longer time. You can make the tea stronger by using more tea leaves. You can stir the tea leaves to make your tea stronger more quickly.

To make a drink using fruit syrup, you add water to the concentrated syrup. When you add water from a tap, the water particles and fruit syrup particles get mixed up. If you add the water slowly and very gently you have to wait for the syrup to diffuse through the water.

Activity 5.3A

What are the factors that speed up or slow down diffusion?

SE

Different factors affect the rate at which particles diffuse.

1. Discuss in your group the factors that might be involved. Some things to think about might be: the size of the particles; the mass of the particles; the state of matter; temperature. Make a list of these factors.
2. In your group, discuss and make a prediction about how each of these factors affects diffusion. For example: I think that if we increase the temperature diffusion will be quicker.
3. In your group, discuss and explain your prediction for each of the factors. For example: I think diffusion will be quicker if we increase the temperature because the particles will have more energy and can move more quickly.

Planning an investigation needs a lot of thought.

Activity 5.3B
Investigating how temperature affects diffusion

SE

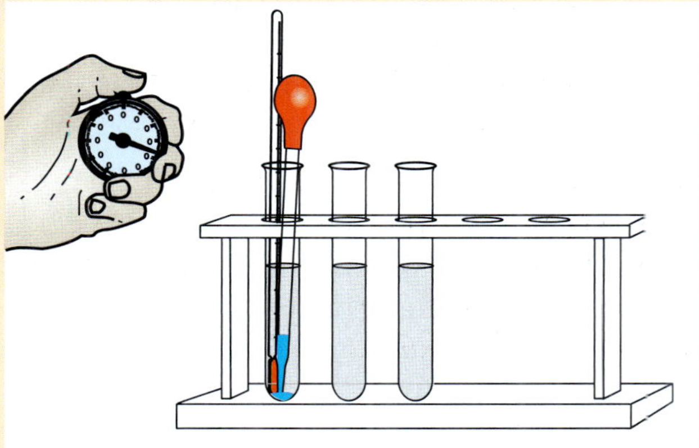

You will use water and ink or food dye. You will very carefully place a drop of ink into a test tube of water and time how long it takes until the water is completely coloured. You will do this with water at different temperatures.

1. Make a prediction about what will happen in your investigation. Explain the reasons for your prediction.
2. Make a list of the equipment you will need.
3. How many different temperatures will you use?
4. What are the highest and lowest temperatures you will use? This is the **range** of temperatures.
5. What **interval** will you use in temperatures between the highest and lowest? The interval is the step between one temperature and the next. Will you go up in 1 °C, 5 °C or 10 °C steps?
6. Which variables will you keep the same?
7. Explain how you will make your investigation a fair test.
8. Explain how you will ensure your results are **reliable**. Reliable means that you would get the same results if you repeat your experiment.
9. Draw a results table.

When you have had your work checked by your teacher you may carry out the investigation.

Questions

A1 Plot a graph of your results. Put the temperature along the horizontal axis and the time along the vertical axis.
A2 What do your results show?
A3 Do you have enough results to form a conclusion?
A4 Was your prediction correct?
A5 Explain your results.

Summary

- The rate of diffusion can be affected by a number of factors such as changes in temperature, concentration and size of particle.

5.4 Brownian motion

Particle theory helps us to explain how diffusion happens. Gases and liquids are made up of tiny particles that move about all the time, bumping into each other and changing direction. Eventually, the random movement of the particles causes them to spread out evenly.

Particle theory can also help us to explain why bigger things – such as pollen grains – jiggle about.

Moving pollen grains

Flowers produce pollen grains to help them to reproduce. Pollen grains are very small, but you can easily see them with a microscope. They are much, much bigger than the tiny particles that are involved in diffusion. Pollen grains cannot move by themselves. They are carried around by air currents, or on insects.

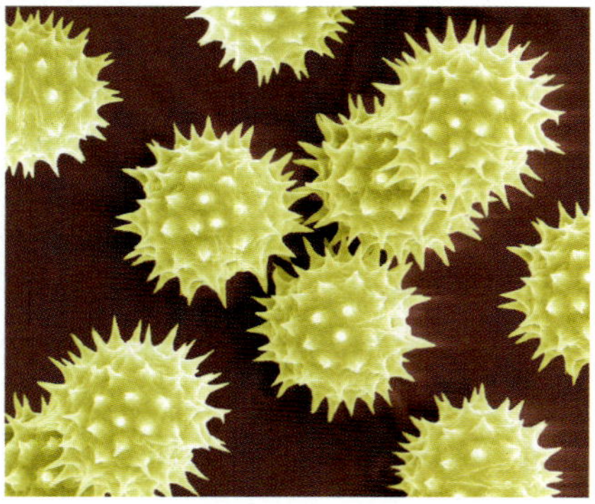
Pollen grains from a sunflower, seen through a microscope.

If you put some pollen grains onto a drop of water on a microscope slide, they float. When you look through the microscope, you will see that the pollen grains are moving about. They jiggle about in random directions. You will see the same effect if you sprinkle some dust on the water.

But we know that pollen grains and dust cannot swim or move by themselves. What makes the pollen grains and dust move?

We can explain the random movement of the pollen grains and the dust using the particle theory. The drop of water is made up of millions and millions of tiny water particles. These are much too small to see. The water particles are always moving. When they bump into the much bigger pollen grains or dust grains, they make them move.

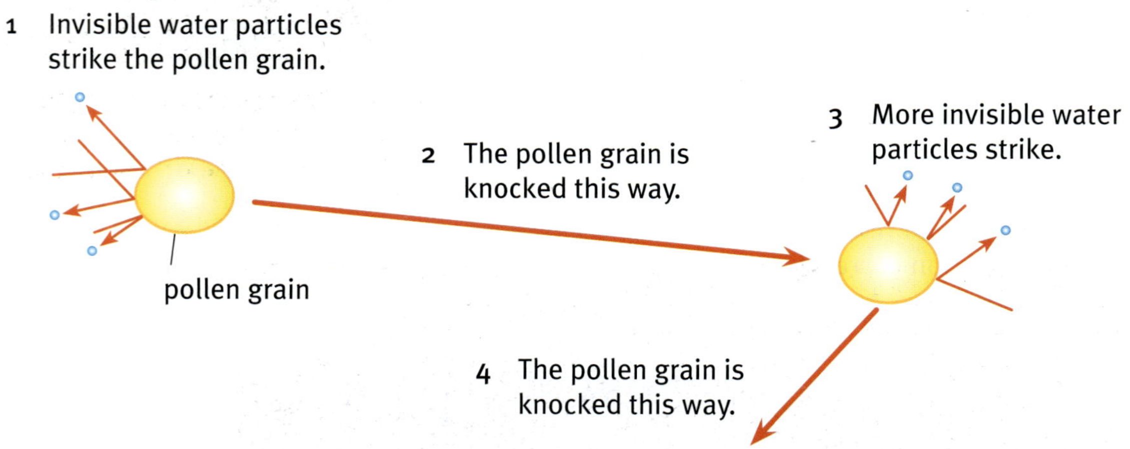

A pollen grain being hit by tiny water particles that are too small to see, making it jiggle about in a random way.

Discoveries about Brownian motion

Robert Brown was a Scottish biologist. In 1827, he watched pollen grains jiggling about under the microscope. He was the first scientist to describe this motion. It was given the name **Brownian motion**.

Robert Brown was puzzled by what he saw. He tried to think of an explanation. He thought that the pollen grains might be moving around actively, swimming in the water.

To test his idea, he watched some flecks of dust in water. The dust moved around just like the pollen grains. Brown knew that the dust was not alive, so he knew that his first idea was wrong.

At the time that Robert Brown lived, no-one knew that substances are made up of tiny particles in constant motion, so they could not explain Brownian motion. The particle theory of matter was first put forward in the 1870s. Only then could scientists explain what was causing Brownian motion.

Robert Brown (1773–1858).

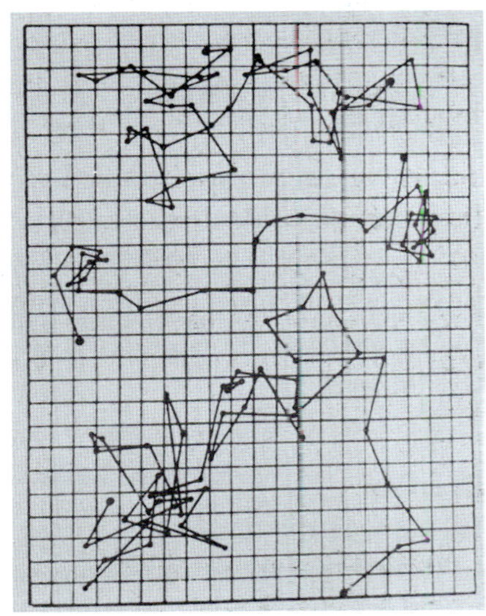

Robert Brown's drawings of the motion of three pollen grains, as he watched them through the microscope.

Questions

1. Describe the observation Robert Brown made.
2. How did Robert Brown explain what he saw?
3. How did he know his explanation was wrong?
4. Use particle theory to explain each of these observations:
   - **a** Pollen grains jiggle about faster when the temperature is higher.
   - **b** Pollen grains move about jerkily, in random directions.

Summary

- When viewed through a microscope, pollen grains and dust in water can be seen moving about randomly. This is called Brownian motion.
- Brownian motion is caused by tiny particles bumping into the pollen grains and dust.

5.5 Gas pressure

Particles in a gas

The particles in a gas are spread out far away from each other. The particles move about randomly all the time. They move very freely.

If the gas is inside a container, then the particles hit the walls of the container as they move around. Each time a particle collides with the wall, it causes a tiny force. There are huge numbers of particles colliding with the wall, and all these tiny forces add up. We call this **gas pressure**.

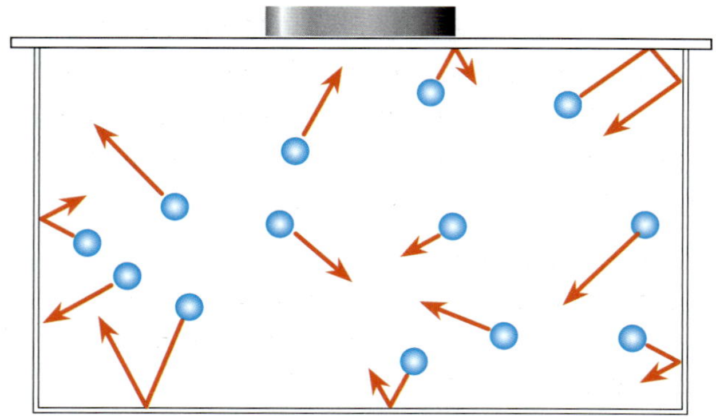

The particles move randomly in all directions. They bounce off all the walls of the container equally. So there is the same pressure on the side walls, the bottom and the top.

Less space, more pressure

What happens if you squeeze the gas particles into a smaller space? There are the same number of gas particles, but they will now hit the walls of their container more often. This makes the gas pressure greater.

The same thing happens when you squeeze **more** gas particles into a space. This is what happens when you inflate a football. You push more air into the space inside the football. There are more air particles inside the football, so there are more particles and more frequent collisions with the walls of the football. This increases the pressure inside the football.

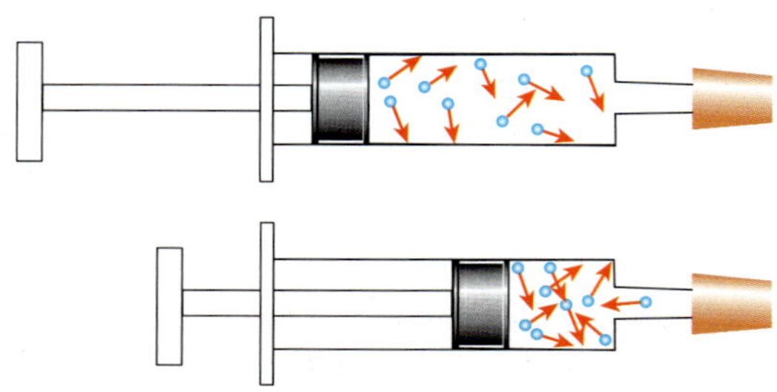

If a gas is squeezed into a smaller space, its particles hit the walls of the container more often, so the gas pressure increases.

Higher temperature, more pressure

If you warm a gas, the particles have more energy so they move about more quickly. They hit the walls of their container more often. This increases the pressure.

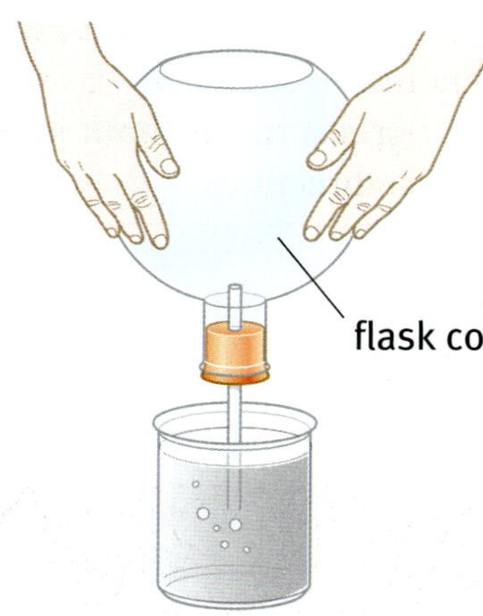

Warmth from your hands makes the air particles move around faster, causing more pressure. The gas forces its way into the water and you can see the bubbles.

Questions

1 What causes gas pressure?

2 If a gas is forced into a small space what happens to the pressure?

A+I 3 Describe what you think will happen to a balloon that has been fully inflated and is put into a hot place. Explain your prediction.

The collapsing bottle experiment

You cannot feel them, but the particles of air around you are bumping into your skin. These moving air particles cause pressure on you and on everything else on Earth.

If you use a vacuum pump to pump air out of a plastic bottle, there are fewer air particles inside the bottle. The frequency of collisions of particles with the walls on the inside of the bottle is less.

On the outside of the bottle there are lots of air particles colliding with the walls of the bottle. The pressure on the outside is greater than the pressure on the inside, so the walls of the bottle are pushed inwards.

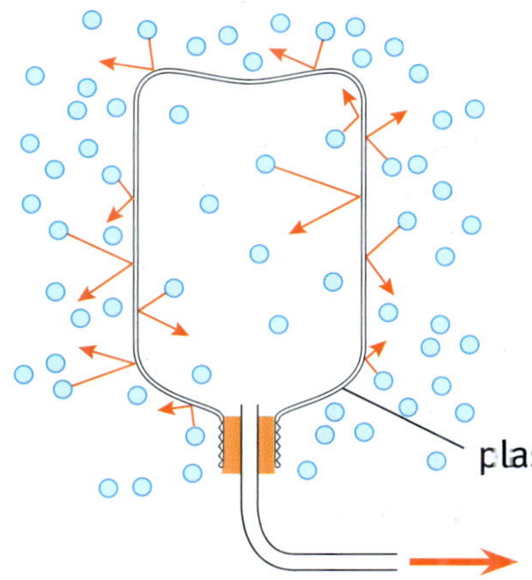

A vacuum pump removes air from the bottle.

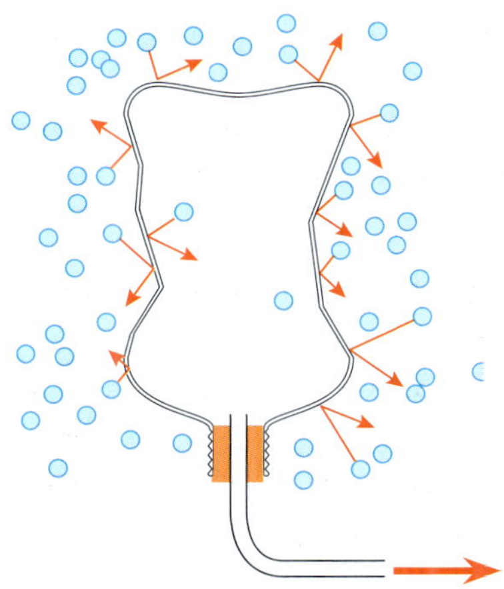
More frequent collisions outside cause the bottle to collapse.

Questions

4 You can buy bottled gas to use for cooking. This gas is squeezed into a small space and is sold in containers that are very strong.

a Explain why the containers need to be very strong.

A+I **b** Explain why the containers are heavy.

A+I **5** Bottled gas is stored outside buildings because there is a danger if they are in a fire. Explain what can happen to full gas bottles if they are involved in a fire.

Summary

- Gas particles move all the time.
- When gas particles bump into the side of their container they cause pressure.
- In a certain amount of space, the pressure is higher when there are more particles and when the temperature is higher.

Unit 5 End of unit questions

5.1 The picture shows a balloon containing air.

a Explain how the particles of air inside the balloon create pressure. [2]

b The air in the balloon is heated up by leaving it in a warm place. Give **two** effects that this has on the air particles. [2]

c Describe **one** way in which the balloon changes when it is left in a warm place. [1]

5.2 Hydrochloric acid produces a gas. So does ammonia solution. These two gases react when they meet to form a white solid called ammonium chloride.
Some cotton wool soaked in hydrochloric acid was placed at one end of a glass tube.
Some cotton wool soaked in ammonia solution was placed at the other end.
The diagram shows what happened.

a What is the name of the process by which the gases move along the tube? [1]

b Explain how this process takes place. [2]

c The particles of hydrochloric acid have a greater mass than the particles of ammonia. Suggest why the ammonium chloride is formed nearer to the hydrochloric acid end of the tube than the ammonia solution end. [2]

5.3 Sunita carries out an experiment to investigate diffusion. She uses water and a food dye to find out how the volume of water used affects the time the dye takes to spread evenly through the water.

Her prediction is that the more water she uses, the longer the time needed for the dye to spread through it.

a Which variable will she change? [1]

b Which variable should she measure? [1]

c State **two** variables that she will need to keep the same. [2]

d How will she ensure her results are reliable? [1]

e Draw a suitable results table for Sunita. [3]

f Sketch a graph to show what the results will look like if Sunita's prediction is true. Label the axes. [2]

6.1 Atoms

What are atoms?

Over 2000 years ago a Greek philosopher called Democritus suggested that everything was made up of tiny pieces. Democritus suggested that, if you could keep on cutting up a substance into smaller and smaller pieces, you would eventually end up with a very small piece that could not be cut up any more.

Democritus called his tiny pieces of matter **atoms**. 'Atom' means 'cannot be divided'.

We now know that atoms really do exist. Today, we can even see some of the larger kinds of atoms, using very special microscopes called scanning tunnelling microscopes. The photograph shows the atoms in some carbon nanotubes. ('Nano' means very, very small.)

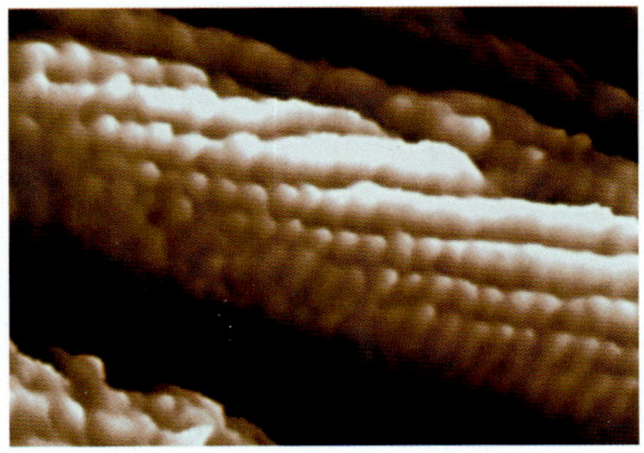

Carbon atoms seen with a scanning tunnelling microscope. Each little round bump is a single carbon atom. The photograph is magnified millions of times.

Different kinds of atoms

There are many different types of atoms. Scientists have discovered 94 different kinds of atoms that occur naturally in the Universe. Another 24 kinds of atoms have been made in laboratories.

Some substances are made up of just a single kind of atom. A substance that is made of just one kind of atom is called an **element**.

For example, carbon is made only of carbon atoms. Gold is made only of gold atoms. Silver is made only of silver atoms. Carbon, gold and silver are examples of elements.

Each type of atom has different properties. This is why different elements have different properties.

These Roman coins are made of pure gold.

If we could see some of the atoms in a coin, they would look something like this.

Questions

1. What are atoms? cannot be divided are small particals
2. If there are 94 different kinds of naturally occurring atoms, how many different naturally occurring elements are there? 94

Atoms joining together

Some substances are made up of individual atoms. For example, a piece of gold is made up of millions of individual gold atoms. Neon – which is a gas – is made of individual neon atoms.

Other substances are made up of little groups of atoms. The atoms join together in groups of two or more.

A group of atoms joined tightly together is called a **molecule**.

Some elements are made up of molecules. For example, in oxygen the atoms are joined together in pairs. A molecule of oxygen is made from two atoms of oxygen joined together.

Sulfur molecules are made up of eight sulfur atoms joined together. They can be joined in slightly different ways.

Atoms of neon.

Molecules of oxygen.

This sulfur molecule is made of eight sulfur atoms.

Activity 6.1
Modelling oxygen molecules

1. Imagine that you and all the other students in your class are oxygen atoms.
2. Form into an oxygen molecule by linking arms with a partner.
3. You are a gas so spread out among the other oxygen molecules and behave as gas molecules at room temperature.
4. Imagine the temperature has dropped so low that the oxygen has become a liquid. Change your arrangement and behaviour to model this.
5. Imagine that the temperature is even lower and that the oxygen has solidified. Change your arrangement and behaviour to model this.

Questions

A1 Describe and explain how molecules of oxygen gas behave when the room temperature falls.

A2 Describe and explain how molecules of oxygen behave when the temperature is so low that the oxygen becomes a liquid.

A3 Describe and explain how molecules of oxygen behave when the temperature is so low that the oxygen solidifies.

Summary

- All substances are made of small particles called atoms.
- Elements are made of one type of atom.
- Molecules are particles made of two or more atoms joined together.

6.2 Atoms and elements

Chemical symbols

We have seen that there are more than 100 different elements (including those that have been made in laboratories). Chemists use a shorthand way of referring to them. They have given each element a **symbol**.

- Sometimes the symbol is the first letter of the English name of the element. For example, the symbol for oxygen is **O**.
- Sometimes the symbol is the first letter of the English name of the element plus another letter from its name. For example, the symbol for helium is **He**.
- Sometimes the symbol is taken from the name of the element in another language. For example, the symbol for sodium is **Na**, from the old Latin name 'natrium'.
- The first letter of the symbol is always upper case. The second letter, if there is one, is always lower case.

The four photographs show four different elements and their symbols.

A flask of chlorine gas, symbol Cl.

Iodine crystals, symbol I.

Mercury, symbol Hg.

Sodium, symbol Na.

Elements on Earth

Some elements, such as copper and gold, have been known for thousands of years. Others, such as radium and aluminium, have only been discovered more recently.

Some elements are very abundant (common) on Earth, and some are rare. The pie chart shows the approximate proportions of the various elements that are found in the Earth's crust.

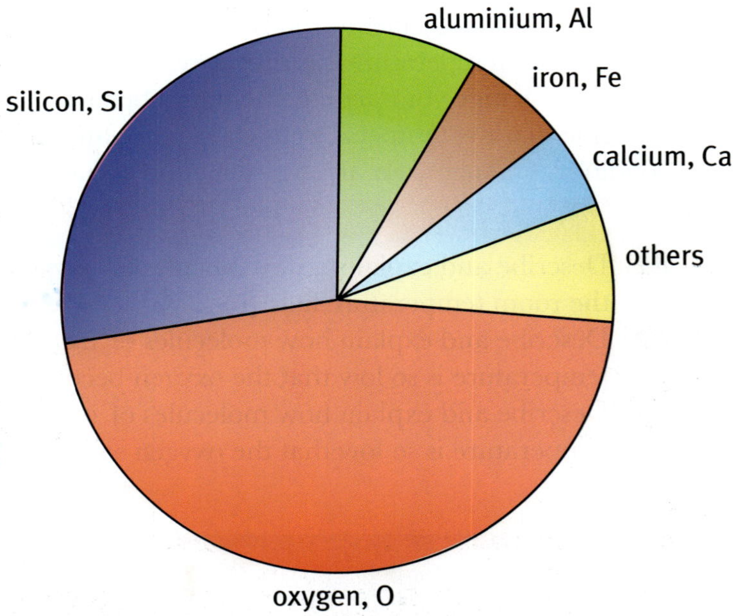

Questions

A+I **1** Which is the most common non-metal found in the Earth's crust?

A+I **2** Which is the most common metal found in the Earth's crust?

Activity 6.2
Researching an element

Choose **one** element. Your teacher may suggest some good ones to choose.

Find out some facts about your element. For example:

- When was the element first discovered? Who discovered it, and how?
- What is the symbol for your element? Why does it have this symbol?
- Where is this element found? Is it rare or abundant on Earth?
- Do humans make use of the element?

Make a short presentation about your element, which you can give to the rest of the class.

Is water an element?

People believed that water was an element until about 1800. It was only then that a scientist passed electricity through water and found that it split up into two gases – hydrogen and oxygen.

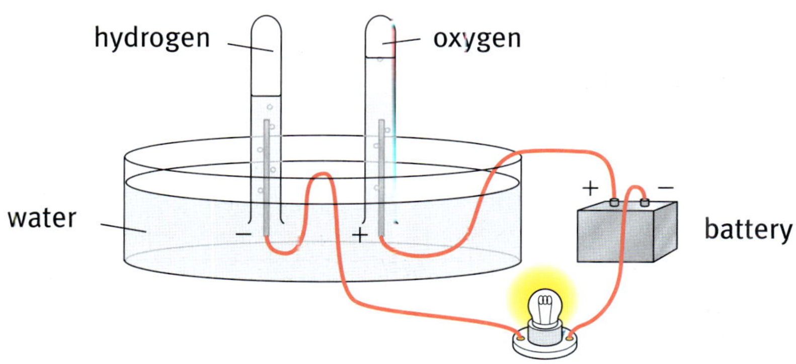

Electricity can be used to split water into the elements hydrogen and oxygen.

Questions

A+I
3 Suggest why people used to believe that water was an element.

4 Explain why the experiment shown in the diagram proves that water is not an element.

A+I
5 a Name **two** gases that are found in air.

b Is air an element? Explain your answer.

Summary

- Each element has its own chemical symbol.
- Some elements are very abundant on Earth, and other elements are rare.

6.3 The Periodic Table

Arranging the elements

Scientists have developed a very useful way of arranging the elements. This is called the **Periodic Table**.

The full Periodic Table, containing all of the 118 known elements, is very large and complex! (You may have one on the wall of your science laboratory.) For now, we will look at just the first 20 elements.

metals

non-metals

H hydrogen							He helium
Li lithium	Be beryllium	B boron	C carbon	N nitrogen	O oxygen	F fluorine	Ne neon
Na sodium	Mg magnesium	Al aluminium	Si silicon	P phosphorus	S sulfur	Cl chlorine	Ar argon
K potassium	Ca calcium						

Questions

1 What are the names of the elements with the symbols Mg, Be, Li and N?

2 Find the symbols for the elements aluminium, boron, fluorine and potassium.

Groups and periods

The Periodic Table is organised in rows and columns. The rows are called **periods**. The columns are called **groups**.

The atoms are organised so that, as you read across each row (period) from left to right, the atoms increase in mass. Hydrogen atoms have the smallest mass, then helium atoms, then lithium atoms.

Questions

3 Which element has atoms with the smallest mass?

4 Which of the first 20 elements in the Periodic Table has atoms with the greatest mass?

5 Give the names (not symbols) of **two** elements in the same period as magnesium.

6 Give the symbols (not names) of **two** elements in the same group as helium.

Metals and non-metals

The Periodic Table is organised so that elements with similar properties are close together.

In the diagram of the Periodic Table on the opposite page, all the elements that are metals are in yellow boxes. All the elements that are non-metals are in blue boxes.

Questions

To answer these questions, you will need to think back to your earlier work on metals and non-metals.

7 Describe **two** properties that the elements in the first two columns of the Periodic Table share with one another.
8 Describe **two** properties that the elements in the last two columns of the Periodic Table share with one another.
9 The photographs show six different elements. For each photograph, decide whether the element is a metal or non-metal. Give a reason for your choice.

A

B

C

D

E

F

Summary

- The elements are arranged in the Periodic Table.
- The elements are arranged in order of the mass of their atoms.
- Metals are towards the left hand side of the table, and non-metals on the right hand side.

6.4 Compounds

What is a compound?

We have seen that some substances are elements. An element is made up of only one kind of atom.

Many substances are made up of more than one kind of atom. If the different sorts of atoms are joined tightly together, then the substance is a **compound**.

The chemical term for two atoms joining tightly together is **bonding**. In a compound, two or more different kinds of atoms are bonded. For example, when sodium atoms bond with chlorine atoms, they form the compound **sodium chloride**.

Properties of elements and compounds

A compound is very different from the elements from which it is made. Once two different elements are bonded, they completely lose the properties of the individual elements. The compound has totally new properties.

The first two photographs show the two elements, sodium and chlorine. The third photograph shows the compound that is made when sodium atoms and chlorine atoms bond together. This compound – sodium chloride – is not at all like either sodium or chlorine.

You may have eaten some sodium chloride today. Sodium chloride is common salt. You would not want to eat any sodium or chlorine, though.

sodium

chlorine

sodium chloride

Questions

1 Describe **two** ways in which sodium chloride is different from sodium.

2 Describe **two** ways in which sodium chloride is different from chlorine.

Naming compounds

Each compound has a chemical name. The chemical name usually tells us the elements that the compound is made from.

There are some important rules to remember when naming compounds.

- If the compound contains a metal, then the name of the metal comes first in the name of the compound.

- If the compound contains a non-metal, the name of the non-metal is usually changed. For example, the compound made from sodium and chlorine is not sodium chlorine, but sodium chlor**ide**.
- When two elements form a compound the name often ends in 'ide'.

Questions

3 Which **two** elements are combined in sodium chloride?
4 Which **two** elements are combined in hydrogen sulfide?
5 Which **two** elements are combined in magnesium oxide?
6 A student wrote this name for a compound made of calcium and sulfur: sulfur calcium. What is wrong with this name? Write the correct name for the compound.

These are crystals of copper sulfate. Copper sulfate is a compound made up of copper, sulfur and oxygen.

Some compounds contain two different elements, plus a third element – oxygen. These compounds often have names ending with 'ate'.

For example, a compound of calcium, carbon and oxygen is called calcium carbonate.

Questions

7 Which **three** elements are combined in calcium nitrate?
8 Which **three** elements are combined in magnesium carbonate?
9 Which **three** elements are combined in lithium sulfate?

Sometimes, the name of a compound tells us how many of each kind of atom are bonded together.

Carbon dioxide is made up of molecules in which one carbon atom is joined to two oxygen atoms. 'Di' means 'two'.

Carbon monoxide is made up of molecules in which one carbon atom is joined to one oxygen atom. 'Mon' or 'mono' means 'one'.

A molecule of carbon dioxide.

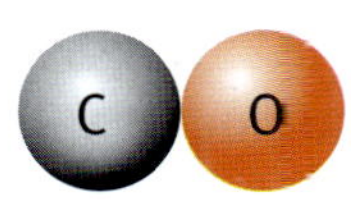

A molecule of carbon monoxide.

Summary

- A compound is formed when atoms of two or more elements bond together.
- A compound has completely different properties from the elements from which it is made.

6.5 Formulae

Particle models

It is easy to decide if a substance is a compound by looking at a particle diagram or model. If there are different kinds of atoms bonded together, then it is a compound.

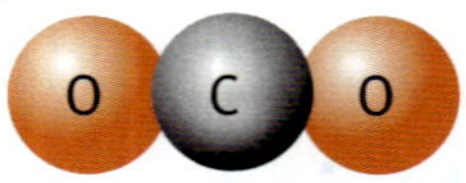

A molecule of carbon dioxide, CO_2.

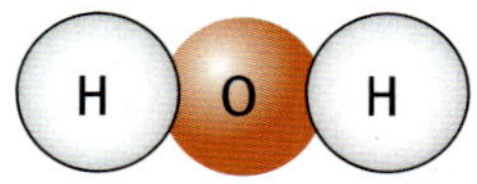

A molecule of water, H_2O.

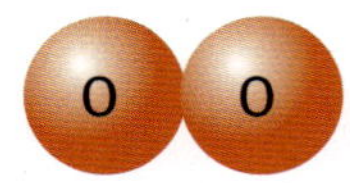

A molecule of oxygen, O_2.

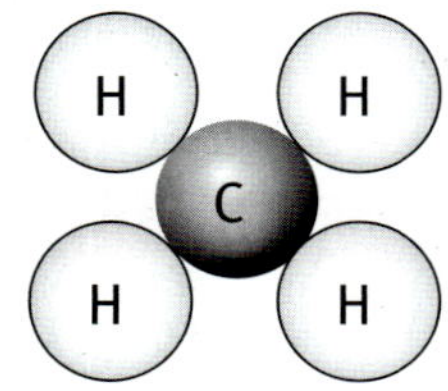

A molecule of methane, CH_4.

Carbon dioxide, water and methane are all compounds because their molecules are made up of different kinds of atoms. Oxygen is an element because the atoms in the molecule are both oxygen atoms.

Using formulae

Every compound has a chemical name. For example, the compound of sodium and chlorine is called sodium chloride.

Some compounds also have everyday names. For example, sodium chloride is also known as common salt.

Every compound also has a **formula**. The formula contains the symbols of the elements that are bonded together in the compound.

The table shows the chemical names and formulae of five compounds.

Chemical name	Formula	What the compound contains
calcium oxide	CaO	one calcium atom bonded to one oxygen atom
carbon dioxide	CO_2	one carbon atom bonded to two oxygen atoms
carbon monoxide	CO	one carbon atom bonded to one oxygen atom
hydrogen sulfide	H_2S	two hydrogen atoms bonded to one sulfur atom
calcium carbonate	$CaCO_3$	one calcium atom, one carbon atom and three oxygen atoms bonded together

Be very careful reading the symbols of the elements. For example, you do not want to confuse the symbol for carbon, C, with the symbol for calcium, Ca.

The little number written below and to the right of some symbols tells you how many atoms of each element are found in one molecule of the compound. If there is no number, that means there is just one atom of that element.

Questions

A+I **1** Which of these substances are elements, and which are compounds? Explain your answer.

K O_2 NaCl Al Ca $CaCl_2$ H_2

A+I **2** The formula for sulfur dioxide is SO_2.

a How many different elements are combined in sulfur dioxide?

b How many atoms of oxygen are combined with each atom of sulfur?

A+I **3** The formula for water is H_2O.

a Which **two** elements are combined in water?

b What does the formula tell you about the numbers of each kind of atom that are combined together?

4 The compound with the formula CO is called carbon monoxide. Suggest why it is not simply called 'carbon oxide'.

A+I **5** Suggest the names of the compounds with these formulae:

a MgO

b NaCl

c $CaCl_2$

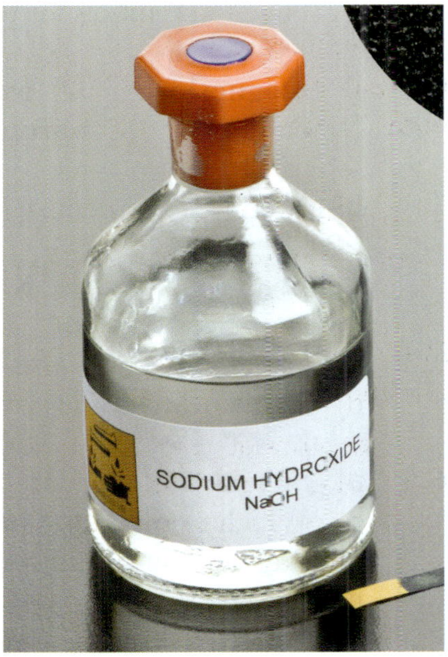

Why do you think bottles of chemicals usually have both their chemical name and their formula on the label?

Hydroxides

There is one more kind of compound that you need to know about. These are the **hydroxides.**

You may remember learning about sodium hydroxide and potassium hydroxide when you studied acids and alkalis. Hydroxides are **alkalis**. Sodium hydroxide and potassium hydroxide are both strong alkalis. When they dissolve in water, they form solutions that can neutralise acids.

The formula for sodium hydroxide is NaOH. The formula for potassium hydroxide is KOH.

Questions

6 Which **two** elements are contained in all hydroxides?

7 What is the name of the compound with the formula LiOH?

A+I **8** How many different elements are combined together in LiOH?

Summary

- Each compound has its own chemical formula.
- The formula tells you which elements the compound contains and how many atoms of each element are combined together.

Unit 6 End of unit questions

6.1 Choose the correct word from the list to match each description.

atom **compound** **element**
group **molecule** **period**

- **a** A substance made up of only one type of atom. [1]
- **b** The tiniest particle of an element that can exist. [1]
- **c** A group of atoms bonded tightly together. [1]
- **d** A substance made of more than one kind of atom bonded together. [1]
- **e** A column in the Periodic Table. [1]
- **f** A row in the Periodic Table. [1]

6.2 **a** Give the symbols for the following elements.

magnesium **oxygen** **hydrogen**
calcium **boron** [5]

b Name the elements with these symbols.

C **Na** **K** **Cl** **Si** [5]

c Explain why scientists use symbols for the elements. [1]

d Explain why some symbols – for example, Cl and Si – have two letters. [1]

6.3 **a** Suggest a name for a compound containing potassium and chlorine. [1]

b Which elements are present in the compound aluminium sulfate? [1]

c Suggest a name for a compound containing calcium, carbon and oxygen. [1]

d What is the difference between a molecule of carbon dioxide and a molecule of carbon monoxide? [2]

6.4 Here are the formulae of four substances.

$MgSO_4$ **H_2O** **N_2** **O_2**

a Name the element that occurs in three of these substances. [1]
b Name the element present in these substances that is a metal. [1]
c Give the chemical symbols for magnesium and hydrogen. [2]
d List the types and numbers of the atoms in one molecule of H_2O. [2]

6.5 The following chemicals are either elements or compounds. Copy the table and tick **one** box for each substance, to show which it is. The first one has been done for you.

Name and formula of substance	Element	Compound
water, H_2O		✓
sulfur dioxide, SO_2		
sodium, Na		
carbon, C		
hydrogen, H_2		

[4]

6.6 The diagrams show the atoms in four different substances. Each circle represents an atom.

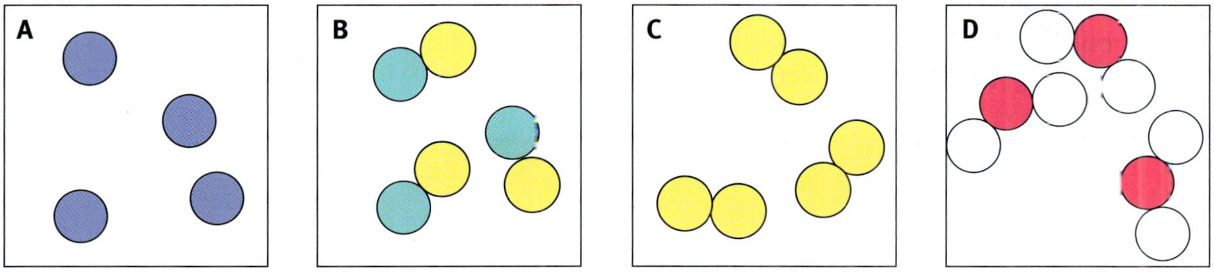

Copy and complete the table, to show which diagrams represent elements and which diagrams represent compounds.

Elements	Compounds

[4]

7.1 Compounds and mixtures

We have seen that, when atoms of elements bond tightly together to form compounds, the properties of the compound are completely different from those of the elements that it is made from.

For example, iron is a metal. It is hard, coloured grey, strong, conducts heat and electricity and is magnetic.

Sulfur is a non-metal. It is yellow, brittle, does not conduct heat or electricity and is not magnetic.

When these two elements are heated they combine together to form the compound iron sulfide. Iron sulfide is not magnetic and does not conduct heat or electricity.

The iron is shown here as small pieces called filings.

The sulfur, shown here as powder, is yellow and not hard.

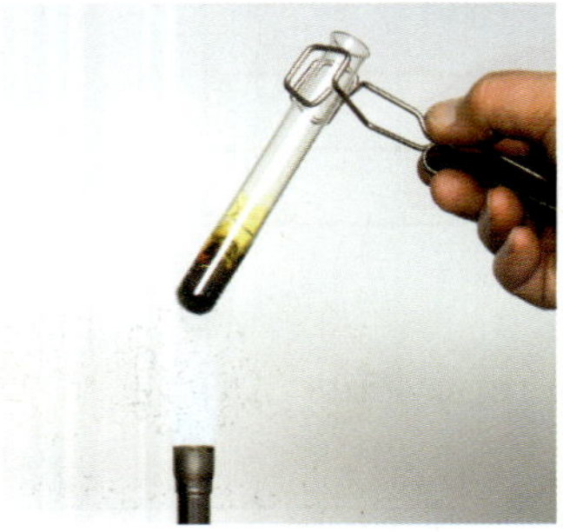

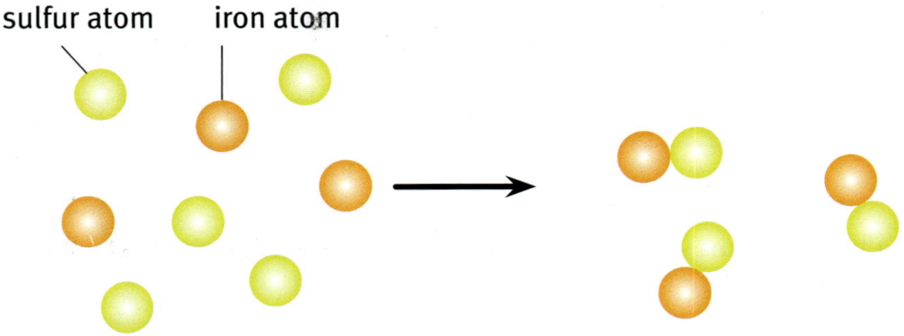

When iron and sulfur are heated together, iron atoms and sulfur atoms bond together to form the compound iron sulfide.

Activity 7.1A

Mixing iron and sulfur

SE

Safety: Do not touch your face or eyes after touching the iron filings. The pieces have sharp edges and can damage your skin and eyes. Wear safety glasses.

1 Place some iron filings in a beaker.
2 Add some yellow powdered sulfur.
3 Stir the mixture.

You now have a mixture of iron and sulfur. The iron and sulfur still have their properties. They have not been changed chemically in any way.

The different properties of the two elements can be used to separate them from the mixture.

4 Use a magnet to remove the iron filings from the sulfur.

Activity 7.1B

Making a compound from iron and sulfur

SE

1. Make a mixture of iron and sulfur.
   Safety: Wear safety glasses. Carry this out in a well-ventilated room.
2. Heat some of the iron and sulfur mixture in a boiling tube, as in the photograph on the opposite page. Stop heating as soon as the mixture starts to glow. The iron and sulfur will combine together and form iron sulfide.
3. Leave the tube to cool.
4. Test with a magnet.

Questions

A1 Describe the appearance of:

a a mixture of iron and sulfur

b the iron sulfide.

A2 Could you remove the iron from the iron sulfide using a magnet? Explain your answer.

Air is a mixture

When you mix iron and sulfur together, you are making a mixture of two elements.

Mixtures can also contain compounds. For example, air is a mixture of several different elements and compounds. Air contains nitrogen, oxygen, carbon dioxide, water vapour and small quantities of some other gases.

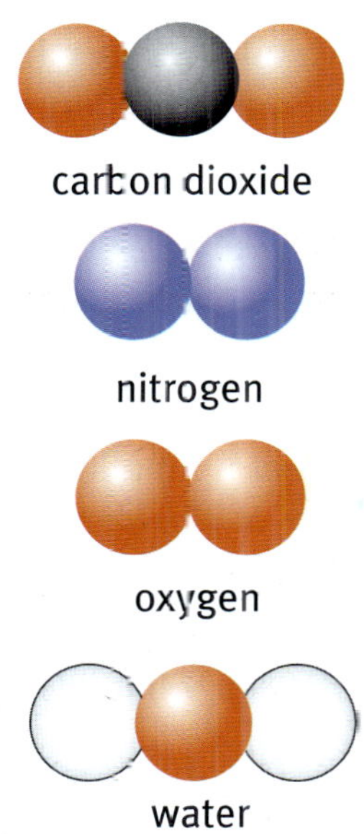

Particle diagrams of some of the gases in air.

Questions

Look at the particle diagrams of the gases in air to answer these questions.

1. List the formulae of the four different gases shown in the diagrams.
2. Which of the gases in air are elements? Explain how you can tell.
3. Which of the gases in air are compounds? Explain how you can tell.
4. Explain why air is a mixture, not a compound.

Summary

- Mixtures contain different elements and/or compounds that are not joined together chemically (bonded).
- A compound has different properties to the elements from which it is formed. In a mixture, each element or compound still has its usual properties.

7.2 More about mixtures

In science the word 'pure' describes something only containing a single substance. Pure water contains just water, with no other substances mixed with it.

A **mixture** is not pure. It is made up of different kinds of particles that are mixed together. The mixture may be of elements, compounds or both. There are solids, liquids and gases that are mixtures.

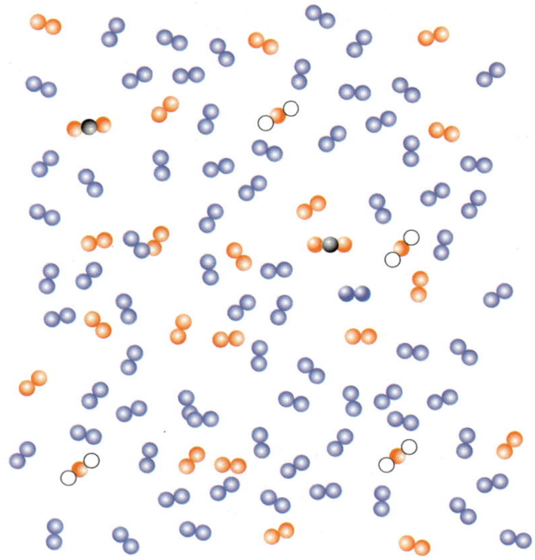

Air is a mixture of several elements and compounds.

Question

1 The diagram on the right shows some particles in air. The orange circles represent oxygen atoms. The blue circles represent nitrogen atoms. The white circles represent hydrogen atoms. The black circles represent carbon atoms.

  a Which is the most common element in air?

  b How many different kinds of molecules are shown in the diagram? Can you name them all?

Metal mixtures

Metal mixtures are called **alloys**. Alloys are made by mixing different metals together and then melting them. The atoms of the different metals mix together, but they do not bond together to form a new compound.

Bronze is an alloy made by mixing copper and tin. Bronze is harder than either copper or tin.

Steel is an alloy, but a rather odd one because one of the elements in the mixture is not a metal. Steel is a mixture of iron and carbon. Sometimes chromium and nickel are also added to steel. This type of steel does not rust and is used for cutlery.

People learnt to melt copper and tin together to make bronze a very long time ago. This bronze helmet was made in what is now Iraq, more than four thousand years ago.

Questions

2 Explain what an alloy is.

3 Give **two** examples of alloys.

4 If you had some copper and tin, how would you make bronze?

5 Suggest why a helmet made of bronze is more useful than a helmet made of copper or tin.

A+I

Mineral water is a mixture

If you look at the label on a bottle of mineral water, you will see that many minerals are listed. There is more than just water in the bottle. The bottle contains a mixture of water and other substances.

These minerals are **dissolved** in the water. The mineral water is a **solution**. A litre of water may have about 0.5 g of minerals dissolved in it. You will find out more about solutions on pages **100–103**.

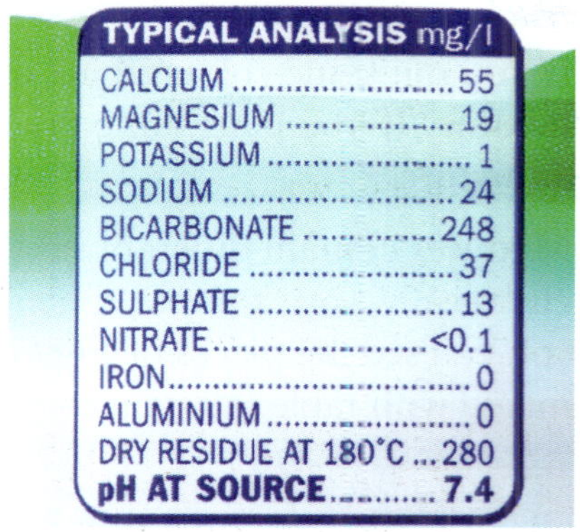

TYPICAL ANALYSIS mg/l	
CALCIUM	55
MAGNESIUM	19
POTASSIUM	1
SODIUM	24
BICARBONATE	248
CHLORIDE	37
SULPHATE	13
NITRATE	<0.1
IRON	0
ALUMINIUM	0
DRY RESIDUE AT 180°C	280
pH AT SOURCE	**7.4**

The label shows the minerals found in mineral water.

Question

6 Look at the picture of the mineral water label. List the **three** most abundant minerals in this bottle of mineral water. Bicarbonate, chloride, Calcium

Activity 7.2
Is it a mixture?

SE

Your teacher will give you a container of water. Your task is to discover if there is any other substance mixed with the water.

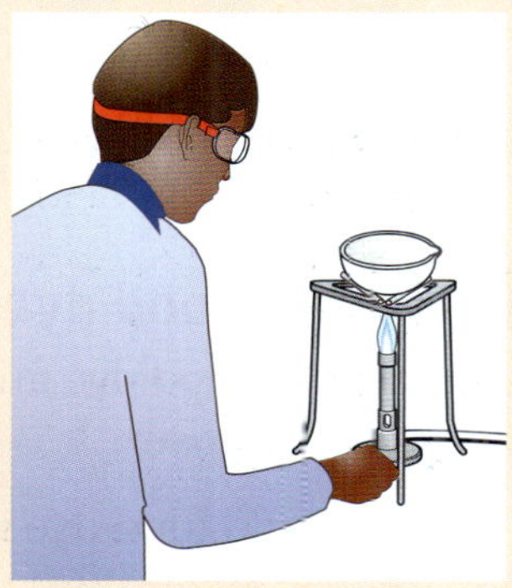

1 Place the water in an evaporating basin and heat until it boils. **Safety**: Wear safety glasses.

2 Continue to heat gently. **Safety**: The solution may start to spit.

3 When you have evaporated off some of the water (or the solution starts to spit) remove from the heat and leave the evaporating basin to cool. **Safety**: Do not touch the evaporating basin with your hands – use tongs.

The water may take a day or two to evaporate completely. It will depend on the temperature.

Questions

A1 Use ideas about particles to explain why the water evaporated.

A2 What was left in the evaporating basin? white layer

A3 Where has this substance come from? from water

A4 Was the water you were given pure water, or was it a mixture of water and other substances? Explain your answer. Because of the white layer on the bottom.

A5 Why did you need to wear safety glasses? So the water doesn't goes into your eyes.

Summary

- Alloys are mixtures of metals.
- Mineral water and sea water are mixtures.

7.3 Separating mixtures

Making mixtures

If you put some coloured ink or food dye into some water, you have made a mixture. If you pour some dried peas and some rice into a pan you have made a mixture.

Mixtures contain different substances that are not combined together chemically. For example, if some iron filings are mixed with powdered sulfur, you can see the pieces of grey iron and yellow sulfur. If powdered carbon is mixed with table salt, you can see the black carbon powder and the white salt.

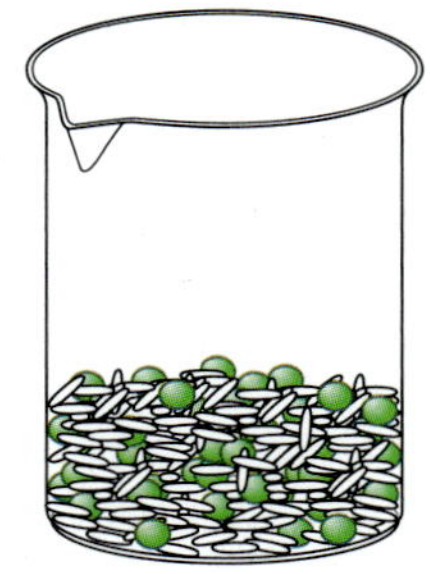

A mixture of rice and peas.

Question

A+I

1 How could you separate the rice and peas?

How can we separate mixtures?

Mixtures can be separated quite easily because the different substances in the mixture have not combined together to make a new substance. They still each have their own properties. To separate the iron and sulfur mixture in Activity **7.1A**, you used a magnet to pick up the iron because iron is magnetic and sulfur is not.

The evaporating dish in the diagram contains a mixture of water and copper sulfate. If it is left in a warm room the water evaporates into the air and leaves the copper sulfate behind in the dish.

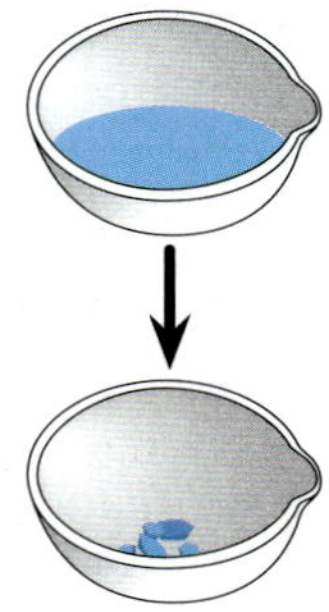

The water evaporates and leaves the copper sulfate in the evaporating dish.

Separating food dye and water

A mixture of food dye and water can be separated using a piece of apparatus called a **condenser**. It is used to separate mixtures of two liquids.

The water and food dye mixture is heated and boils. The liquid water changes to a gas (steam) and this travels along the tube into the condenser.

The cold water that is circulating around the outside of the condenser cools the gas down. This makes the gas condense back to liquid water, which is collected in the beaker. The food dye remains in the heated container.

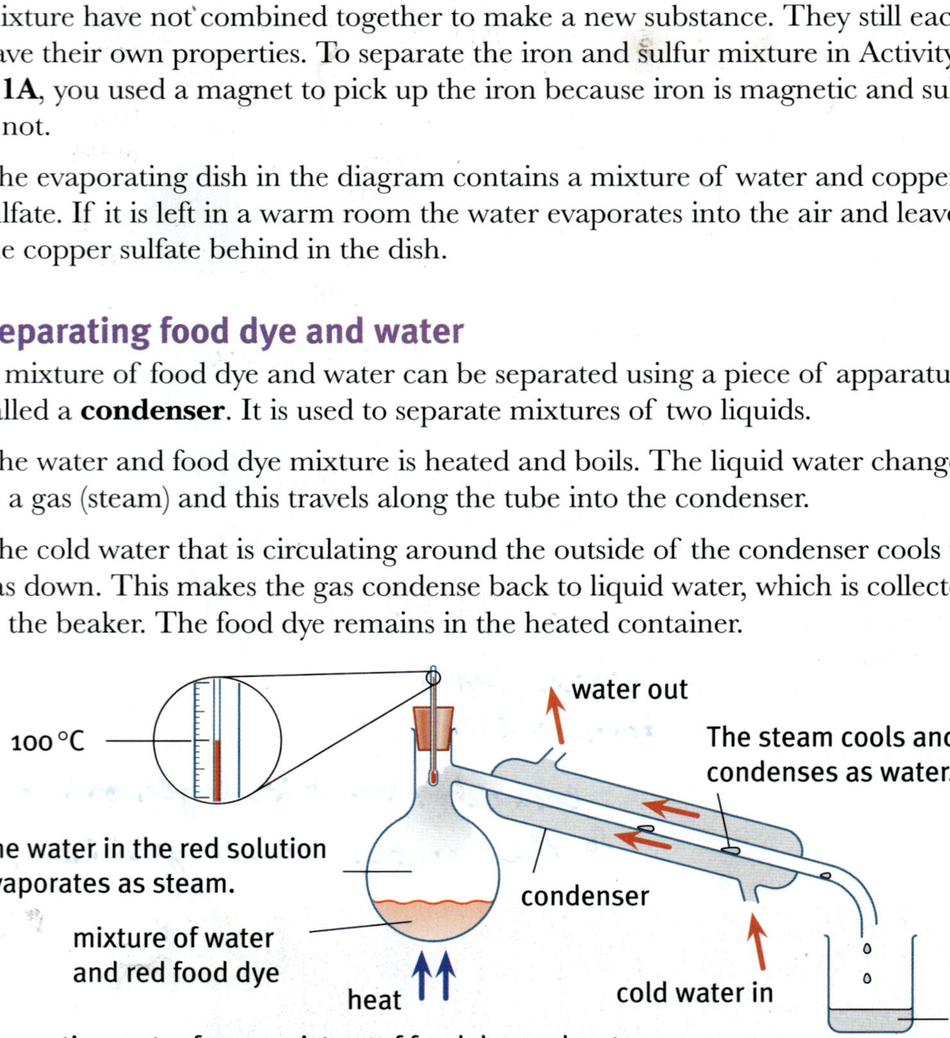

Separating water from a mixture of food dye and water.

Questions

2 Explain how the water in the flask changes to a gas.
3 Explain how the steam changes back into a liquid inside the condenser.

Activity 7.3
Separating sandy, salty water

SE

Your teacher will give you a mixture of water, salt and sand. Your task is to separate the mixture.

1. Prepare a filter paper and place it in a filter funnel. Place the filter funnel in a conical flask. Pour the mixture into the funnel. Take care to add it slowly so that the mixture does not go down the outside of the filter paper. Do not disturb the wet filter paper – it easily tears. When you have filtered all the mixture, leave the filter paper in a warm place to dry.
2. Place the clear liquid (filtrate) from the conical flask in an evaporating basin. Heat this gently. Wear safety glasses. When this liquid starts to spit remove it from the heat and leave in a warm place to evaporate.

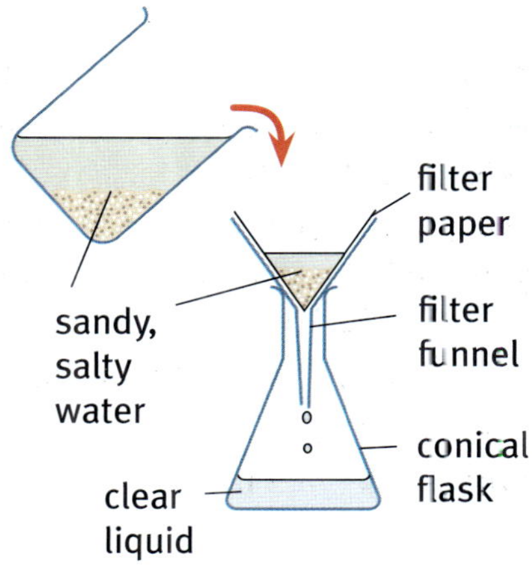

Separating the sand.

Questions

A1 Suggest why the sand remains in the filter paper.
A2 One group of students thought their mixture was taking too long to filter so they used a pencil to stir it up while it was in the filter paper. Explain why this is not a good idea.
A3 What safety precautions should you take when heating the salty water?
A4 How could you obtain the water from your mixture?
A5 The salt left in the evaporating basin is often a little dirty. Suggest what you could do to get cleaner salt.

A+I

Summary
- The properties of the different substances in a mixture can be used to separate them.

7.4 Chromatography

What is chromatography?

Black ink looks as if it is just one colour. In fact, it is a mixture of different colours. You can separate out the different colours using a technique called **chromatography**.

Special paper, rather like filter paper or blotting paper, is used.

Here a small drop of ink has been placed on the paper. The water in the beaker has soaked up into the paper. As the water moves up the paper, the colours in the ink separate out.

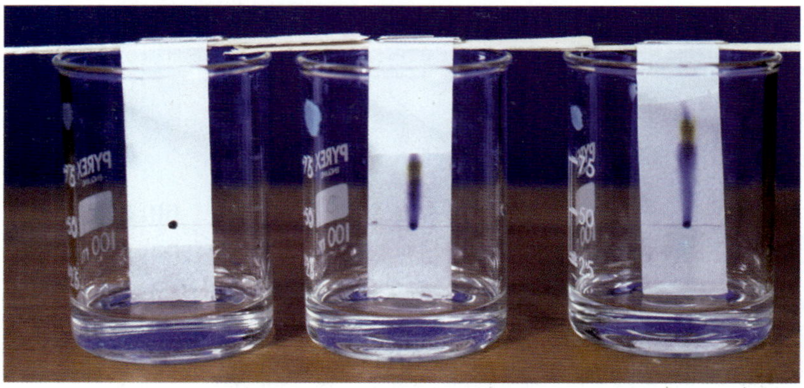

The resulting paper is called a **chromatogram**.

The colours separate because the water dissolves the ink. As the water moves up the paper, it carries the particles of ink with it. Different kinds of ink particles are carried different distances before they get left behind on the paper.

Some ink does not dissolve in water – for example, the ink in a permanent marker pen. To separate the colours you have to use a liquid that the colours do dissolve in – for example, alcohol.

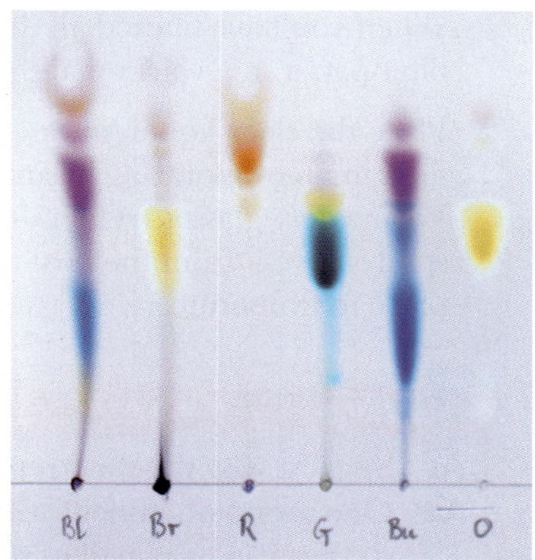

A chromatogram showing the colours in felt tip pens.

Using chromatography

Chromatography is used to study the dyes used in food. Some food dyes contain only one substance. Others contain a mixture of different coloured substances.

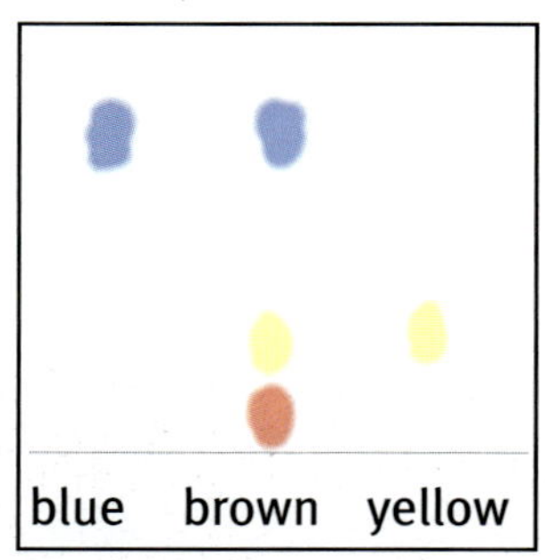

Chromatography results for some food dyes.

Questions

1 Which food dyes in the diagram on the right only contain one colour? Yellow, blue

2 Which food dye contains three colours? Brown

Activity 7.4
Separating the colours in ink

SE

1 Take a strip of chromatography paper.
2 Draw a pencil line about 1 cm from the end of the paper.
3 Place a spot of the ink on the pencil line. The spot should be as small as possible. Dry the spot and then add a little more ink.
4 Place about 2 cm depth of water in the bottom of a beaker.
5 Hang the paper over a spill or glass rod so that the end with the ink spot is just in the water. Make sure that the ink spot stays above the level of the water.
6 Watch what happens as the water moves up the strip of paper.

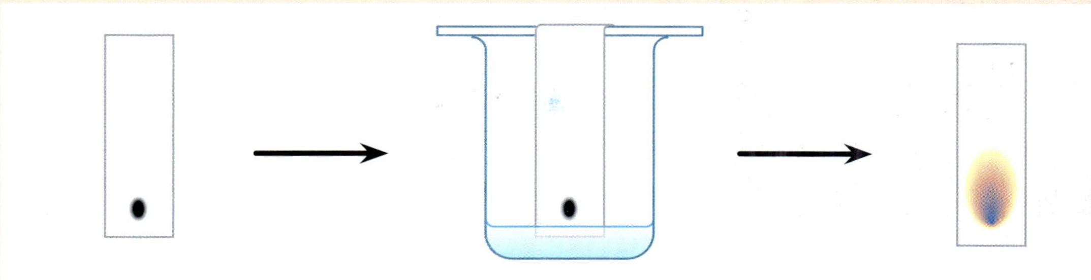

7 Remove the strip of paper carefully before the water reaches the top.
8 Allow the strip to dry and then stick it into your book.

You can try this with all sorts of coloured liquids. Different inks and food dyes, especially from sweets or fruit syrup, are very good.

Questions

A1 Why did you use a line drawn in pencil on the paper?
A2 Why was it important not to let the ink spot be under the level of the water?
A3 Why was it important to remove the strip of paper before the water level reached the end of the strip?
A4 Describe your results.

Summary

- Mixtures of different coloured dyes or inks can be separated using chromatography.
- Chromatography has a wide range of uses.

7.5 Solutions

When you place a lump of sugar or some salt in water it seems to disappear. This is called **dissolving**. You get a colourless **solution**. The substance that dissolves is called the **solute**. The substance that it dissolves into is called the **solvent**.

A solution is a mixture. A sugar solution is a mixture of water and sugar. Although the sugar seems to disappear, it is still there. The sugar molecules have simply spread out among the water molecules.

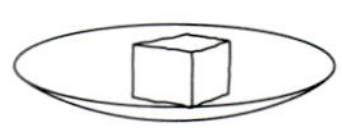

Sugar is the solute.

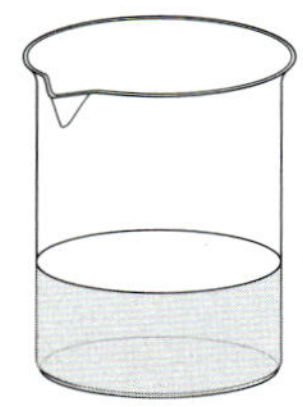

Water is the solvent.

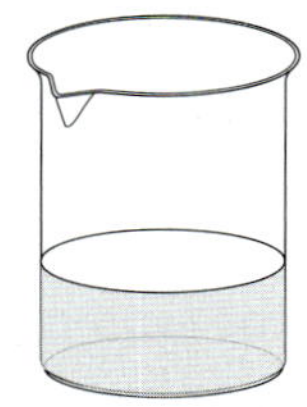

The sugar and water mixture is the solution.

The diagrams below show what happens to sugar molecules when they dissolve.

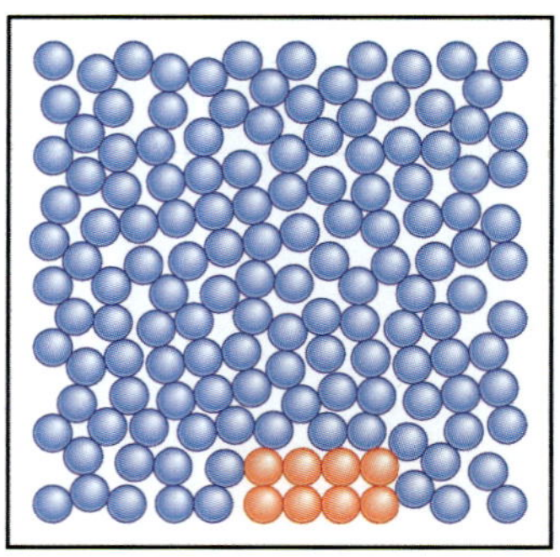

The sugar crystal is visible because the molecules are tightly packed together.

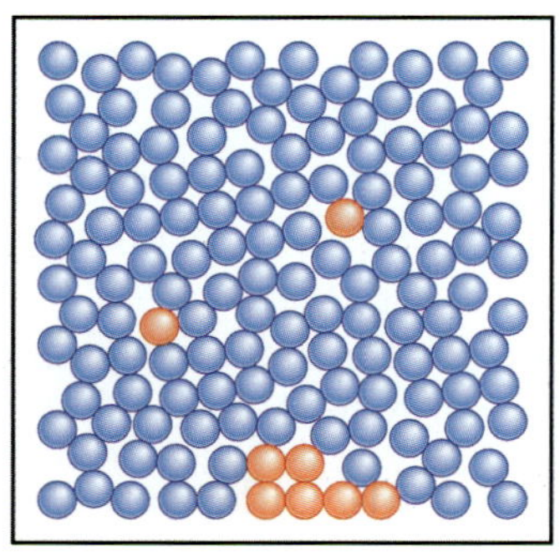

The water molecules bump into the groups of sugar molecules and separate them.

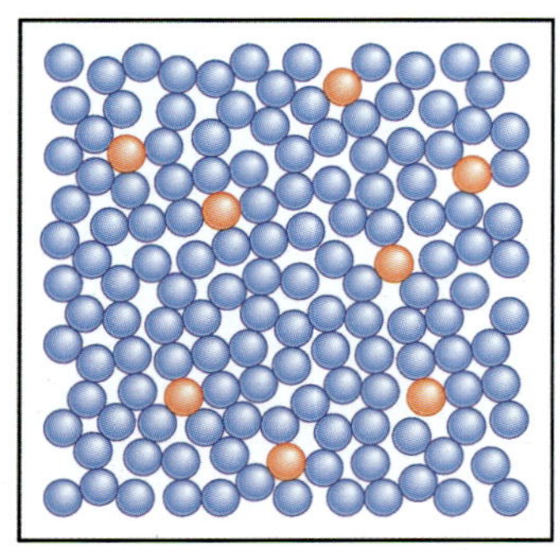

The water molecules separate all the sugar molecules. The molecules are too small to be seen so the solution looks transparent.

If you dissolve a coloured salt such as copper sulfate, the solution formed is coloured.

All solutions are **transparent**. This means you can see through them. A liquid like milk is not a solution because it is not transparent.

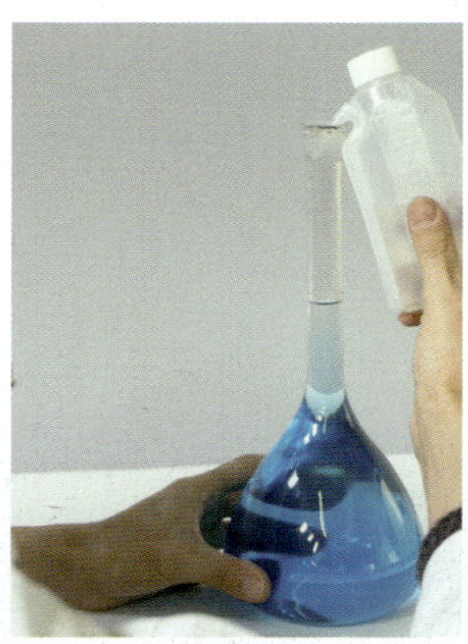

Copper sulfate forms a solution. It is transparent.

Milk is not a solution. You can tell this because it is opaque.

Activity 7.5
Dissolving

SE

1. Place a watch glass or piece of paper on a top pan balan[...] mass. Add some salt. This is the solute. Find the mass of [...] the mass.
2. Remove the salt. Now place a beaker of water on the top [...] find the mass of the water and beaker. The water is the s[...] the mass.
3. Add the salt to the water and find the mass.

Questions

A1 What was the mass of the salt used?
A2 What was the mass of the water and the beaker?
A3 What was the mass of the solution and the beaker?
A4 What does this tell you about the salt solution?

When salt is added to water and it dissolves, it has not disappeared. The salt particles are still in the water. The mass of a solution equals the total mass of the solute and the solvent. This is true for any solution.

mass of solute + mass of solvent = mass of solution

No mass has been lost. This is called **conservation of mass**.

Questions

1. In a solution of sugar and water, which is the solvent and which is the solute?
2. What mass of salt solution is made when 9 g of salt is dissolved in 50 g of water? Explain how you worked out your answer.

A+I

3. A green powder was placed into a beaker of water. After it was stirred the water looked cloudy and lumps of powder could still be seen. Has a solution been formed? Explain your answer.

Summary
- A solute dissolves in a solvent to form a solution.
- A solute does not disappear when a solution is formed. The particles of the solute have been separated and are so small that they cannot be seen.
- Mass is conserved when a solution is formed.

7.6 Solubility

Solutions, solvents and solutes

A solution is made when a solute is dissolved in a solvent. A **concentrated** solution has more particles of the solute dissolved in it than a **dilute** solution.

A solid that dissolves in a solvent such as water is said to be soluble. Sodium chloride (common salt) and sugar are **soluble**.

A solid that will not dissolve in water is **insoluble**. Iron filings are insoluble.

If you keep on adding a soluble solid to a beaker of water, there comes a point when no more of the solid will dissolve. You have made a **saturated solution**.

Some soluble substances are more soluble than others. If you have 100 cm^3 of water, you would be able to dissolve a lot of sodium chloride in it, but only a tiny bit of lead chloride. Sodium chloride has a greater **solubility** than lead chloride.

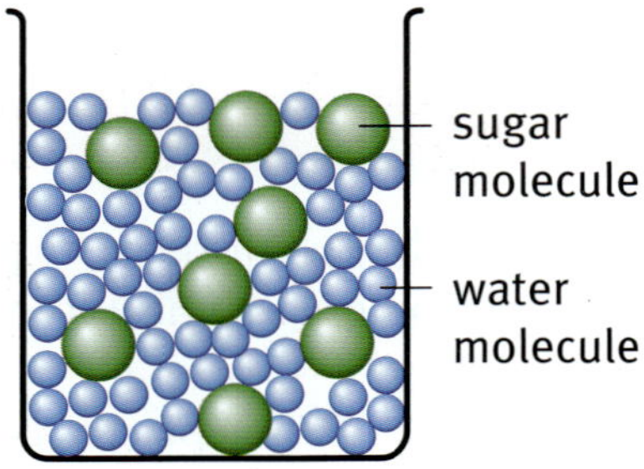

A concentrated solution of sugar has a lot of sugar particles.

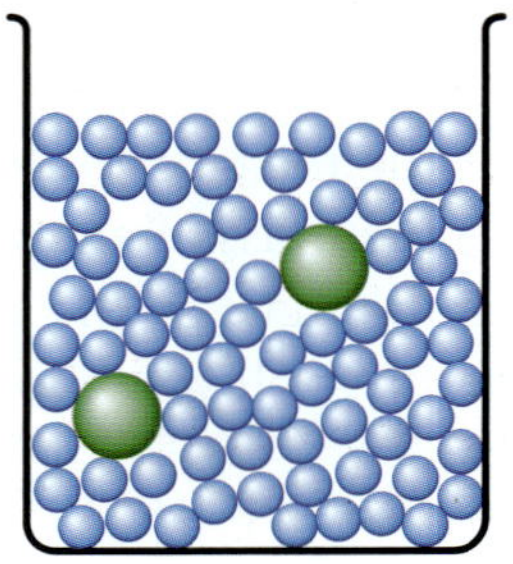

A dilute solution of sugar has fewer sugar particles.

Activity 7.6
Solubility in water

SE

In this activity you will use the various solutes provided and investigate their solubility in water. You will use water at room temperature.

1 Place a measured volume of water in a number of test tubes. Use a different test tube for each of the solutes.
2 Add the first solute to the water. Count how many spatulas you add until no more will dissolve.
3 Repeat for the other solutes.
4 Record your results in a table.

Questions

A1 Which was the most soluble of the solutes you used?
A2 Which was the least soluble of the solutes you used?
A3 In this investigation you used spatulas as a measure of the quantity of solute added. Suggest another way of measuring the solute used which would improve the accuracy of the results.

Solubility

To compare the solubility of different solutes you must measure how much of each solute will dissolve in 100 g of the solvent.

Solute	Solubility / grams of solute in 100 g of water at 20 °C
sodium chloride	36
copper sulfate	32
calcium chloride	74
potassium chlorate	7
lead chloride	1

Questions

1. What is a saturated solution?
2. How much potassium chlorate would dissolve in 200 g water at 20 °C?
3. Use the data in the table to draw a bar chart to show the solubility of the various solutes in water at 20 °C.

Temperature and solubility

Most solutes will dissolve more quickly and easily in hot water than in cold water. You can also dissolve a greater mass of the solute in hot water than in the same volume of cold water. In other words, as temperature increases, the solubility of most solutes also increases.

For example, if you have 100 g of water at 20 °C, you can dissolve 204 g of sugar in it. If you heat the water to 80 °C, you can dissolve 362 g of sugar in it.

Questions

4. How much sugar can be dissolved in 250 g of water at 20 °C?
5. How much more sugar can be dissolved if the 250 g of water is heated to 80 °C?

Water is not the only solvent. Some substances that are insoluble in water will dissolve in other solvents. Some types of ink are soluble in alcohol but not water.

Summary

- Solubility is a measure of how much of a solute will dissolve in a solvent.
- A saturated solution is one that can have no more solute dissolved in it.
- Solubility is affected by temperature.

7.7 Solubility investigation

Dissolving salt in water

These students are discussing ways to investigate how temperature affects the amount of salt that will dissolve in water. They are trying to think of the different things that could affect the results. These are the **variables**.

Questions

SE **1** Which variables have the students identified?

SE **2** How do you think the volume of water will affect the results if it is not kept the same? Explain your answer.

Carrying out the investigation

The students decide to count the number of spatulas of salt that will dissolve in 50 cm^3 of water. They will repeat the experiment at different temperatures from 20 °C to 80 °C.

The variable they change is the temperature of the water.

They will count the number of spatulas of salt that will dissolve. This is the variable that depends on the water temperature.

The volume of water is a variable that the students keep the same so that the test is fair.

The variable you change is called the **independent variable**. The variable you measure as the result is called the **dependent variable**. The variables you keep the same are called the **control variables**.

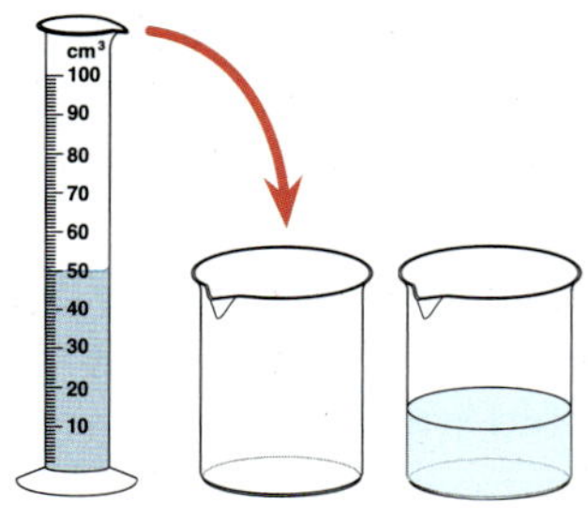

The volume of water is kept the same.

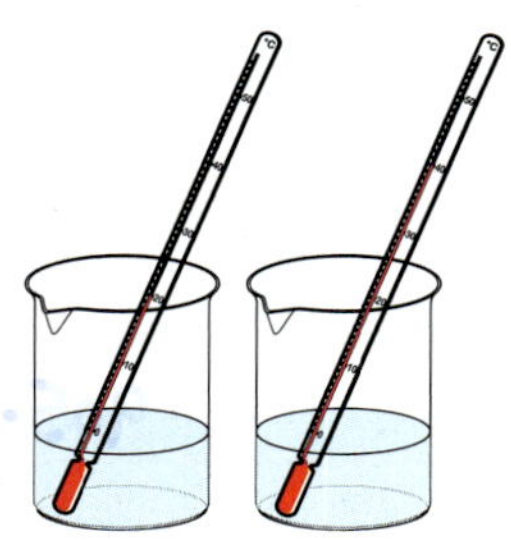

The temperature is changed.

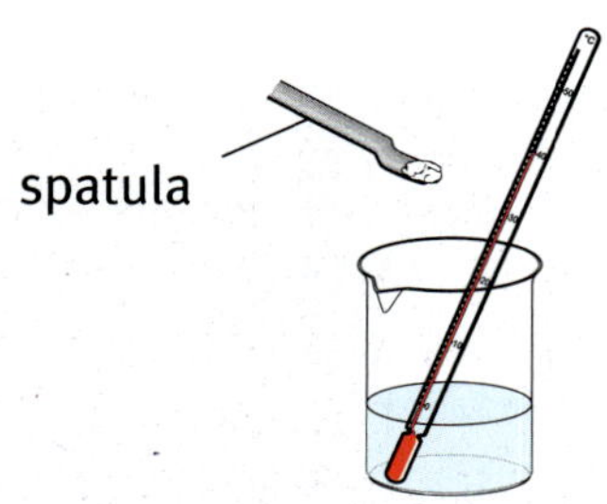

The number of spatulas used is measured.

Plotting a graph of your results

When you plot a graph of your results the independent variable always goes along the horizontal axis.

The dependent variable always goes up the vertical axis.

Questions

SE 3 Which variable is the independent variable in the students' experiment?

SE 4 Which variable is a control variable in the students' experiment? Is there any other variable that needs to be controlled? (Hint: think about the spatula.)

SE 5 Which is the dependent variable in this experiment?

SE 6 What would be the label on the vertical axis of a graph of the results of this experiment?

Activity 7.7A

Planning an investigation

SE You are going to investigate the effect of changing the temperature of water on the amount of salt that can be dissolved in it.

Discuss in your group the plan for your investigation.

You need to consider the variables. You need to consider:

- how you will change the temperature of the water and keep it at that temperature while you add the salt.
- the **range** of temperatures you will use. (The highest and lowest temperatures you will use.)
- the **interval** between the temperatures. (Will you use 10 °C gaps between the temperatures or 5 °C?)

What will you do to keep safe as you do your investigation?

You need to prepare a table for the results.

Discuss the plan with your teacher before you carry it out.

Activity 7.7B

Carrying out the investigation

SE 1 Carry out the investigation.

2 Record the results in a suitable table.

3 Plot an appropriate graph.

4 Explain what you have found out.

Summary

- The independent variable is the variable you change.
- The dependent variable is the one you measure. It changes as a result of the change in the independent variable.
- A control variable is one that you keep the same, to make the investigation fair.

Unit 7 End of unit questions

7.1 The diagrams in the boxes show different arrangements of particles.

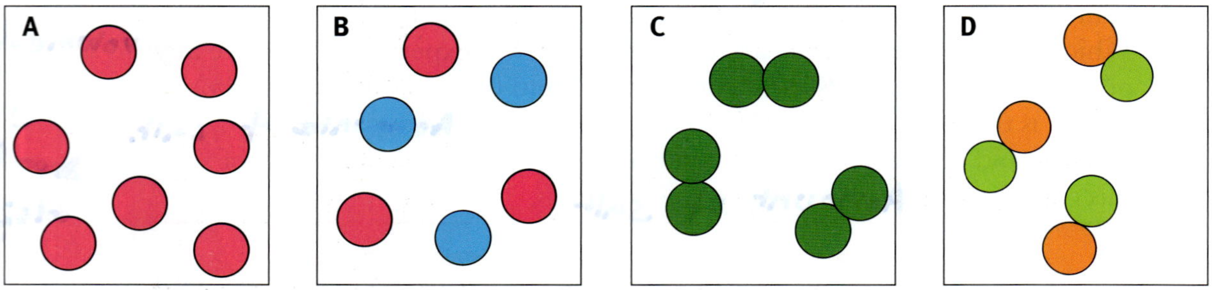

Give the letter of the diagram which represents:

a molecules of a compound [1]

b molecules of an element [1]

c atoms of a mixture [1]

d atoms of an element [1]

7.2 Copy and complete these sentences using words from the list. You may use each word once, more than once or not at all.

dissolve **dissolves** **evaporates** **filtrate** **insoluble**
mixture **saturated** **solid** **solute** **solution**
solvent **temperature** **volume**

Two or more substances mixed together are called a ....**a**......... . A solute is a solid that ....**b**......... in a liquid. The liquid that it dissolves into is called a ....**c**......... . Together they make a ....**d**......... . A solid that does not dissolve in a liquid is called ....**e**......... .

If a solution is left for a few days the water ....**f**......... and a ....**g**......... is left in the container.

If a solid is added to a liquid until no more of the solid will dissolve a ....**h**......... solution is formed.

The solubility of a solid measures how much of the solid will ....**i**......... . When you measure the solubility of a solute you must use the same ....**j**......... and type of the solvent at a given ....**k**......... . [11]

7.3 The table below gives the colours and solubility in water of four compounds.

Name	Colour	Solubility
sodium chloride	white	soluble
zinc carbonate	white	insoluble
iron sulfate	green	soluble
copper carbonate	green	insoluble

The compounds were added to separate beakers of water. There was enough water to completely dissolve the soluble compounds. The contents of each beaker were filtered.

a One of the compounds left a white solid in the filter paper. What is the name of this compound? [1]

b What would be the colour of the filtrate from this beaker? [1]

c Describe how you would obtain pure crystals of iron sulfate from a mixture of copper carbonate and iron sulfate. [3]

7.4 Ibrahim and Emmanuel have been investigating the amount of copper sulfate that can be dissolved in water at different temperatures. They added copper sulfate until no more would dissolve and they carefully measured the mass of the copper sulfate they added. Here are their results.

Temperature of water / °C	20	30	40	50	60	70	80
Mass of copper sulfate dissolved / g	22	24	28	32	30	46	58

a What is the range of temperatures that the boys used? [1]

b What interval did they use for the temperatures? [1]

c Name a variable the boys should have kept the same. [1]

d Which is the independent variable? [1]

e Plot a graph of their results. [5]

f What conclusion can the boys make from their results? [1]

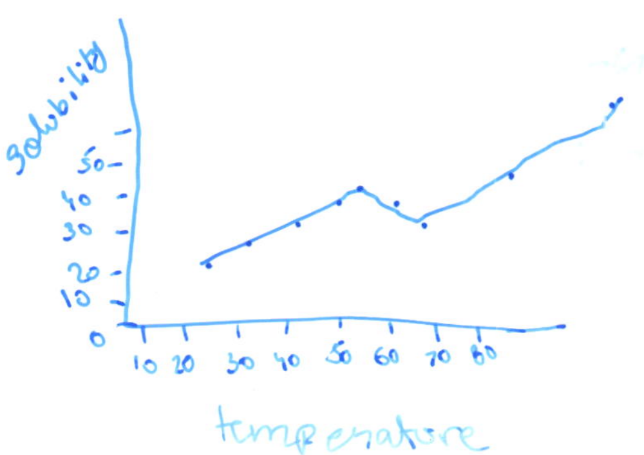

8.1 Physical and chemical changes

Physical changes

When liquid water freezes it becomes a solid. When liquid water evaporates it forms a gas. These are changes of state. They are **physical changes.**

In a physical change, no new substances are formed.

The solid water can be changed back to a liquid by heating it. The gaseous water can be changed back to a liquid by cooling it. All of the time it is still water. It looks different, but it is still the same substance.

Chemical changes

In a **chemical change**, new substances are formed.

For example, when iron is heated with sulfur, a new substance – iron sulfide – is formed. You learnt about this on pages **92–93**.

iron + sulfur → iron sulfide

The iron and sulfur have **reacted** together to form a new substance. A **chemical reaction** has taken place. The iron atoms have bonded with the sulfur atoms.

We can show what happens in a reaction using a **word equation**:

iron + sulfur → iron sulfide

In the equation, the arrow represents the chemical reaction. The **reactants** are the substances that react together. The **products** are the new substances that are made in the reaction.

reactants → products

Questions

1 Imagine that you drop a glass beaker and it breaks.
   - **a** Has a new substance been formed?
   - **b** Is this a physical change, or a chemical change?

2 In the reaction between iron and sulfur, what are the reactants and the products?

Another chemical reaction

In the reaction between iron and sulfur, two reactants join together to form a product. We say that the iron and sulfur **combine** to form iron sulfide.

In some chemical reactions, a substance breaks apart to produce two or more new substances. On page **83**, you saw how electricity can be used to make water split into hydrogen and oxygen.

water → oxygen + hydrogen

Chemical reactions in living organisms

Chemical reactions happen everywhere. They happen in the garden inside plants when they grow and when leaves decay. They happen inside your body to keep you alive – for example, reactions to digest food (see page **22**).

Questions

3 Inside your digestive system, protein molecules are broken down to amino acid molecules. (You can read about digestion on page **28**.)

- **a** Has a new substance been formed?
- **b** Has a chemical reaction taken place?

4 Respiration is a chemical reaction. You can see the word equation for respiration on page **46**.

- **a** What are the reactants in the respiration reaction?
- **b** What are the products in the respiration reaction?

5 Can you name a chemical reaction that happens in plants, but not in animals?

Summary

- In a chemical reaction, new substances are formed.
- We can show what happens during a chemical reaction using a word equation.
- The substances at the start of the reaction are the reactants. The new substances that are formed are the products.

8.2 Burning

Burning is a chemical reaction.

When something burns, it reacts with the oxygen in the air. Sometimes, ashes are formed. The ashes contain new substances. The new substances in the ashes are oxides.

When charcoal burns, ash is left behind.

When magnesium metal is burnt a white powder is formed. This powder is magnesium oxide. A new substance has been formed from magnesium and oxygen.

Magnesium and oxygen are the **reactants**. Magnesium oxide is the **product**.

magnesium + oxygen → magnesium oxide

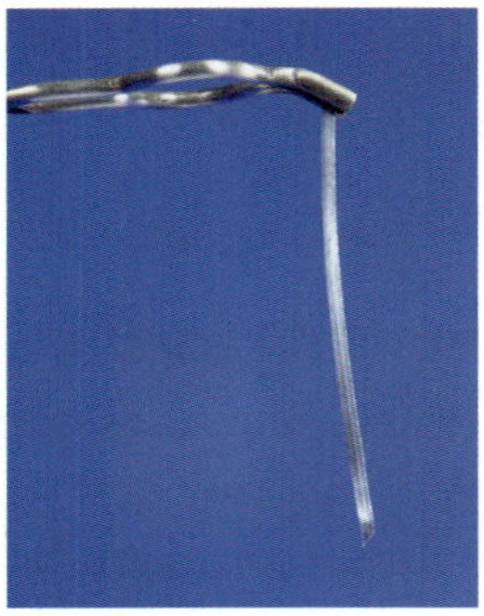

Magnesium ribbon.

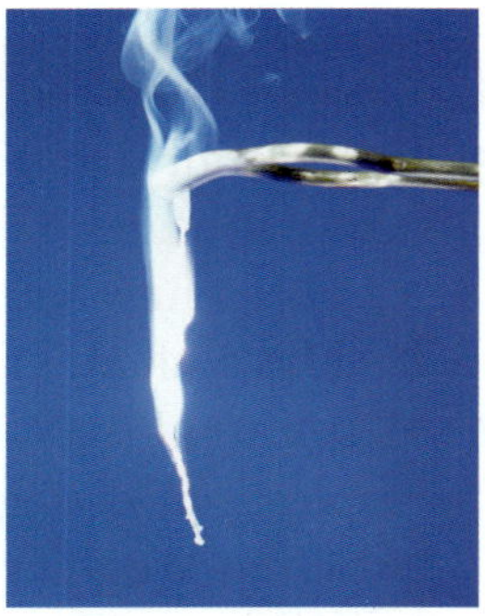

Burning magnesium ribbon.

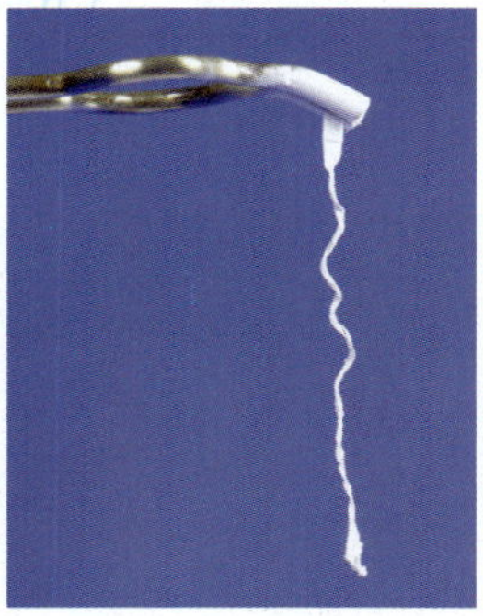

Magnesium oxide.

Activity 8.2
Burning magnesium

SE

1. Set up a Bunsen burner on a heat-proof mat. Wear safety glasses.
2. Take a small piece of magnesium ribbon and place it in some tongs.
3. Hold the tongs at arm's length and place the magnesium ribbon in the Bunsen flame.
4. Once the magnesium ribbon has caught fire remove it from the flame.
   Whilst the magnesium is burning **do not look directly at the flame**. Magnesium burns very brightly and the light could harm your eyes.

Questions

A1 Describe what happens to the magnesium ribbon.

A2 Describe what has been formed.

A3 Name the reactants in this chemical reaction.

A4 List all the safety precautions you need to take while carrying out this experiment.

Looking at the reactants and products

The table compares the properties of the reactants and product when you burn magnesium. You can see that the properties of the product are different from those of the reactants.

	Magnesium (reactant)	Oxygen (reactant)	Magnesium oxide (product)
Element or compound?	element	element	compound
State at room temperature	solid	gas	solid
Appearance	soft, shiny, malleable	colourless, has no smell	white, powdery
Conducts electricity?	yes	no	no
Melting point / °C	651	214	2800

Questions

1. Compare the melting points of magnesium, oxygen and magnesium oxide.
2. Find one similarity between magnesium oxide and one of the reactants.
3. For each of the photographs below, say if it is a physical change or a chemical reaction and explain why you think this.

a Making toast.

b Melting chocolate.

c Fireworks going off.

d Ice melting.

e Coal burning.

f Copper roof turning green.

Summary

- Burning is a chemical reaction. The substance that is burnt combines with oxygen.
- The products formed in a chemical reaction have different properties from the reactants.

8.3 Reactions with acids

Magnesium in acid.

Reactions between metals and acids

When magnesium is placed in hydrochloric acid, bubbles of gas are given off. The gas is hydrogen.

magnesium + hydrochloric acid → magnesium chloride + hydrogen

Other metals and acids can react together in the same type of reaction

zinc + sulfuric acid → zinc sulfate + hydrogen

Questions

1 What are the reactants in the first word equation above? magnesium + hydrochloric acid.
2 What are the products formed when you react zinc with sulfuric acid? zinc sulfate + hydrogen.

Testing for hydrogen

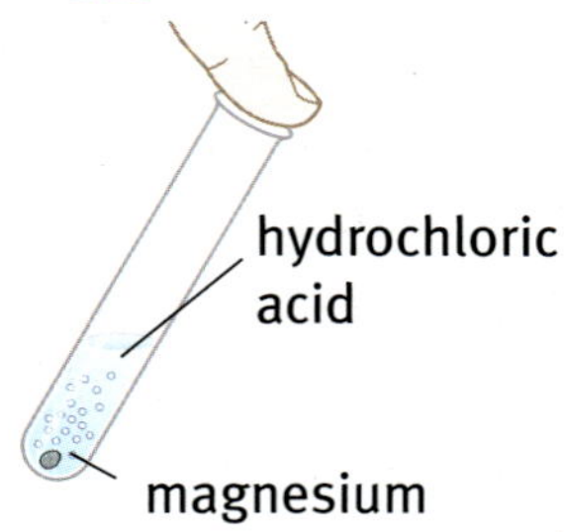

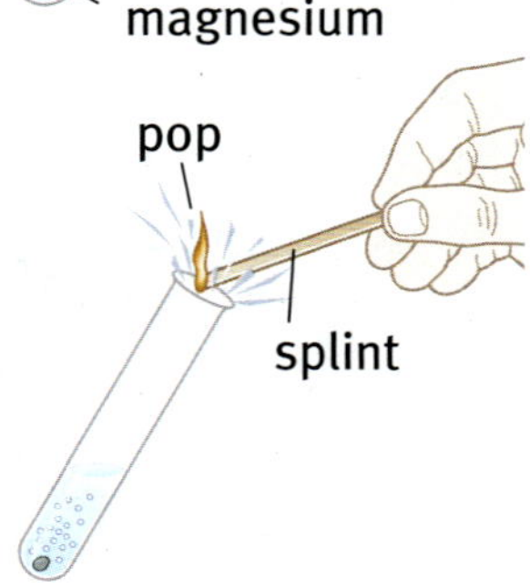

When we see bubbles forming during a chemical reaction, we know that a gas is being produced. But we cannot tell what kind of gas it is.

The diagram shows how you can test a gas to find out if it is hydrogen. Hydrogen gas burns with a squeaky pop. To carry out the test you light a splint and place it in the mouth of the tube. You need to keep your finger over the end of the test tube until the last moment or you will have no hydrogen left to test. This is because hydrogen gas is a lot lighter than air.

When the hydrogen pops, it is reacting with oxygen in the air, to form water.

hydrogen + oxygen → water

Activity 8.3

Metals and acid

SE

1 Put a small piece of each of the metals you are given into a different test tube.
2 Take one tube at a time, and add hydrochloric acid so that the test tube is half full.
3 If you see bubbles given off, test for hydrogen gas.
4 Record your observations and findings in a table.

Questions

A1 Write a word equation for each of the reactions you carried out.
A2 List any safety precautions you took.
A3 Explain how you tested for hydrogen gas. Comment on any difficulties you had doing this test.

Reactions between carbonates and acids

In Stage **7**, you learnt that limestone is affected by hydrochloric acid. The calcium carbonate in the limestone reacts with hydrochloric acid. The products are calcium chloride, water and carbon dioxide.

The word equation shows what happens when calcium carbonate reacts with hydrochloric acid.

calcium carbonate + hydrochloric acid → calcium chloride + water + carbon dioxide

There is the same pattern of reaction when you use other carbonates.

Green copper carbonate powder reacts with hydrochloric acid. There is a lot of fizzing as carbon dioxide gas is given off. The equation for this reaction is:

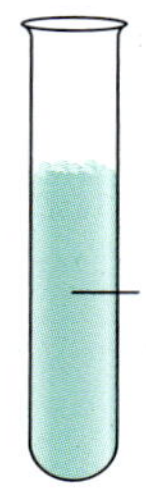

copper carbonate + hydrochloric acid → copper chloride + water + carbon dioxide

Testing for carbon dioxide

You can also test for carbon dioxide with a lighted splint. Carbon dioxide will make the splint go out.

An even better way to test for carbon dioxide is to use limewater. Carbon dioxide makes limewater go cloudy.

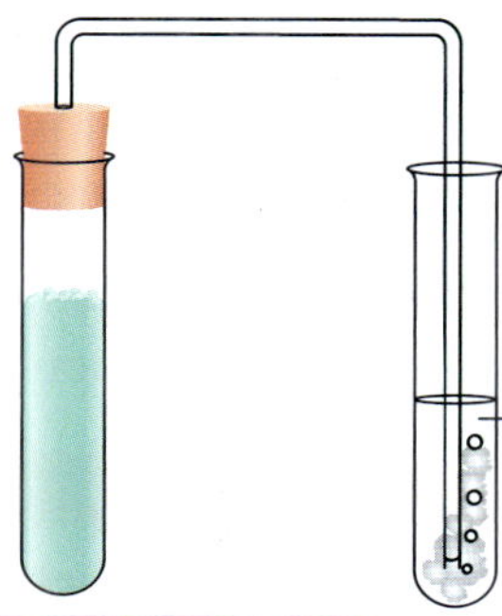

Questions

3 List the reactants when limestone reacts to produce calcium chloride, water and carbon dioxide.

4 Which products are the same in both the copper carbonate and the calcium carbonate reactions shown above?

5 Write a word equation for the reaction between magnesium carbonate and hydrochloric acid.

Summary

- Some metals react with acids, producing hydrogen gas.
- Carbonates react with acids, producing carbon dioxide gas.

8.4 Rearranging atoms

What happens in a chemical reaction?

In a chemical reaction, atoms form new combinations. Atoms that are on their own may join together with other atoms. Atoms that are bonded with other atoms may separate, forming new combinations with other atoms.

In the reaction between iron and sulfur, the iron and sulfur atoms that were there at the start of the reaction are still there at the end. They have just rearranged themselves.

iron + sulfur → iron sulfide

In a chemical reaction, no atoms are lost. No new atoms are produced. The atoms are simply rearranged into new combinations.

When you look at any of the equations for the reactions in this topic you can see that the elements that are present in the reactants are also present in the products.

Here is the equation for the reaction between magnesium and hydrochloric acid.

magnesium + hydrochloric acid → magnesium chloride + hydrogen

Magnesium metal is a reactant. The magnesium is still present in the products as part of the compound magnesium chloride.

The element hydrogen is present in the reactants as part of the compound hydrochloric acid. In the products, it is present as hydrogen gas.

This is an important idea. No element that is present in the reactants disappears from the products. No new element appears in the products.

Questions

1 Look back at the reaction between calcium carbonate and hydrochloric acid, on page **113**.

- **a** Which product of this reaction contains the element calcium?
- **b** Which reactant contains the element hydrogen?
- **c** Which product contains the element hydrogen?
- **d** Which reactant contains the element carbon?
- **e** Which product contains the element carbon?

2 Look at the reaction in which water is broken down to hydrogen and oxygen, on page **83**.

- **a** What kind of atoms are present at the start of the reaction?
- **b** How many of each kind of atom are present at the start of the reaction?
- **c** What kind of atoms are present at the end of the reaction?
- **d** How many of each kind of atom are present at the end of the reaction?

Conservation of mass

Atoms have mass. If no atoms are gained or lost during a chemical reaction, then no mass is gained or lost either.

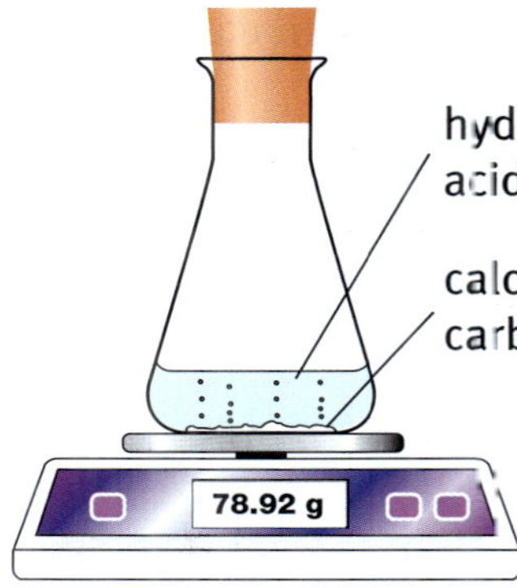

Brad, Rafaela and Tian-ning carry out the reaction between calcium carbonate and hydrochloric acid.

They place some calcium carbonate in a flask, add the hydrochloric acid and place a stopper in the top of the flask. They place the flask on a top pan balance. They each have different ideas about what will happen to the mass of the flask as the reaction takes place.

Rafaela Tian-ning Brad

When the three students carry out the reaction they find that the mass has not changed. Brad's idea was correct and so was his reason.

In chemical reactions the elements you begin the reaction with are the ones you end the reaction with. Nothing is added or taken away. The mass you begin with is the mass you end with.

This important idea is called **the conservation of mass.**

Question

A+I

3 a Chinua reacts 37 g of magnesium with 150 g of sulfuric acid. What will be the total mass of the products of this reaction?

b If Chinua starts with 10 g of magnesium, how much magnesium will be present in the magnesium sulfate?

Summary

- When a chemical reaction takes place, no new atoms or elements are formed or lost.
- The total mass of the reactants equals the total mass of the products.

8.5 More about conservation of mass

When you add calcium carbonate to hydrochloric acid, there is a chemical reaction.

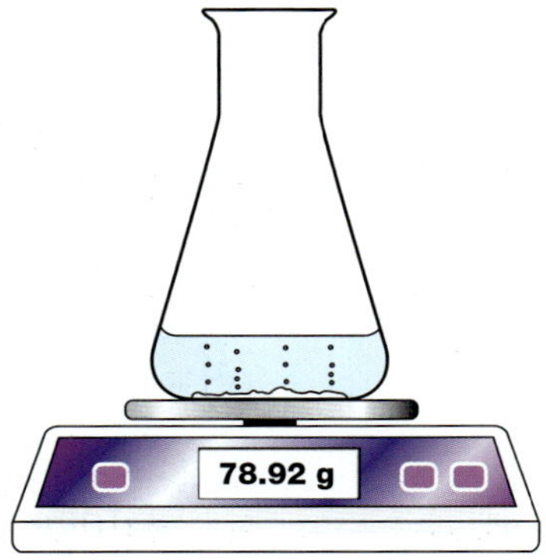

Mariam places a flask of hydrochloric acid on a top pan balance and carefully adds calcium carbonate. She measures the mass of the flask and the contents at the beginning of the reaction and after ten minutes. These are her results:

Time / minutes	Mass of flask and contents / g
0	250
10	207

Not what you expect?

The law of conservation of mass tells you that there must be the same mass at the end of a reaction as at the start. But in Mariam's experiment the mass appears to decrease. Why is this?

The word equation for this reaction is:

calcium carbonate + hydrochloric acid → calcium chloride + water + carbon dioxide

The carbon dioxide gas escapes into the air because the flask is open. You then cannot measure its mass. So it appears as if the mass decreases as the reaction continues.

The elements present in the reactants are all present in the products. Remember that water is made from hydrogen and oxygen atoms.

Questions

1 In the reaction between calcium carbonate and hydrochloric acid:

- **a** Which **one** of the reactants contains the element oxygen? calcium carbonate
- **b** Which **two** of the products contain the element oxygen? carbon-dioxide and water
- **c** Where does the element hydrogen in the water come from in this reaction? hydrochloric acid

2 Explain why the mass decreased in Mariam's experiment. carbon-dioxide escape

Another surprising result

Here is another reaction that produces a result which is a surprise to some people.

Some magnesium is placed in a crucible, and the mass of the crucible with the magnesium is recorded. The crucible is then heated very carefully. The lid of the crucible is lifted from time to time during the heating to allow the air in. After heating, the mass of the crucible with contents is found again.

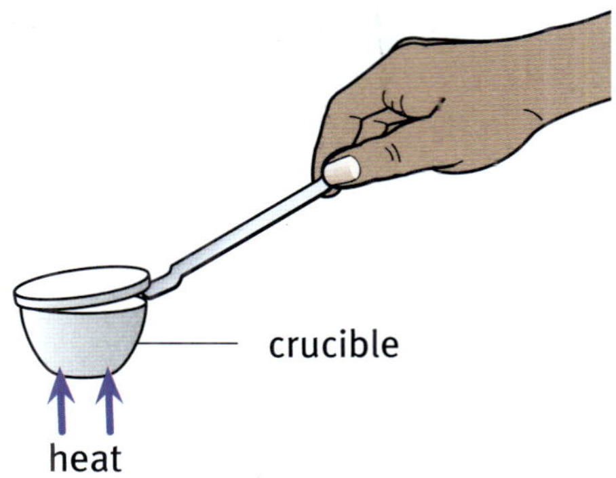

While heating the magnesium, lift the lid to allow the oxygen in.

A reaction takes place when the magnesium is heated. After the reaction, the crucible contains white ashes. The mass of the ashes is more than the mass of the magnesium at the start of the reaction.

Some people think that the ashes will be lighter because the ashes look smaller than the magnesium. They see flames escaping from the crucible, so they think something has been lost.

However, the word equation explains the situation.

magnesium + oxygen → magnesium oxide

There is an increase in mass because oxygen from the air has combined with the magnesium.

A French scientist called Antoine Lavoisier carried out this experiment in 1772. He repeated it many times and found he had an increase in mass every time. He could not explain why this happened. Finally he came up with the idea that when something burns it combines with a gas from the air. He also found that the gas from the air that is involved in burning is involved in respiration as well. He named this gas oxygen.

Antoine Lavoisier.

Question

3 What type of change takes place in the crucible experiment described above?

Summary

- Sometimes results in experiments are unexpected.
- Finding explanations for unexpected results can lead to new ideas about science.

8.6 Detecting chemical reactions

In a chemical reaction, new products are formed from the reactants. How can you tell this has happened? There are a few clues you can look out for that might mean a reaction has taken place.

Copper oxide reacting with sulfuric acid.

A colour change

Gently heating black copper oxide with sulfuric acid produces a blue solution of copper sulfate.

copper oxide + sulfuric acid → copper sulfate + water
(black) (blue)

A gas is given off

When magnesium is placed in hydrochloric acid, bubbles of hydrogen gas are given off.

magnesium + hydrochloric acid → magnesium chloride + hydrogen

Magnesium reacting with hydrochloric acid.

Heat is produced

When potassium is placed in water, hydrogen gas is given off. The reaction produces so much heat that the gas burns.

The word equation for this reaction is:

potassium + water → potassium hydroxide + hydrogen

Potassium reacting with water.

A change in pH

If you add potassium to water that contains Universal Indicator, you see the indicator change colour from green to purple. This shows that the solution has become alkaline. The pH has changed.

When an acid is used to neutralise an alkali, there is also a change in pH. This is a type of reaction called a **neutralisation reaction**.

The neutralisation reaction between sodium hydroxide and hydrochloric acid can be described by the word equation:

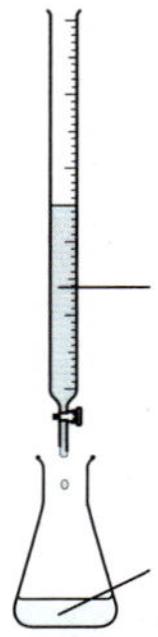

In this reaction, sodium chloride and water are produced.

sodium hydroxide + hydrochloric acid → sodium chloride + water

A precipitate is formed

If you mix solutions of silver nitrate and calcium chloride, a chemical reaction takes place. In the reaction, an insoluble solid is formed. This is called a **precipitate**. The solid is silver chloride.

silver nitrate + calcium chloride → silver chloride + calcium nitrate

When silver nitrate and calcium chloride react a precipitate is produced.

You might have used limewater to detect carbon dioxide. Limewater is a solution of calcium hydroxide. Carbon dioxide makes limewater turn cloudy because a precipitate of calcium carbonate forms.

calcium hydroxide + carbon dioxide → calcium carbonate + water

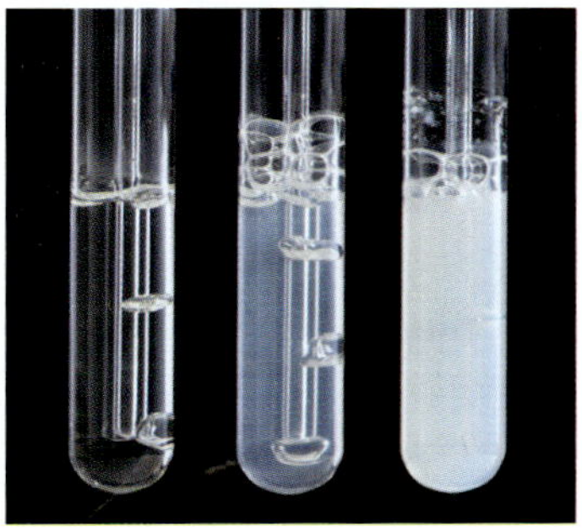

As carbon dioxide is bubbled into the limewater a precipitate is formed.

Questions

1 Name **two** things you might look for to see if a chemical reaction has taken place.
2 Potassium is called an 'alkali metal'. Suggest a reason for this.
3 What is the name of the compound formed when oxygen reacts with magnesium?
A+I 4 Suggest what happens when carbon burns in oxygen. Write a word equation for this reaction.

Activity 8.6
Has a chemical reaction taken place?

SE

You will be given a series of experiments to do. Your aim is to carry them out according to the instructions, and to observe and record what happens. Pay attention to any safety instructions.

For each experiment decide if there is a chemical change or a physical change. Give a reason for your choice.

Summary

- A chemical reaction could be indicated by a colour change, gas being produced, a change of temperature, a change in pH, or the formation of a precipitate.

8.7 Rusting

A lot of chemical reactions are useful – for example, cooking and the reactions that happen inside your body. But some reactions are not very useful. An example of a reaction that is not useful is **rusting**.

When iron is left out in damp air it rusts. Iron reacts with substances in the air to form an orange-brown solid.

This new iron horseshoe is shiny.

What is rust?

Rust is formed when iron reacts with oxygen in the air. The product is iron oxide, which is commonly known as rust.

iron + oxygen → iron oxide

This means that the iron changes and no longer has the same properties. A strong iron girder can become rusted and fall apart. This could mean that a building collapses.

Rust is only formed when both oxygen and water are present. Water is not part of the equation above but it is needed for the reaction to happen.

The iron sheets in this old bush hut have rusted.

What causes iron to rust?

A new iron nail is placed in each of four test tubes, as in the diagram to the right.

Test tube 1 contains nothing apart from the nail, and is open to the air.

Test tube 2 contains water and the nail is half in the water. The tube is open to the air. So this tube has water and air.

Test tube 3 has calcium chloride in the bottom. The calcium chloride absorbs water so the air inside the tube is dry. There is no water in this tube. The tube is stoppered.

Test tube 4 has water that has been boiled to remove as much dissolved gas as possible. On the top of the boiled water is a layer of oil. This stops any air entering the water. The tube is stoppered.

Changes in all metals, such as when a copper roof turns green, are chemical changes but they are not called rusting.

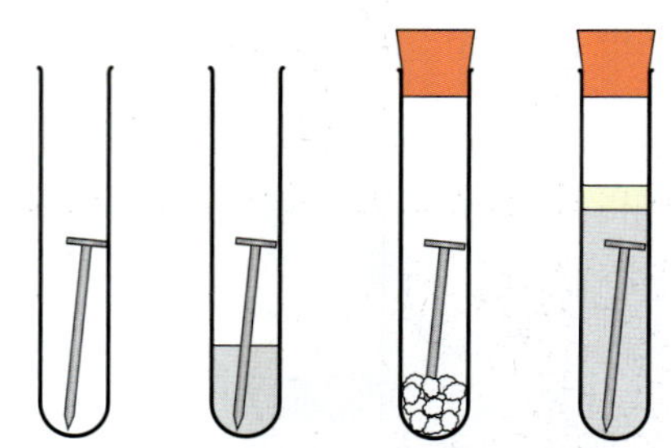

After a few weeks the experiment looks like this.

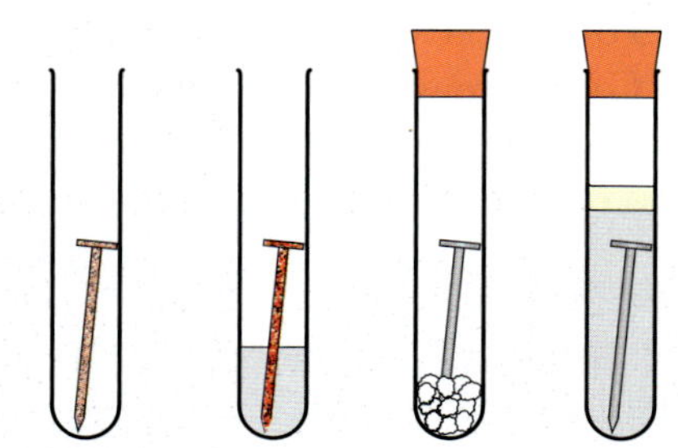

Tube number	Contains	Result
1	moist air	nail is rusted
2	water and air	nail is very rusty
3	dry air	no rust
4	boiled water covered with oil, no air	small amount of rust

Questions

1. What conditions are needed to **prevent** iron from rusting?
2. Which test tube and which conditions caused the iron nail to rust most quickly?
3. Why is the same type of nail used in all test tubes?
4. How is the air in tube 3 dried?
5. How is the air in tube 4 kept out of contact with the nail?

How can iron be protected?

There are ways that the iron can be protected so it does not rust.

- The iron can be painted. This stops the oxygen in the air reaching the iron.
- The iron can be galvanised. This means covering the iron with a layer of zinc. This again prevents the oxygen reaching the iron.

The layer of zinc on this fence stops it from rusting.

The paint on this park gate stops it from rusting.

Summary

- Some reactions are not useful.
- Rust is formed when iron reacts with oxygen in damp conditions.

Unit 8 End of unit questions

8.1 The diagram shows an experiment where zinc metal is added to sulfuric acid.

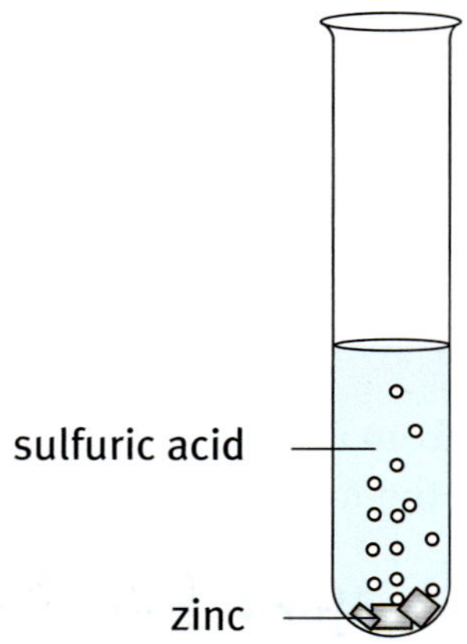

- **a** What is the name of the gas given off in this reaction? [1]
- **b** How do you test for this gas? [2]
- **c** What products are formed in this reaction? [1]
- **d** How do you know when all of the acid has reacted? [1]
- **e** Write the word equation for this reaction. [2]

8.2 For each of the following, state if it is a physical change or a chemical reaction.

- **a** burning a piece of wood
- **b** melting chocolate
- **c** cooking an egg
- **d** heating glass and bending it
- **e** baking a cake. [5]

8.3 Magnesium ribbon burns in air.

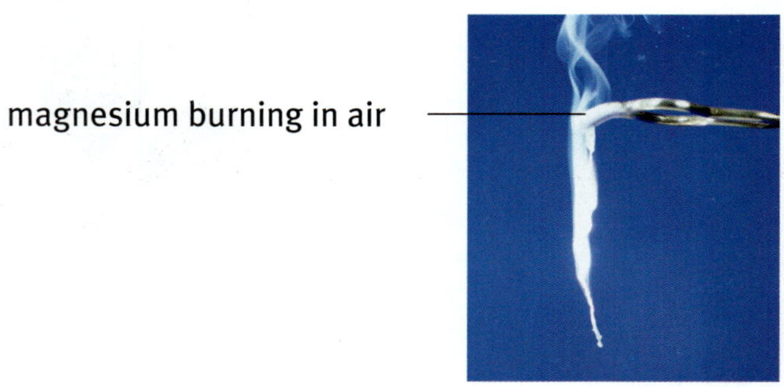

- **a** Write the chemical symbol for magnesium. [1]
- **b** Name the element in the air that reacts with magnesium when it burns. [1]
- **c** Name the compound formed when this element reacts with magnesium. [1]
- **d** Magnesium also reacts with chlorine. Write the word equation that describes this reaction. [2]

8.4 Rust is found on a garden fork that has been left outside.

a Which of the following metals has the main part of the garden fork been made from?

aluminium **iron** **copper** **zinc** [1]

b What is the chemical name for rust? [1]

c Suggest **one** way of preventing the fork from rusting. [1]

8.5 Look at the following equations.

A carbon + oxygen → carbon dioxide

B sodium hydroxide + hydrochloric acid → sodium chloride + water

C potassium + water → potassium hydroxide + hydrogen

D copper carbonate → copper oxide + carbon dioxide

Write the **letter** for the equation that:

a produces a metal oxide [1]

b is a neutralisation reaction [1]

c is a burning reaction. [1]

Copy and complete the following equations:

d sodium + water → .... + hydrogen [1]

e copper carbonate + sulfuric acid → .... + ... + water [2]

f sulfur + ... → sulfur dioxide [1]

9.1 How fast? – Measuring speed

The traffic in the photograph is moving along a busy motorway. The drivers have to be careful to avoid collisions.

Some vehicles move faster than others. They have different **speeds**.

Drivers on a motorway must obey the speed limit. There are signs along the motorway which show the speed limit.

The sign in the photograph shows that the speed limit is 130 kilometres per hour in dry weather.

Traffic on a motorway.

A speed limit sign on a motorway.

Question

A+I

1 a Look at the speed limit sign in the photograph. What is the speed limit in wet weather?

b In Stage **7**, you learnt about forces and motion. Use what you learnt to explain why cars should travel more slowly in wet weather.

What is speed?

Speed is the quantity that tells us how fast something is moving. For example, we might say:

'The car's speed was 50 kilometres per hour when it hit the wall.'

Remember that, when we give a measurement, we give its value including the unit. In this example, the unit is kilometres per hour, usually written as km/h.

A speed of 50 km/h means that the car would travel 50 km in one hour if it kept moving at that speed.

In science, we usually measure speed in metres per second (m/s).

So we might say:

'The sprinter's speed was 10 m/s.'

Distance and time

How can we measure a runner's speed? There is a clue in the units. We need to find how many metres a runner travels in each second. So we need to measure two quantities:

- distance travelled (in metres, m)
- time taken (in seconds, s).

The trainer checks how quickly the athletes can run 100 m.

Then we calculate speed like this:

$$\text{average speed} = \frac{\text{distance travelled}}{\text{time taken}}$$

Or simply:

$$\text{speed} = \frac{\text{distance}}{\text{time}}$$

We have to say **average speed** because the runner's speed may be changing as they run – they may be speeding up or slowing down.

Calculating speed

Here is an example. A runner completes a 200 m race in 25 s. What is her average speed?

The distance travelled is 200 m and the time taken is 25 s. So:

$$\text{speed} = \frac{\text{distance}}{\text{time}} = \frac{200\,\text{m}}{25\,\text{s}} = 8\,\text{m/s}$$

Questions

2 A car travels 100 m in 5 s. What is its average speed?

3 A red car travels 400 m in 20 s. A blue car travels 660 m in 30 s. Which car has the greater average speed?

Activity 9.1

The speed of runners

In this activity, you are going to measure the average speed of a runner. They will run between two marked points. Your task is to make measurements so that you can calculate their speed.

- You can measure the distance between the two points using a tape measure.
- You can measure the time taken using a stopwatch.

When you have made your measurements, calculate the runner's average speed.

Next, think up some other speeds you can measure. Check your ideas with your teacher before you carry them out.

Summary

- Speed is a measure of how fast an object is moving.
- $\text{average speed} = \dfrac{\text{distance travelled}}{\text{time taken}}$

9.2 Speed check

Road traffic must obey the speed limit, for the safety of everyone. Speed cameras may be used to check that drivers are not going too fast.

A speed camera stands at the side of the road. It measures the speed of each vehicle as it passes. It takes a photograph of any car which is speeding (going faster than the speed limit). Then the driver can be identified from the registration number.

One type of camera works like this:

- There are two detector strips in the road. They are a known distance apart.
- The camera detects the car as it passes over each strip. A timer in the camera measures the time taken by the car to travel from one strip to the next.
- A mini-computer calculates the speed of the car. If the car is speeding, the camera takes a photograph of it.

This speed camera detects any cars that are travelling faster than the allowed speed, and photographs them.

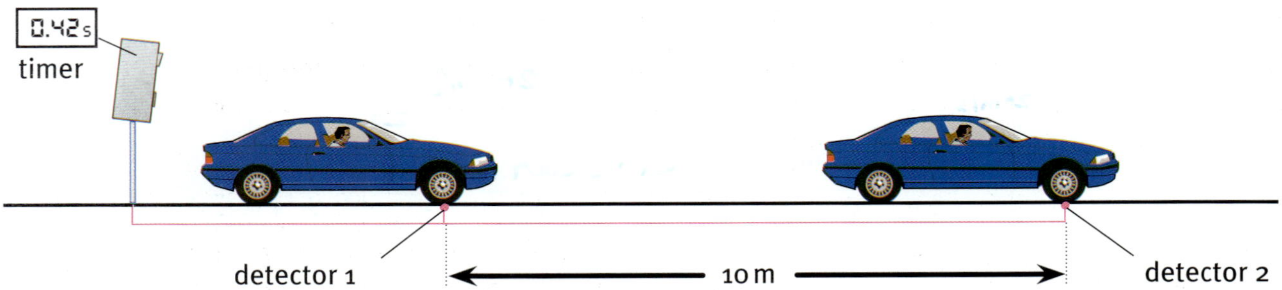

$$\text{speed} = \frac{10.0\,\text{m}}{0.42\,\text{s}} = 24\,\text{m/s}$$

A speed camera calculates the speed of each passing car.

Question

1 a A car is detected by a speed camera. The two detectors are separated by 5.0 m. The car travels this distance in 0.2 s. What is its speed?

b If the speed limit is 22 m/s, is the car travelling too fast?

Light gates

In the laboratory you can use **light gates** to measure the speed of a moving object. A light gate is similar to a speed camera on the road.

The picture shows one way to use two light gates to measure the speed of a moving trolley.

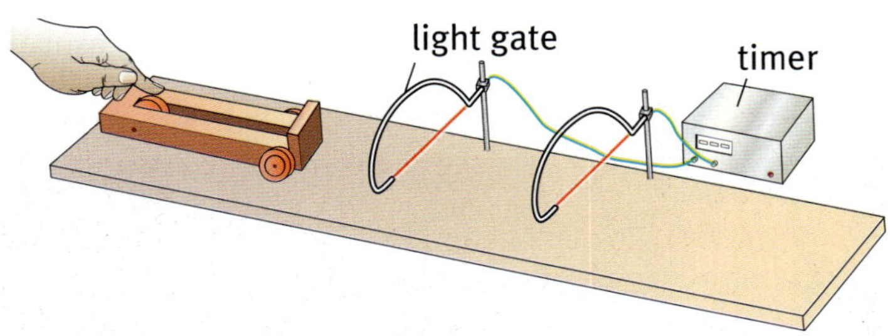

One light gate starts the timer. The other stops it.

Each light gate has an invisible beam of infrared light. When anything breaks the beam, the light gate sends a pulse of electricity to the timer.

- One light gate is connected to the START terminal of an electronic timer.
- The other light gate is connected to the STOP terminal.

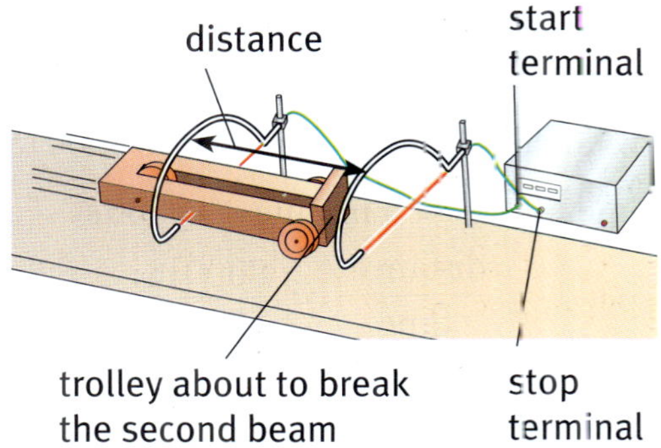

The picture shows a trolley running past the light gates. It breaks the first beam; this starts the timer. Then it breaks the second beam; this stops the timer.

The timer shows how long it took for the trolley to move between the two light gates. We can measure the distance between the two light gates. Then we can calculate the trolley's average speed:

$$\text{speed} = \frac{\text{distance}}{\text{time}}$$

Fractions of a second

Light gates are useful because they can measure very short time intervals – less than a second. You cannot use a stopwatch to measure times less than one second.

Light gates can be connected to a computer instead of a timer. Then the computer can calculate the speed of the moving object. Before it can do this, you need to tell it the distance between the two light gates.

Question

2 The distance between two light gates is 12.0 cm. A trolley passes between them. The timer shows that it takes 0.60 s. What is its speed? Give your answer in cm/s.

Activity 9.2

Using light gates

In this activity, you are going to find out more about using light gates to measure the speed of a moving object.

- You can measure the speed of a moving trolley or toy car.
- You can measure the speed of a falling object.
- You can find out how to measure the speed of an object using a single light gate.

Summary

- **Light gates can be used to measure the time taken by an object to move between two points.**
- **If we know the distance between the two points, we can calculate the object's speed.**

9.3 Speed calculations

Skidoo racing is a popular sport in many countries. It takes about 5 minutes to travel 8 km along the track.

We can use this information to calculate the skidoo's speed. Take care! We need to work in the correct units – metres and seconds.

distance travelled = 8 km = 8000 m

time taken = 5 minutes = 300 s

$$\text{speed} = \frac{\text{distance}}{\text{time}} = \frac{8000\,\text{m}}{300\,\text{s}} = 26.7\,\text{m/s}$$

A skidoo race.

Question

1 In the Olympic Games, a female athlete ran 5 km in 14 minutes. What was her average speed during the race?

How far?

The faster you run and the longer you run for, the farther you will get. You can work out how far using the equation for speed.

The equation must be rearranged like this:

distance travelled = average speed × time taken

Or simply:

distance = speed × time

Here is an example:

A bus is travelling along a road. Its speed is 25 m/s. How far will it travel in one minute (60 s)?

distance travelled = speed × time taken
= 25 m/s × 60 s
= 1500 m

So the bus will travel 1500 m (1.5 km) in one minute.

A bus carrying pilgrims in India.

Question

2 A migrating bird can travel at a speed of 30 m/s. How far will it travel in 25 minutes at this speed? Give your answer in metres (m), and in kilometres (km).

How long?

You can also use the equation for speed to calculate the time a moving object's journey will take. The equation must be rearranged like this:

$$\text{time taken} = \frac{\text{distance travelled}}{\text{average speed}}$$

Or simply:

$$\text{time} = \frac{\text{distance}}{\text{speed}}$$

Here is an example:

An aircraft flies at an average speed of 250 m/s. How long will it take to fly between two airports 750 km apart?

$$\text{time taken} = \frac{\text{distance travelled}}{\text{average speed}} = \frac{750\,000\text{ m}}{250\text{ m/s}} = 3000\text{ s}$$

So the aircraft will take 3000 s, which is 50 minutes.

A passenger aircraft like this can fly at 300 m/s.

Question

3 A cargo ship travels at an average speed of 12 m/s. How long will it take to travel between two ports which are 600 km apart?

Activity 9.3
Speedy sums

Make up **three** questions like the ones in this topic.

- In one question, you need to calculate average speed.
- In one question, you need to calculate distance travelled.
- In one question, you need to calculate time taken.

Make sure that you can answer the questions. Keep your answers secret.

Exchange your questions with a partner. Solve each other's questions. Do you get the same answers?

Summary

- $\text{speed} = \frac{\text{distance}}{\text{time}}$
- $\text{distance} = \text{speed} \times \text{time}$
- $\text{time} = \frac{\text{distance}}{\text{speed}}$

9.4 Patterns of movement

The train in the photograph is moving. You can tell this because it looks blurred. The grass is not blurred because it is stationary.

The train looks blurred because it takes the camera a fraction of a second to take the picture. During this time, the train moves.

A fast-moving train.

Question

1 A photographer takes a picture of a train which is travelling at 40 m/s. If the camera takes 0.01 s to take the picture, how far does the train travel in this time?

Constant speed, changing speed

The next photograph shows an owl flying. There is only one owl, not five. The camera has taken five pictures, one after the other. They were taken at equal intervals of time.

An owl flying at a steady speed.

From the photograph, you can tell that the owl is flying from left to right. You can also tell that it is flying at a constant speed, because the pictures are equally spaced.

The next photograph shows a steel ball bearing rolling down a slope. The images of the ball bearing get farther apart as it runs down the slope. This shows that the ball bearing is speeding up.

A ball bearing rolling down a slope.

So equal spacings tell us that an object is moving at a steady speed. Increasing spacings tell us that it is speeding up.

Question

2 Imagine that you are able to take a photograph of a rolling ball which is slowing down. What pattern would you expect to see? Make a sketch to show your idea.

Activity 9.4
Ticker timer

A ticker timer is a piece of apparatus which records how something is moving. The moving object pulls a long paper tape behind it. The ticker timer prints dots on the tape at equal intervals of time.

Use a ticker timer to record the motion of some moving objects. Make tapes that show the patterns of movement of objects which are travelling at a steady speed, speeding up, and slowing down.

Distance/time graphs

Another way to show how an object is moving is to draw a distance/time graph. Distance is shown on the y-axis and time on the x-axis.

If an object is moving at a steady speed, the graph will be a straight line sloping upwards – see Graph **A**. This shows that the object's distance from the starting point increases at a steady rate. It is travelling equal distances in equal times.

Graph **B** shows the distance/time graphs for two cars. The red car is going faster than the blue one. Its graph line slopes upwards more steeply, because it travels a greater distance in each second.

Graph **C** is for an object which is speeding up. Its distance/time graph curves upwards.

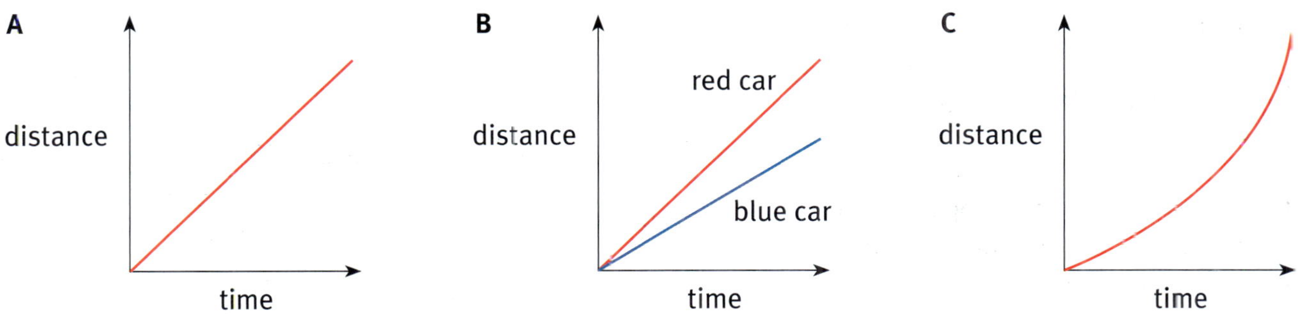

Distance/time graphs for some moving objects.

Question

A+I

3 Imagine that you are walking along slowly. Then you start to run fast. Make a sketch of a distance/time graph to represent this movement.

Summary

- We use a distance/time graph to record the pattern of movement of a moving object.

9.5 Distance/time graphs

The car and the truck in the picture pass the lamp-post at the same time. After 1 s, the car has travelled 15 m. The truck has travelled 10 m.

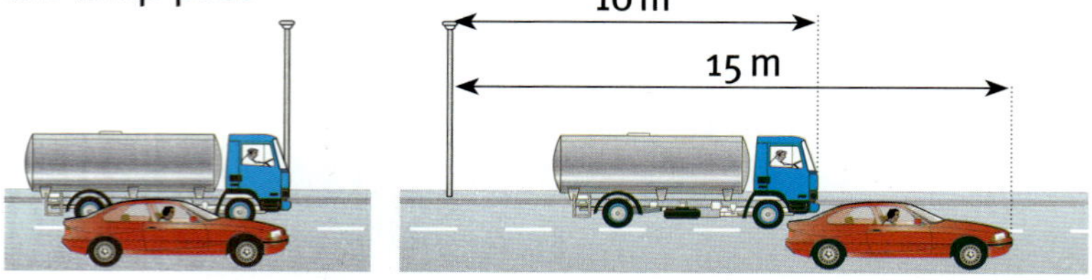

The car is moving faster than the truck.

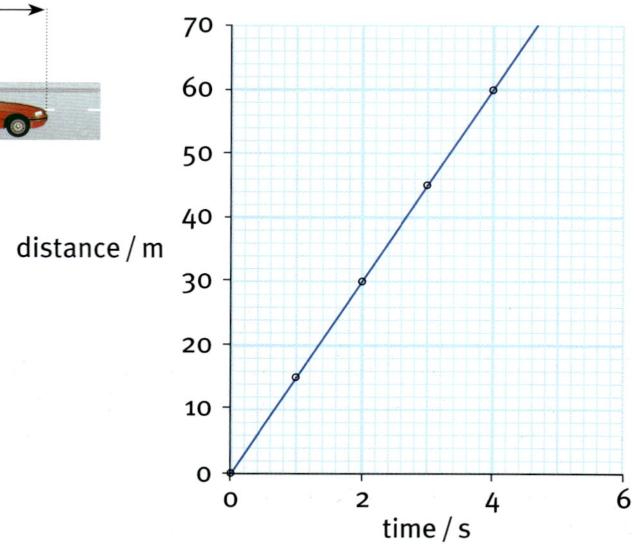

This distance/time graph shows that the car is travelling 15 m every second.

Question

1 **a** Copy the distance/time graph for the car. On the same graph, draw a distance/time graph for the truck. It travels 10 m every second.

b From your graph, work out how long it takes the truck to travel 50 m.

Drawing distance/time graphs

We can draw a distance/time graph to represent a journey. Here is an example.

A cyclist rode up a steep hill and then down the other side. The journey is divided into five sections, A–E. The table shows how far he had travelled at the end of each stage. The information in the table has been used to draw the graph.

Section of journey	Time / s	Distance / m
Start	0	0
A	50	500
B	150	900
C	200	900
D	250	1000
E	300	2000

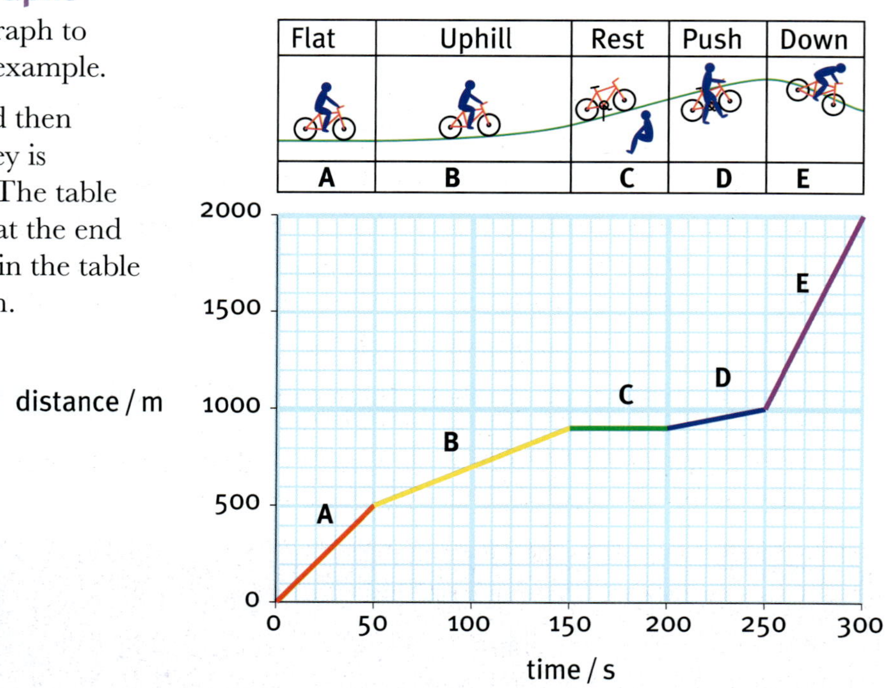

Using distance/time graphs

We can use a distance/time graph to answer questions about an object's movement. Here is an example.

The graph shows the movement of a runner in a race.

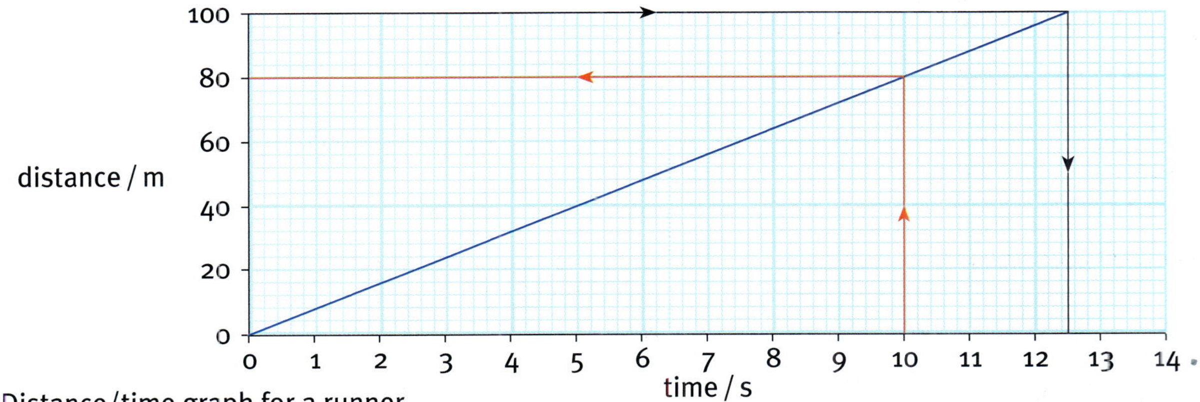

Distance/time graph for a runner.

Question 1: How far has the runner travelled after 10 s? Find 10 s on the time axis. Draw a line straight up from this point until it reaches the graph line, as shown. Now draw horizontally across to the distance axis. The answer is 80 m.

Question 2: How long does the runner take to travel 100 m? Find 100 m on the distance axis. Draw a line horizontally from this point until it reaches the graph line, as shown. Now draw vertically down to the time axis. The answer is 12.5 s.

Activity 11.5
Journey graphs

1 Here is some information about Mina's journey to the market. Use the information to draw up a table showing how far she had walked at different points in the journey. Then draw a distance/time graph.

Mina left home, walking slowly. After 10 minutes, she had walked 1000 m. Then she met a friend. They stood and talked for 4 minutes. Mina realised she might be late. She ran the next 2000 m to the market and arrived there 30 minutes after leaving home.

2 Draw a distance/time graph for a journey similar to Mina's. It might be a journey on a bus or plane. Swap your graph with a partner. From your partner's graph, draw a table of distances and times for the journey. Then write a description of the journey, in words.

Summary

- A distance/time graph can be used to find out distances travelled and times taken during a journey.

Unit 9 End of unit questions

9.1 **a** A red car travels 120 km in one hour. A blue car travels 130 km in the same time. Which car has the greater average speed? [1]

b Runner A takes 45 s to run 400 m. Runner B takes 48 s to run the same distance. Which runner has the greater average speed? [1]

c A bus travels a distance of 100 km in 2.5 h. Calculate its average speed. Give your answer in km/h. [1]

9.2 A driver can work out her average speed using the instruments in her car. The picture shows the clock and the distance meter at the beginning of a journey, and at the end. The distance meter gives the total distance travelled by the car in its lifetime, in kilometres.

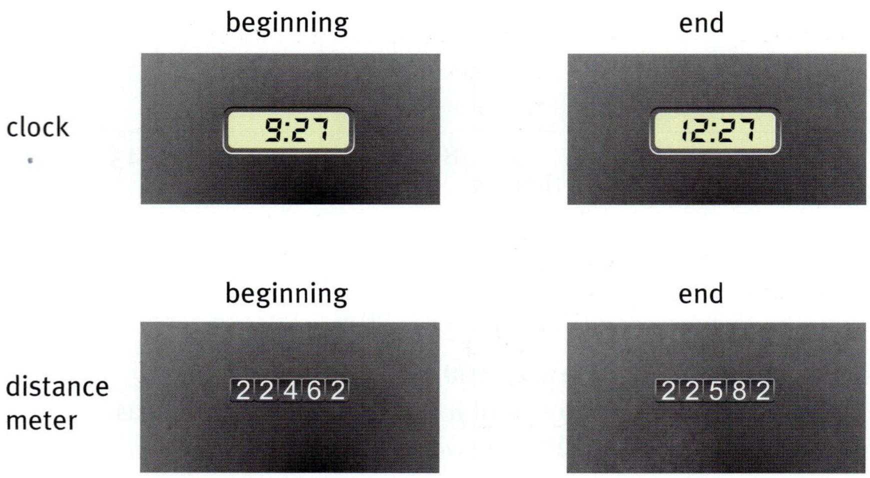

a How much time has passed between the beginning and end of the journey? [1]

b How far has the car travelled in this time? [1]

c Calculate the car's average speed during the journey. Show your working. [2]

9.3 A train is travelling at an average speed of 150 km/h.

a How far will it travel in 2.4 hours? Show your working. [2]

b How long will it take to travel between two stations 525 km apart? Show your working. [2]

9.4 Here are three distance/time graphs, **A–C**.

A

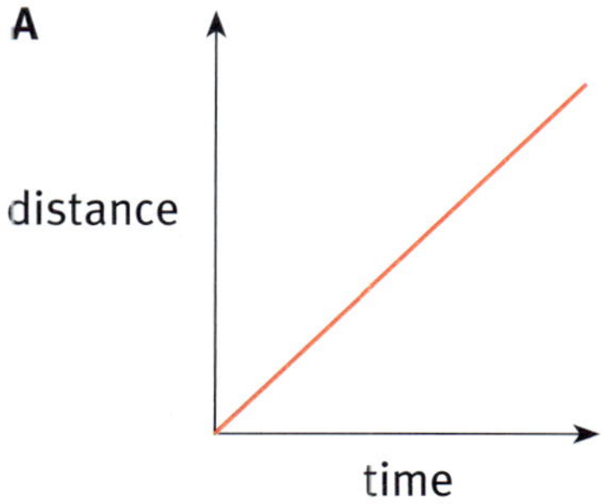

B

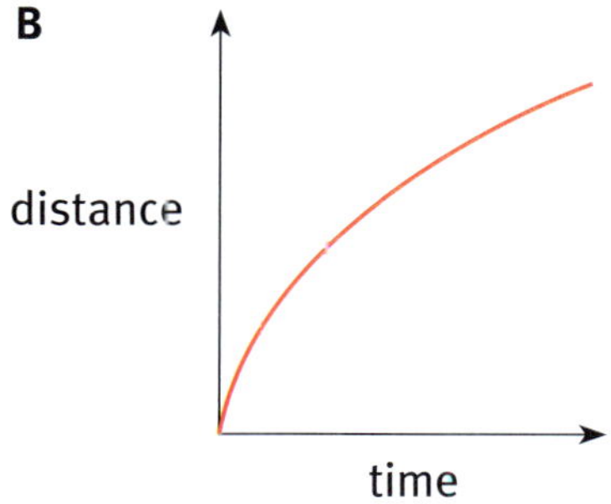

C

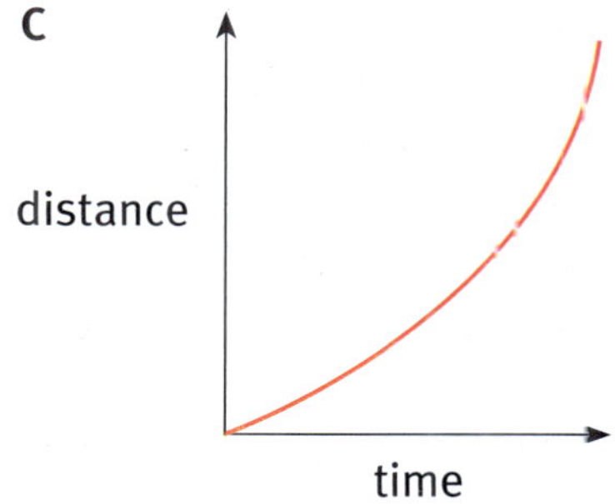

a Which graph represents the journey of a car moving at a steady speed? [1]

b Which graph represents the journey of a car whose speed is increasing? [1]

c The distance/time graph below represents the movement of two cars, blue and red.

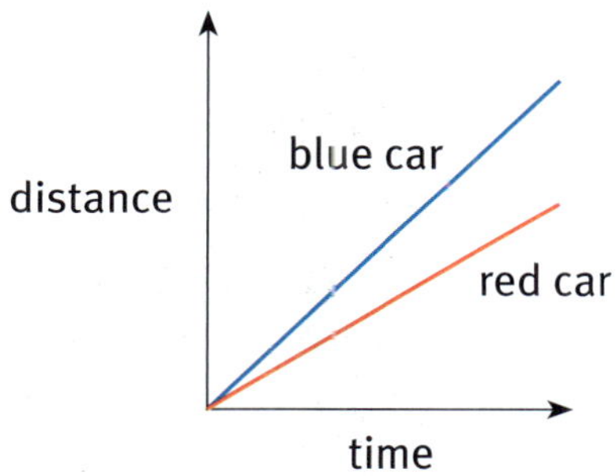

Which car has the greater speed? Explain how you can tell. [1]

9.5 The distance/time graph below represents part of the journey of a train. Study the graph and answer the questions that follow.

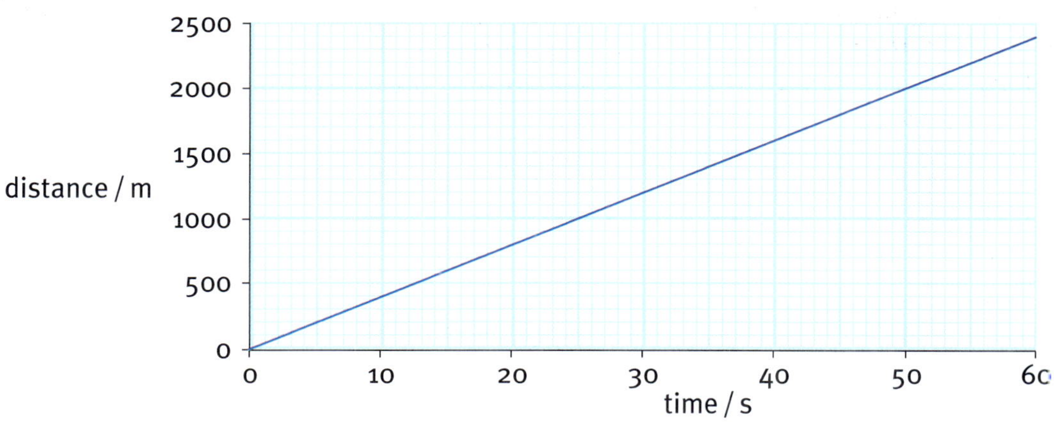

a How far did the train travel in 50 s? [1]

b Calculate the train's average speed. Show your working. [2]

10.1 Changing sounds

It's easy to make a sound. Hit a box with a stick. Blow into a tube. Pluck a rubber band.

We can make sounds with our vocal cords. Try placing your thumb and fingers gently on your throat while you are talking or singing. You should be able to feel **vibrations**.

All sounds come from sources which vibrate (move back and forth). You may be able to see the vibrations of a guitar string. You can't see the air inside a saxophone vibrating.

The air inside the saxophone vibrates when you blow. The guitar strings vibrate when you pluck them.

Loudness and pitch

There are three types of musical instruments: stringed instruments (with strings that vibrate), wind instruments (ones that you blow into), and percussion instruments (that you strike).

Musicians learn to make different sounds with their instruments. There are two things they can change:

- They can make the sound of their instrument louder or softer. They can control its **loudness**.
- They can make the note higher or lower. They can change its **pitch**.

This drummer hits, or strikes, the drum as he accompanies a dance performance. A drum is a percussion instrument.

Question

1 Loudness and pitch are two important properties of a musical sound.

a If a musician plays a softer note, which property has been changed, loudness or pitch?

b If the musician makes the note lower, which property has been changed, loudness or pitch?

Activity 10.1

Loud and soft, high and low

In this activity, you are going to look at some musical instruments and consider how the sounds they produce can be changed. If you play a musical instrument, you may be able to contribute more to this activity.

Watch different instruments being played. Suggest how the note can be made louder, and how its pitch can be made higher. Test your ideas.

Show your findings in a table.

Loudspeakers

Loudspeakers are used to produce sounds from computers, radios and television sets.

Inside a loudspeaker is a paper cone. This cone vibrates back and forth to make the sounds that we hear.

In the photograph, some small plastic balls are bouncing up and down on the cone as it makes a sound.

The cone vibrates up and down more when it produces a louder sound. It vibrates up and down more frequently when the pitch of the note is higher. ('More frequently' means more times each second.)

A loudspeaker, showing its vibrating cone.

Question

2 Imagine that a loudspeaker is producing a quiet note with a low pitch. How will its vibrations change:

a if the pitch of the note becomes higher?

b if the note becomes louder?

Summary

- Sounds are produced by vibrating objects.
- Bigger vibrations give louder sounds.
- Faster (more frequent) vibrations give sounds of higher pitch.

10.2 Looking at vibrations

Amplitude and frequency of vibrations

When you pluck a guitar string, it vibrates very rapidly. It may vibrate hundreds or thousands of times each second. This is too fast to see clearly.

The picture shows one way to observe slow vibrations. A metre rule is clamped to the bench. A weight is taped to the free end.

When you pull the end downwards and let it go, the weight vibrates up and down. If you do this with a short ruler, you can make a 'twanging' sound.

The picture shows the **amplitude** of the vibration. It tells you the maximum distance the vibrating object moves from its rest position before it started vibrating.

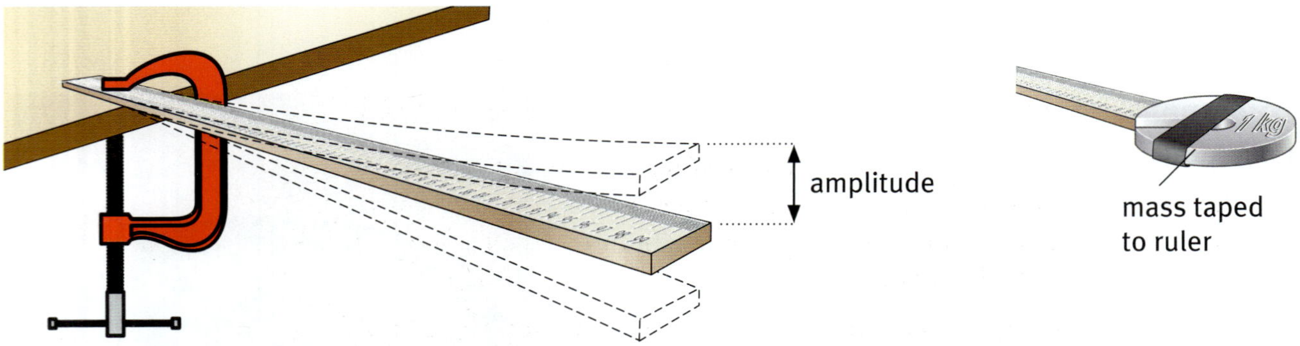

The metre rule vibrates up and down.

The number of vibrations per second is called the **frequency** of vibration. If an object vibrates 20 times each second, we say that its frequency is 20 Hz. The symbol Hz stands for **hertz**, the unit of frequency.

1 hertz = 1 Hz = 1 vibration per second

To measure the frequency of a vibration, you may have to time a large number of complete vibrations – say, 20 or 50 – and then calculate how many vibrations there are in 1 s. This is like taking your pulse; you can't time a single heartbeat accurately.

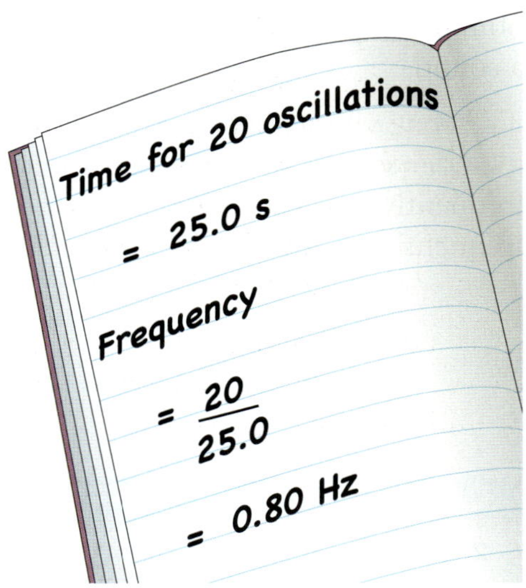

Calculating frequency.

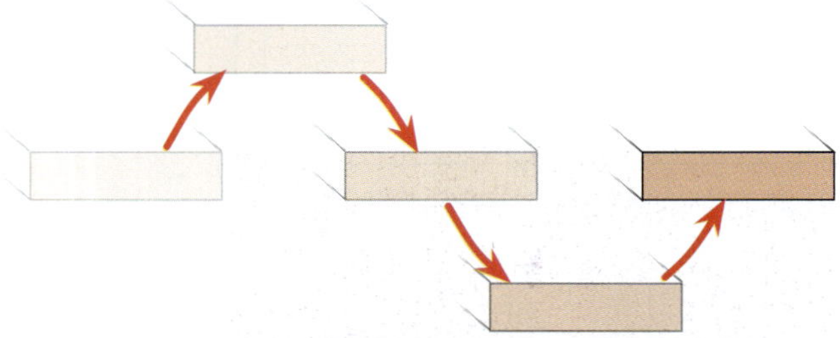

A complete vibration – the object moves up from its rest position, then down, and then back to its rest position.

Questions

1 a If a guitar string vibrates 250 times each second, what is its frequency?
  b If a drum skin vibrates with a frequency of 100 Hz, how many times does it move up and down each second?

2 If a bird flaps its wings up and down 50 times in 20 s, what is the frequency of its flapping?

Activity 10.2

Studying vibrations

SE

You are going to investigate the vibrations of a ruler which has been clamped at one end. Firstly, you will need to decide how to measure the frequency of its vibrations. Discuss your ideas with your partners and then share your best idea with the rest of the class.

Secondly, choose a question to investigate. Write a plan and check it with your teacher before you start.

- How will the frequency of the vibrations change if you make the ruler longer or shorter?
- How will the frequency of the vibrations change if you make the ruler vibrate up and down with a greater amplitude?
- How will the frequency of the vibrations change if you change the weight attached to its end?

You may be able to think of a question of your own to investigate. Before you carry out your investigation, write a prediction: what do you think you will find? Give a reason to support your prediction.

Summary

- The amplitude of a vibration is the greatest distance the object moves from its rest position.
- Frequency is the number of vibrations per second.
- Frequency is measured in hertz (Hz).

10.3 How sound travels

When a musician plays, sounds spread outwards from their instrument. Anyone nearby can hear the sounds. This shows that sound can travel through air.

Sound can also travel through solids and liquids. For example, place your ear against a table. Ask someone to tap the table – you will hear the tapping sound very clearly.

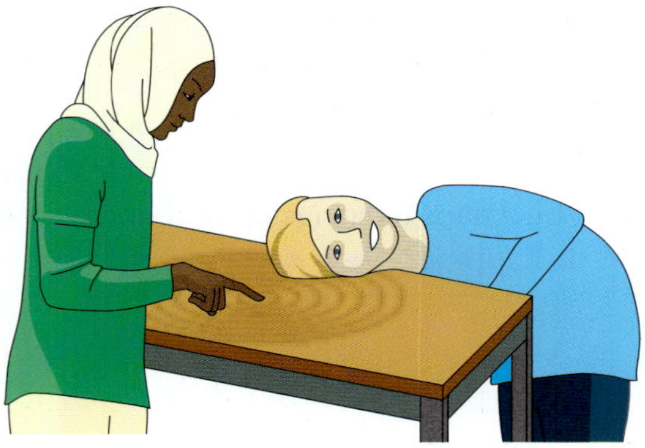

The sounds made by tapping the table travel through the wood.

Question

A+I

1 How could you show that sound travels through water?

Sound and a vacuum

The picture shows an experiment to find out whether sound can travel through a **vacuum** (an empty space, with no air in it). An electric bell is hanging in a glass bell-jar. At first, the girl can hear it ringing.

Then the air is pumped out of the jar, so there is a vacuum in the jar. Now the girl cannot hear the bell. She can see that it is still ringing.

Sound needs a material to travel through. The material can be solid, liquid or gas. Sound cannot travel through a vacuum.

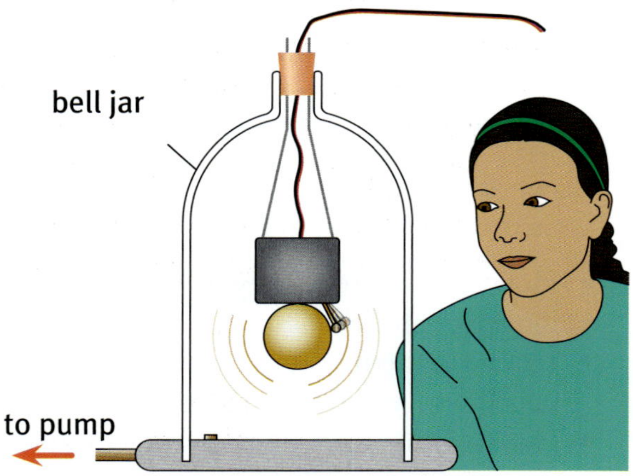

Can sound travel through a vacuum?

Questions

2 Explain how this experiment shows that light can travel through a vacuum.

A+I

3 We can see the Sun but we cannot hear it. Explain these two observations.

Sound travelling

You should remember that air is made up of tiny particles called molecules. By thinking about these particles, we can explain how sound travels.

Vibrations of the loudspeaker create a sound wave in air.

When a loudspeaker makes a sound, its cone vibrates back and forth. This pushes the air molecules next to the cone so that they move back and forth with the same frequency. These molecules then push on the next layer of molecules so that they also start to vibrate.

These molecules push on the next ones, and so on. The molecules only vibrate from side to side, but the vibration travels outwards through the air. We call this a **sound wave**.

Take care! Molecules of the air do not travel all the way from the loudspeaker to your ear. You hear the sound because the vibrations are passed along from one molecule to the next.

Activity 10.3

Sound waves

Try out some simple experiments which show how sound waves travel.

- Watch a candle flame moving in front of a loudspeaker.
- Use a long spring to show how a vibration can move.
- Test whether sound waves can be reflected by a hard surface.
- Measure the time taken for sound to reach you.

For each experiment, write one sentence to describe what you saw. Write a second sentence to explain what you saw.

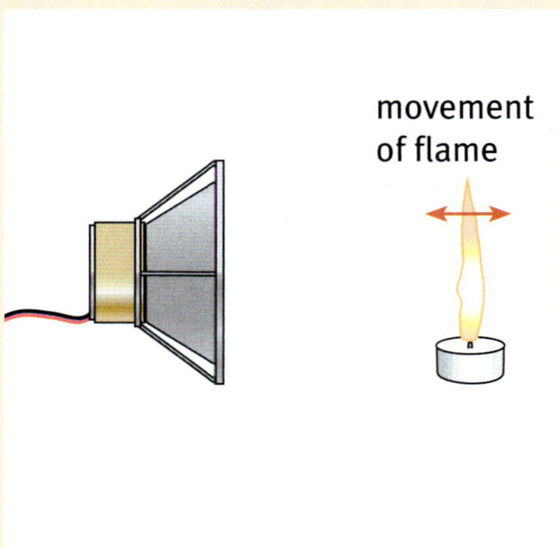

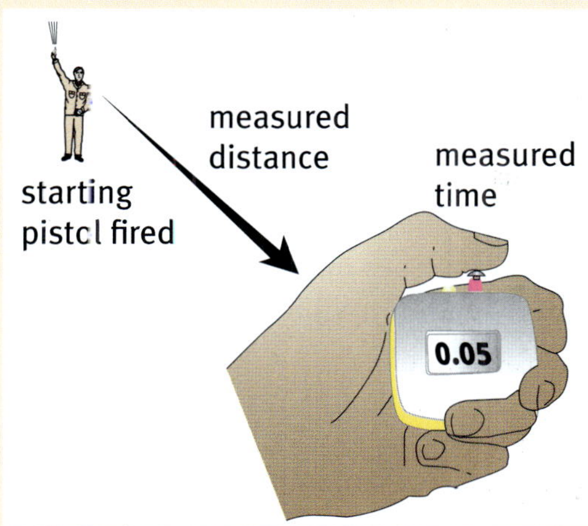

Summary

- Sound needs a material to travel through. Sound cannot travel through a vacuum.
- Sound travels when particles push each other back and forth. This is a sound wave.

10.4 Sounds on a screen

A sound wave is a vibration travelling through the air, or through another material. We cannot see a sound wave.

A microphone can detect sound waves. It changes them into electrical vibrations.

Question

A+I

1 Who might use a microphone in their work? What would they use it for?

Seeing a trace

If you connect a microphone to an **oscilloscope**, it will allow you to see a picture of the sound wave, as a line on the screen. The line is called a trace.

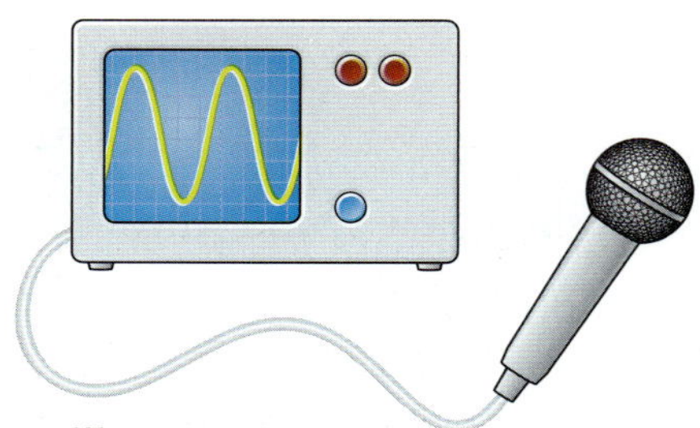

A microphone connected to an oscilloscope.

Changing amplitude

The pictures on the right show what happens to the trace on the oscilloscope screen when the loudness of the sound changes.

- When there is no sound (silence), the trace is a flat line. The air molecules are not vibrating.

Silence.

- With a quiet sound, the trace goes up and down a bit in the shape of a wave. It has a small amplitude.

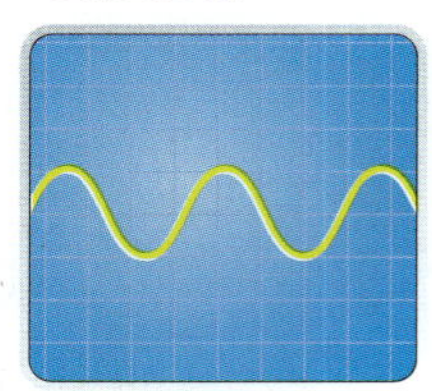

Quiet sound.

- With a loud sound, the trace goes up and down much more. Its amplitude is greater.

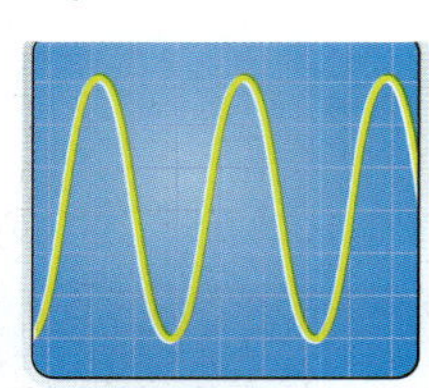

Loud sound.

Remember that we measure the amplitude from the middle of the trace to the peak (the highest point).

Question

2 Draw a diagram to show what is meant by the amplitude of a trace on an oscilloscope screen.

Changing pitch

The pitch of a sound tells you how high or low it is. The two traces shown here are for a high-pitched sound and for a low-pitched sound.

- You can see that, for a high-pitched sound, the waves shown by the trace are closer together. This is because the sound has a higher frequency. The molecules of the air are vibrating more times each second.
- For a low-pitched sound, the waves are more spread out. They don't go up and down so often because the sound has a lower frequency.

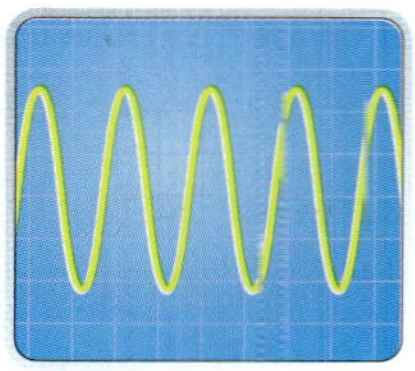

High-pitched sound.

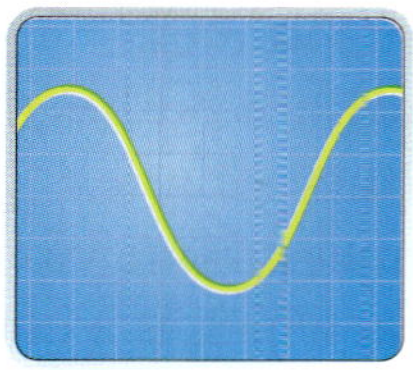

Low-pitched sound.

Question

3 Draw **two** oscilloscope traces, side-by-side, to show the following:
   a a quiet sound with a low pitch
   b a loud sound with a high pitch.

Activity 10.4
Screen sounds

SE

Your teacher will show you a microphone connected to an oscilloscope. Your task is to predict:

- what you will hear
- what you will see on the screen

when you try each of the following.

1. A quiet sound gets louder and then quieter again.
2. The frequency of a sound is increased and then decreased.
3. The microphone is moved closer to the loudspeaker, and then further away again.
4. Someone plays a note on a musical instrument.

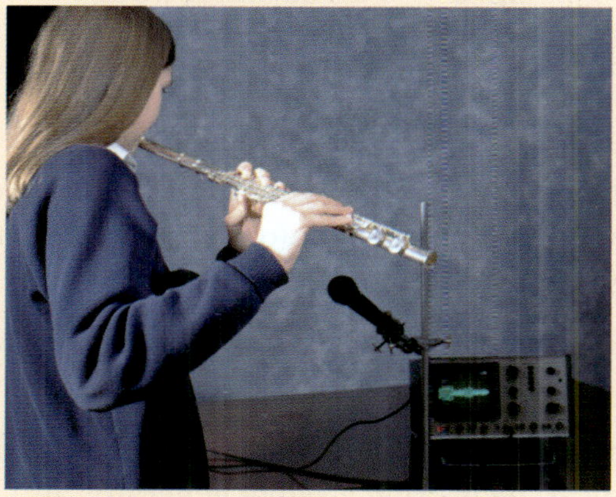

Summary

- An oscilloscope can be used to display traces representing sound waves.
- Louder sounds have waves with a greater amplitude.
- High-pitched sounds have waves squashed more closely together.

10.5 How we hear

Sound waves are vibrations moving through the air. How do we hear these waves?

Our ears are our 'sound detectors'. The diagram shows the structure of an ear.

- The vibrations travel down the ear canal.
- The vibrating air pushes on the **eardrum** so that it vibrates.
- The eardrum pushes the three small bones so that they vibrate.
- The smallest bone vibrates against the **cochlea**, which is a curled-up tube filled with liquid.
- The vibrations travel through the liquid, stimulating the nerve cells inside the cochlea. These send electrical signals along the nerve to the brain.

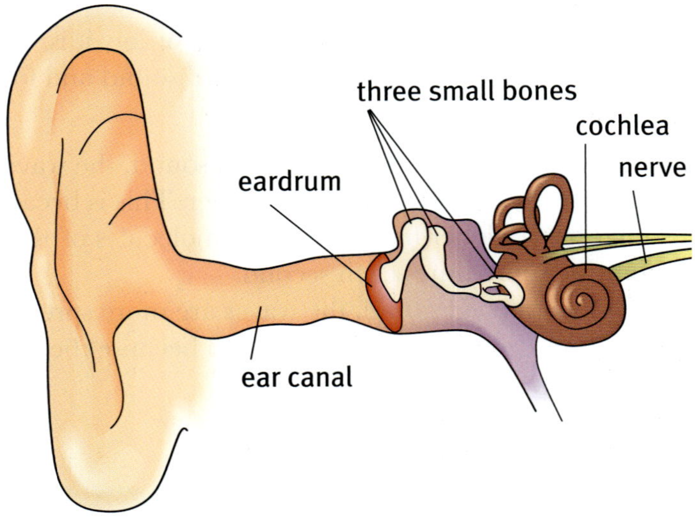

The structure of the human ear.

Question

1 The list below shows the parts of the ear. List them in the correct order to show how the vibrations of a sound wave eventually reach the brain.

cochlea **three small bones** **nerve**
ear canal **eardrum** **brain**

Hearing high and low

When you are young, you probably have good hearing. You can hear very faint (quiet) sounds. You can hear very high-pitched sounds.

Older people gradually lose the ability to hear the faintest sounds and the highest sounds.

You can find out which are the highest and lowest notes you can hear using a signal generator and a loudspeaker.

The signal generator can make sounds with different frequencies.

Activity 10.5
Hearing test

Your teacher will use the signal generator to make sounds with different frequencies.

What is the highest frequency you can hear? What is the lowest frequency?

Range of hearing

Most people can hear sounds with frequencies as low as 20 Hz. Young people (aged under 20) can usually hear sounds of up to about 20 000 Hz.

As people get older, their hearing deteriorates. By the time they are 50, they may not hear sounds above 15 000 Hz.

Sounds above 20 000 Hz are beyond the range of human hearing. Such sounds are known as **ultrasound**. Many animals can hear ultrasound.

Bats use ultrasound to find their way around. They emit high-pitched squeaks and listen to the reflected waves.

The bat listens for reflected ultrasound waves. In this way, it can tell how far it is from the wall.

Question

2 Which of the following frequencies would you expect a young person to be able to hear? 500 Hz, 6000 Hz, 25 000 Hz, 15 Hz, 15 000 Hz

Noise annoys

There are many sounds we don't want to hear. Unwanted sound is called **noise**.

Loud sounds can damage our ears. Listening to music through headphones can be harmful if you have the volume turned up too high.

Keep the volume down or you may damage your hearing.

Often there are laws to protect workers who work in noisy places. They should wear ear protectors so that they do not become deaf.

The chainsaw is noisy so the woodworker wears ear protectors.

Question

A+I

3 Suggest some jobs where people have to work in a noisy environment.

Summary

- Our ears convert sound waves into nerve signals to the brain.
- Young people can usually hear sounds whose frequencies lie between 20 Hz and 20 000 Hz.
- Loud sounds can damage our hearing.

Unit 10 End of unit questions

10.1 Write down whether each of the following statements about sound is true or false.

- **a** Sounds are produced by sources which vibrate. [1]
- **b** Sounds are carried by air which moves from the source to our ears. [1]
- **c** The frequency of a sound is the number of vibrations each second. [1]
- **d** A sound with a higher frequency is louder than one with a lower frequency. [1]
- **e** Sound can travel through solids, liquids and gases. [1]
- **f** Sound can travel through a vacuum. [1]
- **g** Sound waves travelling down the ear canal push on the cochlea. [1]

10.2 Loudspeaker **A** vibrates 200 times each second. Loudspeaker **B** vibrates 400 times each second.

- **a** What is the frequency of the sound produced by loudspeaker **A**? Give the value and the unit. [2]
- **b** Which loudspeaker produces the note with the lower pitch? [1]
- **c** A ruler vibrates 70 times in 20 seconds. What is the frequency of its vibration? [3]

10.3 The diagram below shows a trace which represents a sound wave.

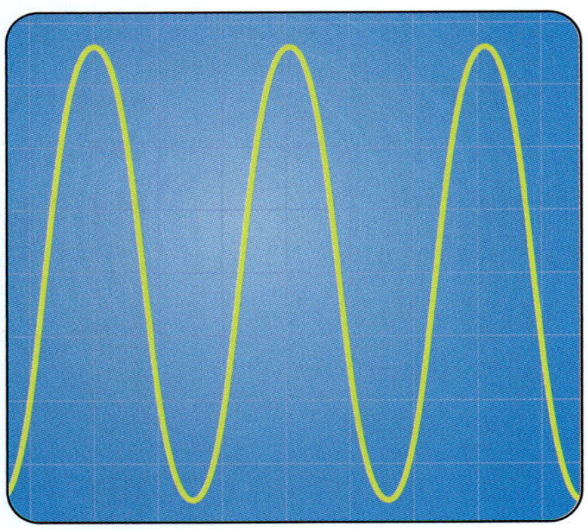

Copy the trace.

- **a** On your copy, mark the amplitude of the wave. [1]
- **b** Add a second trace to show a wave which has the same amplitude as the wave shown but a higher frequency. [2]

10.4 The trace below represents a sound wave which is changing.

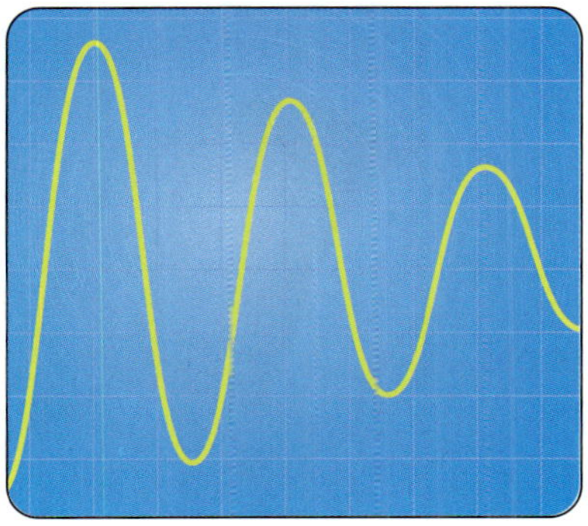

a State whether the frequency of the wave is increasing, decreasing or staying the same. [1]

b State whether the pitch of the sound is increasing, decreasing or staying the same. [1]

c State whether the loudness of the wave is increasing, decreasing or staying the same. Explain your answer. [2]

11.1 How light travels

Light is important to us. We see things because light from them enters our eyes.

Sight is one of our most important senses. We use it to find out about the world around us.

This baby is just a few weeks old. She is undergoing an eye test.

Sources of light

A **light source** is an object that emits its own light. Hot objects such as flames and the Sun are light sources. A torch bulb has a hot filament, so it is also a light source.

Some light sources are not hot – for example, a computer screen.

A torch bulb is a source of light.

Question

1 Give **four** examples of objects that are light sources.

Straight lines

The photograph of the Sun behind the clouds shows us how light travels. You can see the straight **rays** of light spreading out from the Sun in the photograph. This tells us that light travels in straight lines.

The Sun is hidden behind the clou
but we can see its rays.

Question

A+I **2** Look again at the photograph. You cannot see the Sun, but you can easily work out where it is in the sky. Explain how you could use a ruler to work out the Sun's position in the sky. Make a sketch to show your idea.

Activity 11.1

Light travelling in straight lines

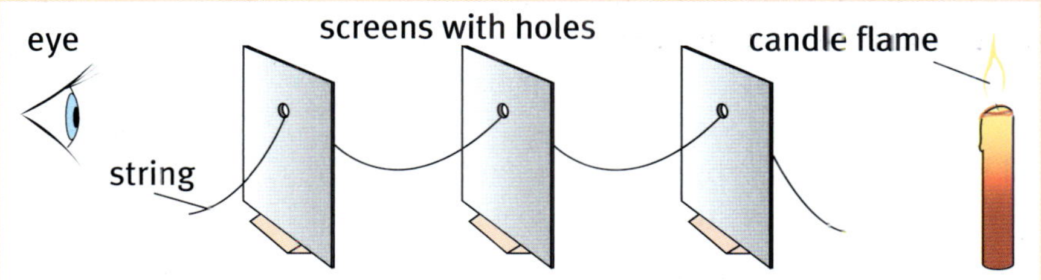

Here is one way to show that light travels in straight lines.

Each of the three cards has a small hole in it. Pull the string so that it is taut (tight and straight). Then the three holes will be arranged in a straight line.

Look through the holes and you will see the candle flame. Light from the flame passes through the three holes, one after another.

Make a prediction: what will happen if you move one of the cards sideways? Does it matter which card you move? Test your ideas.

Luminous and non-luminous

An object which is a source of light is described as **luminous**. An object which is not a source of light is described as **non-luminous**.

We see non-luminous objects because they reflect light to our eyes. For example, the chair in the diagram is a non-luminous object. The person can see it because light from the lamp reflects off it.

In the diagram, we show the light from the lamp travelling in straight lines.

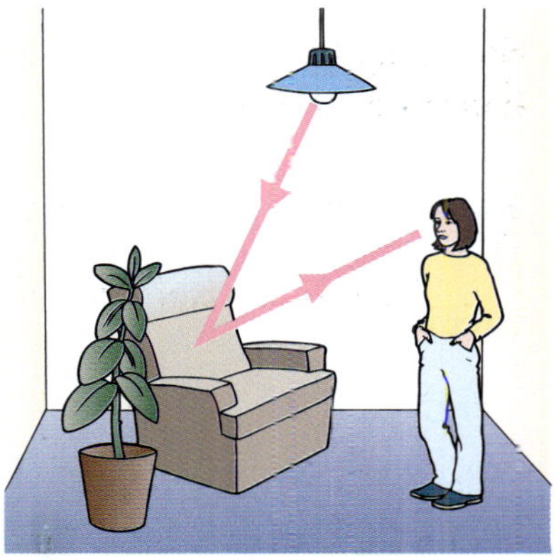

The chair is non-luminous. We need a source of light to see it.

Questions

A+I

3 Imagine that you are reading a book. A lamp is nearby to help you see the pages. Draw a diagram to show how light from the lamp makes it possible for you to read the book.

4 In Stage **7** Unit **11**, you learnt that we see the Moon and planets by reflected light.

a What is the source of this light?

b Is the Moon a luminous or non-luminous object?

c Draw a diagram to show how someone on Earth sees the Moon by reflected light.

Summary

- Light travels in straight lines.
- We see luminous objects because they are light sources.
- We see non-luminous objects because they reflect light to our eyes.

11.2 How shadows form

When light strikes an object, different things can happen. It depends on the material the object is made of.

- The light may pass straight through the object. We say that it has been **transmitted**. The material is **transparent**.
- The light may be absorbed by the object. (The object gets a little warmer.) The material is **opaque**.
- The light may bounce off the object. We say that it has been **reflected.**

Sometimes two of these things can happen, or all three. For example, glass transmits light but it may also reflect some of it.

In the shade

On a sunny day, you may want to stay in the shade. You need to find somewhere where the Sun's hot rays cannot reach you.

A shadow forms when light from a light source is blocked by an opaque object. The area where there is a shadow is darker because less light is reaching it.

These children are staying in the shade while two of their friends are playing in the sunlight – you can see their shadows on the ground.

Forming a shadow

A shadow forms when an opaque object blocks the light. It forms because light travels in straight lines – it cannot bend round corners.

The diagram shows one way to understand this. A pencil stands in front of a white card screen.

When light from a torch is directed at the pencil, the shadow of the pencil appears on the screen.

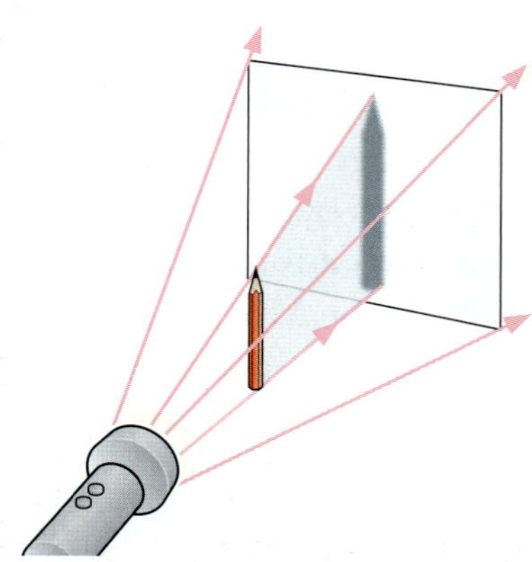

Because light travels in straight lines, it cannot bend round the pencil.

Questions

1. The pencil has a shadow. Is the pencil opaque or transparent?
2. A shiny object reflects light. Will a shiny object make a shadow when light shines on it? Explain your answer.

Rays of light

When we want to understand light, we often draw diagrams with straight lines, showing the paths of the light rays.

To understand where the tree's shadow will fall, we need to draw lots of rays of light, all coming from the Sun. Then we can see which rays are blocked by the tree. This will show us where the tree's shadow will be.

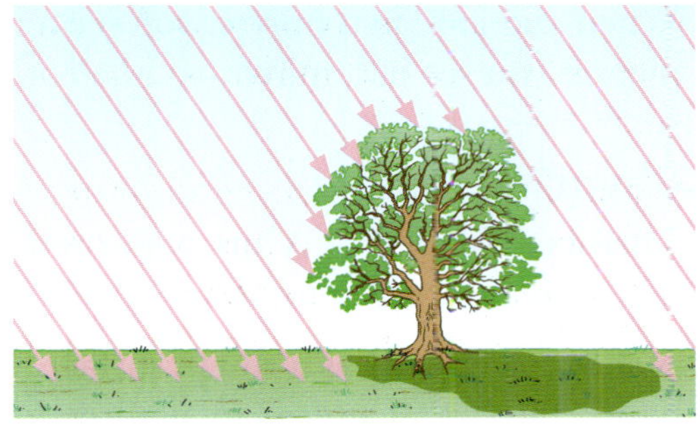

The tree blocks some of the Sun's rays.

Questions

3 Explain why we draw straight lines to show rays of light.

A+I

4 Look again at the diagram of the tree and its shadow. Later in the day, the Sun will move round so that it is shining from the top right-hand corner of the diagram. Redraw the diagram with the Sun's rays coming from the top right and work out where the tree's shadow will be.

Activity 11.2

Shadows large and small

SE

Shadows change during the day as the Sun moves across the sky. Their direction changes and their size changes.

Look at the photograph of the lemurs. They have long tails, but the shadows of their tails are even longer. How can this be?

Explain why shadows change their size, according to the Sun's position in the sky. Here are some things you might use to investigate this:

- a toy animal or doll
- a bright light
- a ruler, pencil and protractor
- a sheet of paper.

You could demonstrate your ideas to the rest of the class. You could make diagrams to show your ideas.

Summary

- A ray is a straight line which shows the path of light.
- A shadow forms when an opaque object blocks light.

11.3 How reflections form

When you look in a mirror, you see a clear reflection of yourself. The picture you see in a mirror is called an **image**.

A mirror gives a clear image of whatever is in front of it.

Bouncing light

Mirrors reflect light. White paper reflects light. Why do we see a clear image in a mirror but not in a sheet of paper?

A sheet of paper has a rough surface. When rays of light strike the paper, they are scattered in all directions.

A mirror has a very flat, smooth surface. Rays of light bounce off a mirror without being scattered.

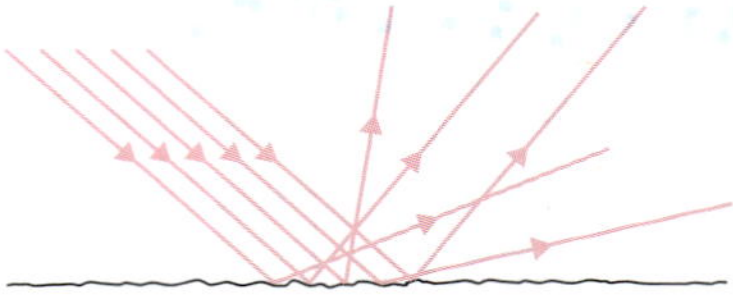

A piece of paper scatters light in all directions.

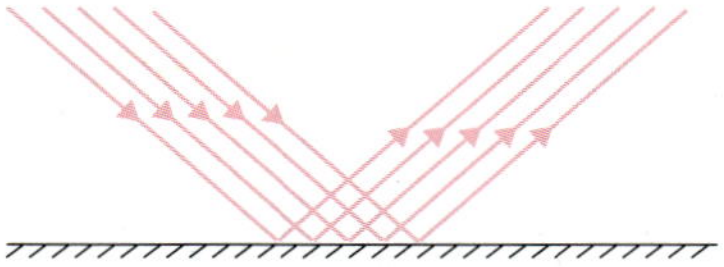

A mirror reflects all the light in the same direction.

Predicting the path of light

If you shine a ray of light at a mirror, it reflects off the mirror. The **law of reflection** tells us about the direction in which the ray is reflected. The diagram on the right shows this.

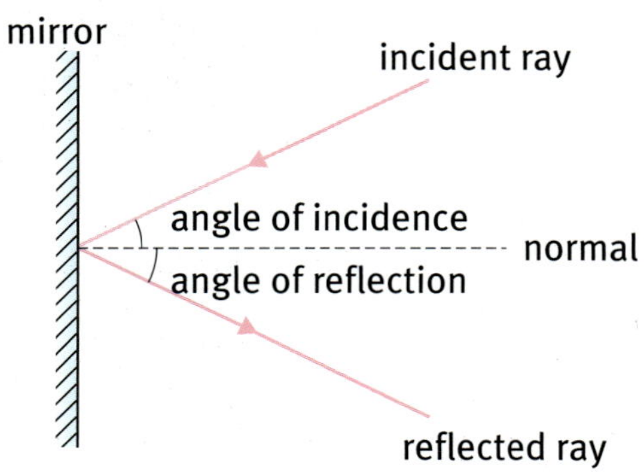

Diagram showing the law of reflection of light.

Here is how to understand this diagram:

- The mirror is represented by a straight line; the shading shows the back of the mirror.
- The ray of light coming in is called the **incident ray**. The ray of light going out is the **reflected ray**.
- To predict the direction of the reflected ray, we need to draw the **normal** to the surface of the mirror. The normal is a straight line drawn at right angles (90°) to the mirror at the point where the ray is reflected.

The law of reflection of light says that the two angles marked in the diagram are equal. (Note that each of the angles is measured from the normal to the ray, not from the ray to the mirror.)

Law of reflection:

angle of incidence = angle of reflection

Questions

A+I

1 Give **three** uses of mirrors in everyday life.
2 If you look into a pond or a calm river, you may see a clear reflection of yourself. What does this tell you about the surface of the water?
3 Make a copy of the diagram showing the law of reflection. Use a ruler to draw the rays and the mirror. Use a protractor to make sure that you draw the normal at 90° to the mirror. Draw the angles of incidence and reflection with values of 30°. Label your diagram fully.
4 If a ray of light strikes a mirror with an angle of incidence of 60°, what will be the angle of reflection? Sketch a diagram of this situation.

Activity 11.3
Law of reflection

SE

You can use a ray box and a plane (flat) mirror to show that the law of reflection is correct.

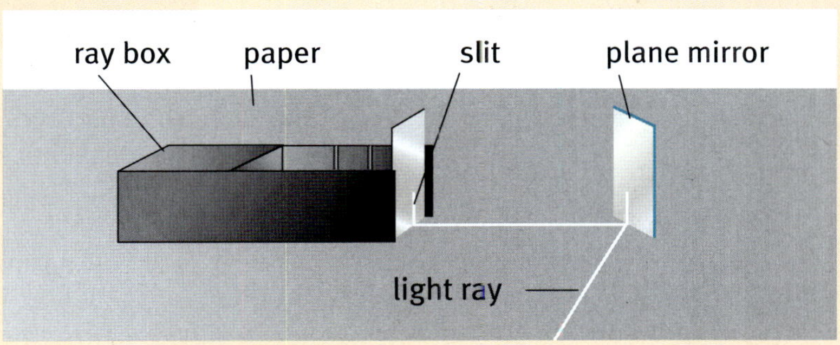

Testing the law of reflection.

1 Stand the mirror on a sheet of white paper. Using a pencil, draw a line along the back of the mirror (where its reflecting surface is).
2 Direct a ray of light at the mirror. Look for the reflected ray.
3 Mark two dots on the incident ray and two dots on the reflected ray.
4 Now remove the sheet of paper. Using a ruler, draw the paths of the two rays. The dots will show you their paths. Use a protractor to help you draw in the normal. Mark the angle of incidence and angle of reflection and measure them with a protractor. Are they equal?
5 Repeat this with the ray striking the mirror at a different angle.

Summary

- Smooth surfaces reflect light according to the law of reflection.
- Law of reflection: angle of incidence = angle of reflection.

11.4 How light bends

The photograph shows a pencil standing in a beaker of water. The pencil looks as if it is broken at the point where it enters the water.

You may have noticed other strange effects when looking through water or glass – a river or pool may look shallower than it really is, for example.

The pencil looks broken – we see the lower half of it through water.

Transparent materials

Water and glass are transparent materials. Light can pass through them, but something happens when light enters or leaves such a material.

We need to follow the path of a ray to see what happens. The photograph shows how a ray of light bends when it enters a glass block. It bends again when it leaves the block.

The change of direction of a light ray when it enters or leaves a transparent material is called **refraction**.

The light ray is refracted when it enters and leaves the glass block.

Question

1 Look at the photograph of the ray of light travelling through the glass block. Where does the ray bend? What path does it follow inside the glass block?

Rays changing direction

The diagram shows how someone can see a coin lying at the bottom of a pool of water. How does a ray of light travel from the coin to the person's eye?

The ray travels in a straight line to the surface of the water. This is where it bends.

The straight ray then travels to the eye.

To understand how it bends, we draw the normal to the surface at the point where the ray bends. The normal is drawn at 90° to the surface.

We can see that the ray bends away from the normal as it leaves the water.

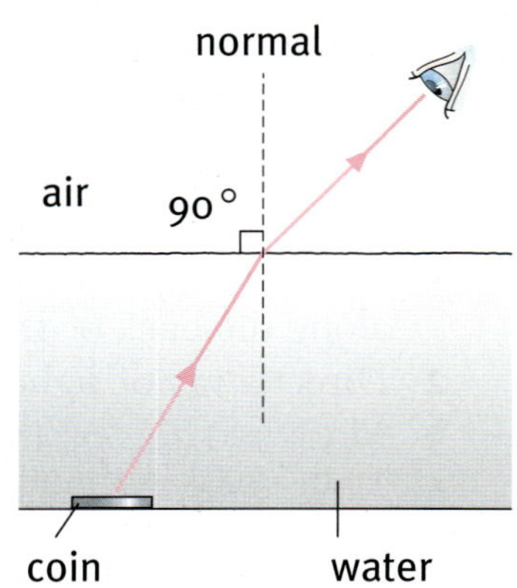

The ray bends as it leaves the water.

Question

2 Look at the photograph above which shows the light ray passing through the glass block.

a Find the point where the ray leaves the glass. Does it bend away from the normal?

b Which way does the ray bend when it enters the glass?

Activity 11.4
Refracted rays

The diagrams show how a ray of light bends when it enters a glass block.

Check that these diagrams show correctly what happens when a ray of light is refracted by glass.

If a ray enters the glass along the normal, it does not bend. Is this correct?

If a ray enters the glass at bigger angle, it bends more. Is this correct?

(Take care! The angles are measured between the ray and the normal.)

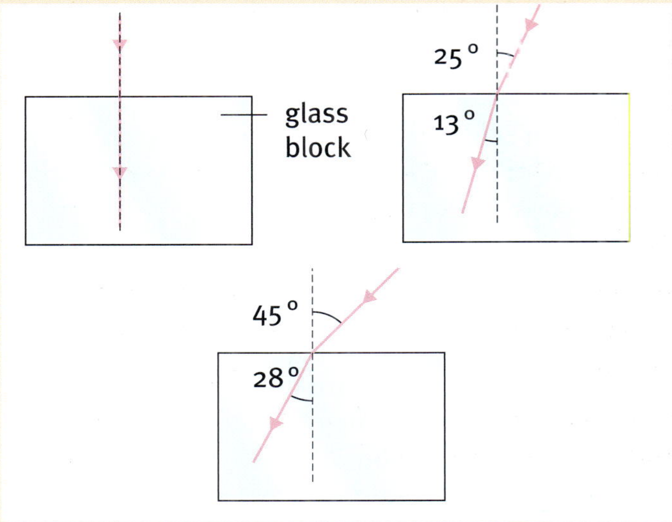

The hidden coin

The picture shows a trick you can perform that makes use of refraction. A coin is placed in the bottom of a can. Move your head so that the coin is just hidden behind the rim of the can.

Now ask someone to carefully pour water into the can. The coin appears!

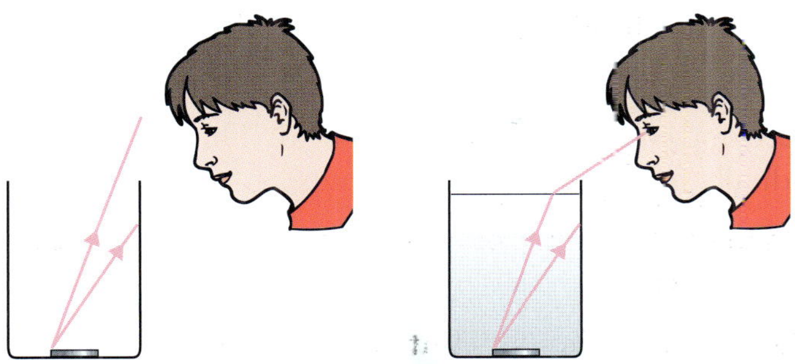

With water in the can, the coin can be seen.

Question

A+I

3 Use the idea of refraction to explain why the coin can be seen when there is water in the can.

Summary

- Light is refracted when it enters or leaves a transparent material.
- A light ray bends towards the normal when it passes from air into a transparent material.
- A light ray bends away from the normal when it passes from a transparent material into air.

11.5 The spectrum of white light

Sometimes, if it rains and the Sun shines at the same time, you may see a rainbow. You have to stand with your back to the Sun; you will see an arch of beautiful colours looking as though it is hanging in the air.

A rainbow over a village in Tibet.

Splitting light

You can see the colours of the rainbow for yourself by sending a ray of white light into a glass prism. (A prism is a triangular glass block.)

When the light enters the prism it bends – it is refracted. It also bends as it leaves the prism.

Something else happens. The white light is split up into a **spectrum** of colours. They are the same colours as you see in a rainbow. The splitting up of white light into separate colours is called **dispersion**.

The colours of the spectrum always appear in the same order:

red orange yellow green blue indigo violet

(Indigo is a dark blue-purple colour.) Although we say there are seven colours in the spectrum, there are no dividing lines where one colour changes to the next. The colour changes gradually from one shade to the next.

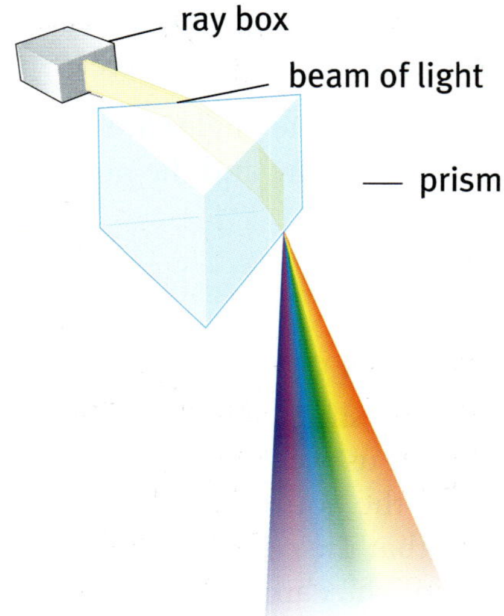

Making a spectrum using a prism.

The colours of the spectrum.

Questions

1. Look at the diagram of the spectrum being formed by a prism. Which colour is refracted most as it passes through the prism? Which colour is refracted least? Red least and violet more
2. A rainbow appears when sunlight is dispersed to form a spectrum. What is the transparent material that causes this? water droplets or water vapoor.
3. To remember the colours in the spectrum, some people write this: Roy G. Biv. It looks like someone's name. How will this help them to remember the order of the colours? It is the names of rainbow colour.

Explaining dispersion

Because a spectrum appears when light passes through a glass prism, some people imagined that it was the glass that gave the colours to the light. Isaac Newton realised that this was incorrect. He showed that white light (such as light from the Sun) is a mixture of all the different colours of the spectrum.

Dispersion happens because of refraction. When white light enters a block of glass, some colours bend more than others. Violet bends the most, red the least. This means that the different colours travel off in different directions, and so we can see them separately.

Question

A+I

4 Which colour of light is refracted more by a prism, green or blue? Explain how you can tell. Blue, because it has shorter wave lenght.

Activity 11.5

A rainbow in the lab

1. Place the prism on a piece of white paper. Draw around it with a pencil to mark its position.
2. Shine a ray of light from a ray box or a torch into the prism. Aim for a point near one corner of the prism.
3. Adjust the position of the ray until you get a clear spectrum emerging from the prism.
4. On the paper, mark two dots on the ray going into the prism. Mark the positions of the red and violet rays coming from the prism.
5. Remove the prism and the light source. Draw in the rays and label your diagram.

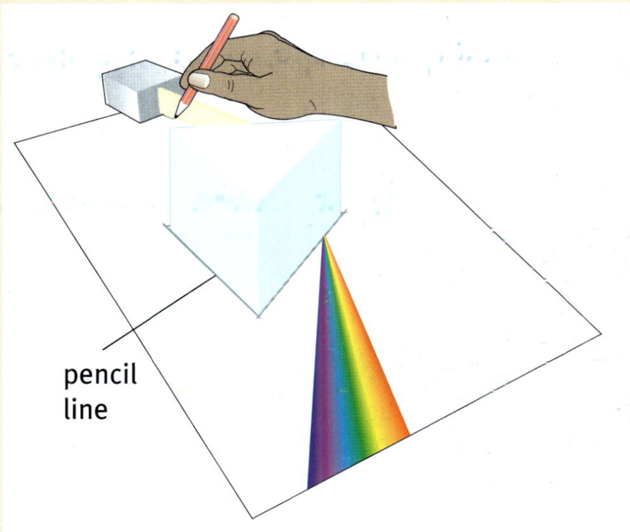

Summary

- White light is made up of all the colours of the spectrum, from red to violet.
- White light can be split up into these colours using a prism; this is called dispersion.
- Dispersion happens because some colours of light are refracted more than others.

11.6 Coloured light

In the theatre, coloured lights are used to make interesting effects. To make coloured light, a filter is placed in front of a bright white light.

A **filter** is a piece of coloured plastic or glass. It only lets through some of the colours which make up white light. It absorbs the other colours.

For example, a red filter lets through red light (and a bit of orange). It absorbs yellow, green, blue, indigo and violet.

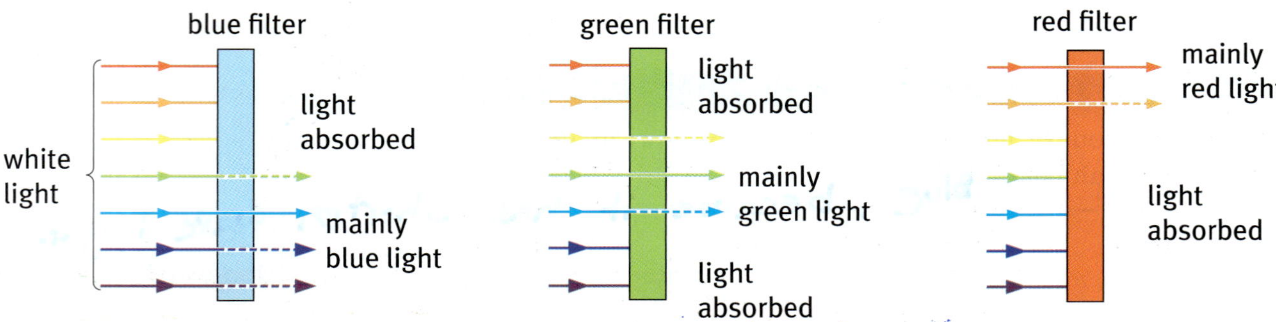

How coloured filters make light of different colours.

Questions

1 Which colours can pass through a blue filter? Which colours are absorbed?

A+I 2 Imagine that you put a green filter next to a blue filter, so that white light had to pass through one filter after the other. Would any light come through?

A+I 3 Which **two** filters, if placed together, would absorb all colours of light?

Adding coloured light

A prism divides white light into a spectrum. Here is how to put white light back together again.

Put red, green and blue filters on three torches. Shine them so that their different colours overlap. Where all three meet, you will see white. This is because each filter lets through one third of the spectrum. When you use them together, all colours of the spectrum are present and they add up to give white.

Red, green and blue are called the **primary colours** of light. When two or more colours of light are mixed together, this is called colour addition.

Coloured lights can add together to make other colours.

Reflecting coloured light

Grass is green. When you see grass, green light from the grass is entering your eye.

Grass is green because it reflects green light from the Sun. It absorbs all of the other colours of sunlight. The grass has removed most of the colours of the sunlight. This is called colour subtraction. Other colours work the same way. For example, a red object reflects red light and absorbs all other colours. White objects reflect all colours of light and black objects absorb all colours.

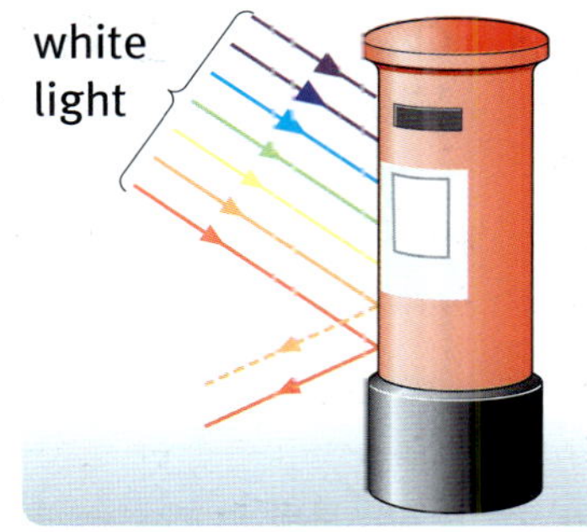

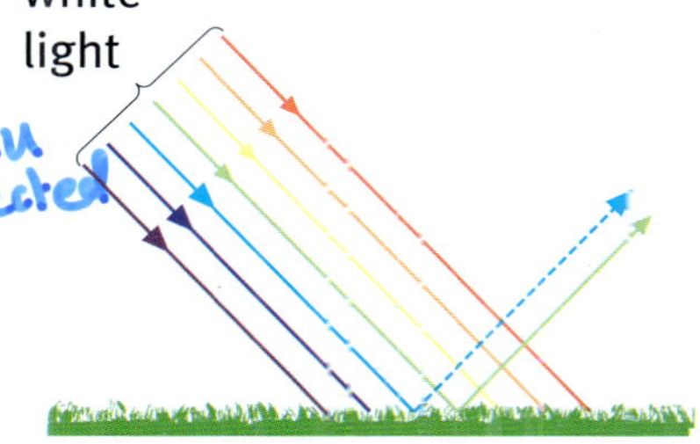

Questions

4 Which colours of light are reflected by a black object? no light will be reflected

5 Look at the diagram of the postbox. It is painted with red paint. Explain why it looks red when white light shines on it. Use the words 'reflected' and 'absorbed' in your explanation.

when it reflected the colour will be orange and red will be reflected. Indigo, violent, blue, green, yellow will be reflected.

Activity 11.6
Colour changes

Grass does not always look green. At night it looks black because no light is falling on it, so no light is reflected to our eyes.

1 The picture shows a postbox with grass around it. The scene looks different when red light is shone on it, and when green light is shone on it.
With a partner, discuss why the appearance of the scene changes. When you have decided on your explanation, compare your ideas with another pair.

2 Now try to decide what the scene will look like if yellow and green light are shone on it.

3 Use coloured pens or pencils to draw a simple scene. Shine coloured light on your scene. Does it look different if you change the colour of the light?

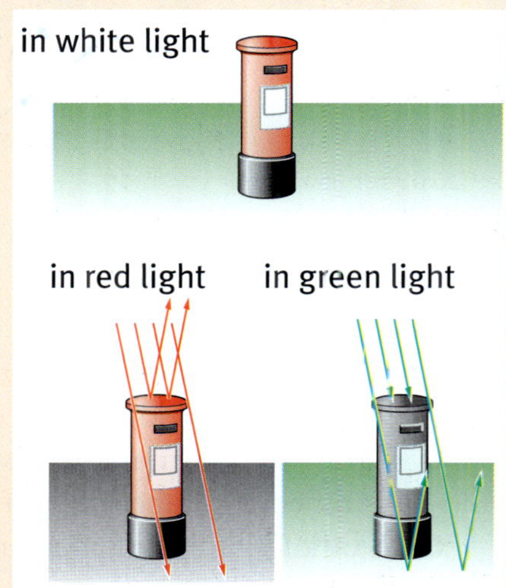

Summary

- Coloured filters transmit some colours of light and absorb others.
- The primary colours of light (red, green and blue) add to make white light.
- Objects look different colours because they reflect some colours of light and absorb others.

Unit 11 End of unit questions

11.1 Copy the table below. Use words from the list to fill the first column of your table. You may use each word once, more than once, or not at all.

opaque **image** **transparent** **non-luminous** **shadow** **mirror**

	What you see when you look in a mirror
	A region where no light falls
	Describes an object that blocks light
	Describes a material that allows light to pass through
	Describes an object that we see because it reflects light

11.2 A student drew this diagram to show how a ray of light is reflected by a flat mirror.

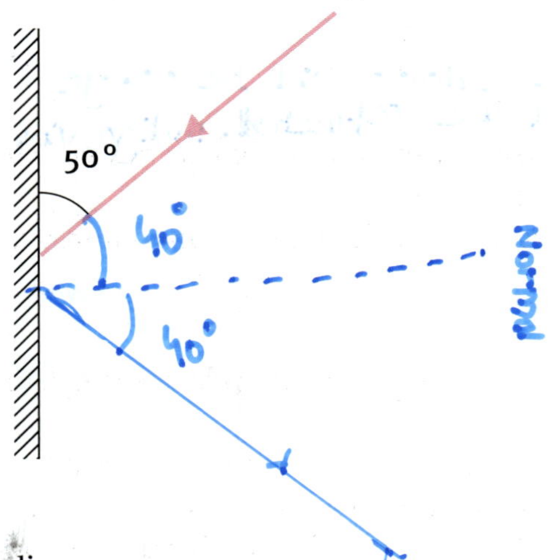

Make a copy of the diagram.

a On your copy of the diagram draw the reflected ray. Label the mirror, the incident ray and the reflected ray. [1]

b Draw the normal to the surface of the mirror at the point where the ray is reflected. Label the normal. [1]

c Mark the angle of incidence and the angle of reflection. Label them **I** and **R**. [2]

d Calculate the value of the angle of incidence. [1]

e Use the law of reflection to determine the value of the angle of reflection. [1]

11.3 The diagram shows a ray of light passing from air into a glass block.

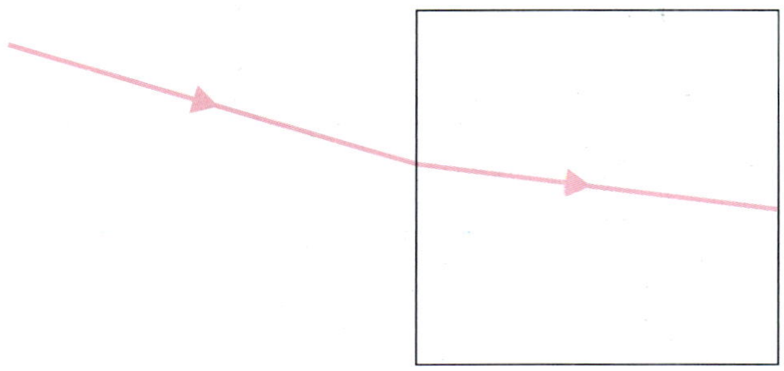

- **a** What name is given to the bending of light when it travels from one material into another? [1]
- **b** Does the ray bend towards the normal or away from the normal when it enters glass from air? [1]
- **c** State how a ray of light can travel from air into glass without bending. Illustrate your answer with a diagram. [1]
- **d** Draw a diagram to show how a ray of light bends when it travels from glass into air. [1]

11.4 When white light passes through a prism, it is split up into a spectrum of different colours.

- **a** What name is given to the forming of a spectrum by a prism? [1]
- **b** Which colour of the spectrum is refracted most by a prism? [1]
- **c** Which colour lies between yellow and blue in the spectrum of white light? [1]
- **d** A student shines a mixture of red and blue light onto a blue toy car. What colour will the car appear to have? Explain your answer. [2]

12.1 Magnets and magnetic materials

Magnets are useful things.

- Magnets can be used to hold cupboard doors shut.
- They are used in electric motors and generators.
- They are used in headphones and loudspeakers.
- They have fun uses – for example, magnetic letters.

This child is learning to spell using magnetic letters on the board.

Question

1 Think about your own home. Can you suggest some other uses for magnets?

Permanent magnets

Permanent magnets come in different shapes and sizes. They can be used to attract other objects – for example, paper clips made of steel.

A permanent magnet is an object which stays **magnetised** for a long time. It doesn't stop being a magnet after it has been used.

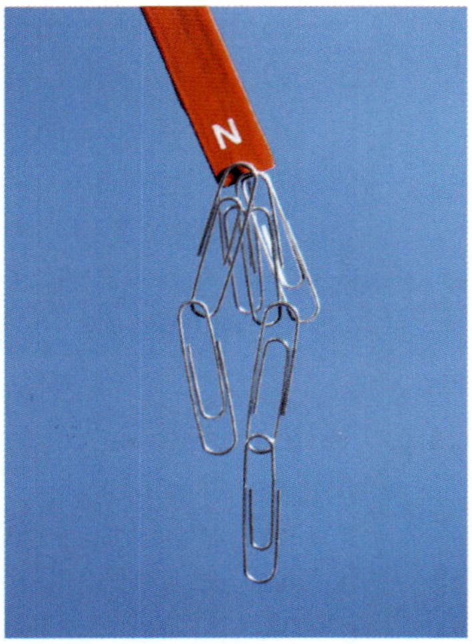

Permanent magnets come in different shapes. This shape is a bar magnet.

Magnetic materials

Some materials are attracted by magnets. Other materials are not.

A material which is attracted by a magnet is called a **magnetic material**.

Question

2 Paper clips are made from a magnetic material. What material is this? (You will find the answer higher up on this page.)

Activity 12.1A
Magnetic and non-magnetic materials

Some people imagine that all metals are magnetic materials. Are they correct?

Use a permanent magnet to test a number of different materials. Which are attracted by the magnet?

Show your results in two lists: **magnetic materials** and **non-magnetic materials**.

Iron and steel

Iron is a magnetic material. Steel is mostly made of iron, so most types of steel are also magnetic.

Nickel and cobalt are two other magnetic metals. Nowadays many small, strong magnets are made using a metal called neodymium.

Other metals such as aluminium and tin are non-magnetic. The picture shows how steel and aluminium cans can be separated using a powerful magnet.

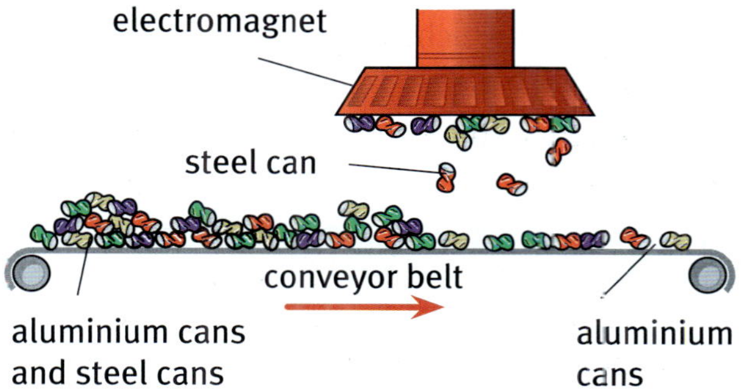

Questions

3 **a** Are steel cans magnetic or non-magnetic?
b Are aluminium cans magnetic or non-magnetic?

A+I **4** It is important to recycle cans because they are made from valuable materials. Write a paragraph to describe how steel and aluminium cans can be separated using a magnet, as shown in the diagram.

Activity 12.1B
Comparing magnets

SE Some permanent magnets are stronger than others. They attract magnetic materials with a stronger force.

Compare **three** permanent magnets. Devise your own method to decide which is the strongest and which is the weakest.

When you have completed your work, compare your method with the methods used by others in the class. Which do you consider the best, and why?

Summary

- A permanent magnet remains magnetic after it has been used.
- Magnetic materials are attracted by permanent magnets.

12.2 Magnetic poles

Magnets attract magnetic materials. There is a **magnetic force** which pulls on a piece of steel when a magnet attracts it.

You may have noticed that the force is strongest if you use the end of the magnet. A bar magnet's magnetism is strongest at the ends. The ends of the magnet are called its **magnetic poles**.

The poles are called the north pole (N) and the south pole (S). Why is this?

If you hang up a bar magnet so that it is free to turn around, it will turn until one end points towards the north – this end is the north pole of the magnet. The south pole points towards the south.

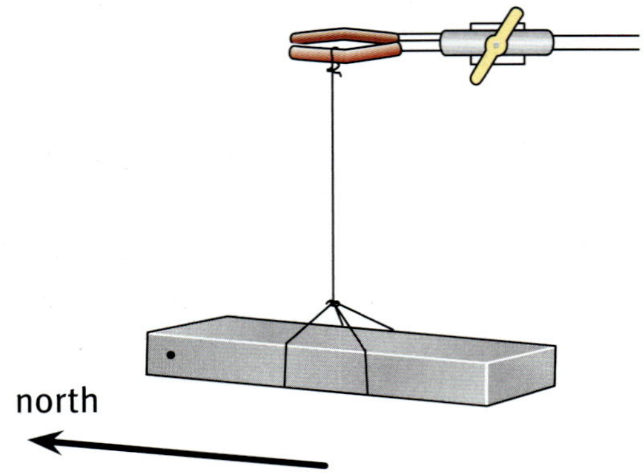

A bar magnet turns until it points north–south.

Two magnets

The diagram shows what happens when the poles of two magnets are close together. They may **attract** each other, or they may **repel** each other (push each other away). The arrows show the direction of the force on each magnet.

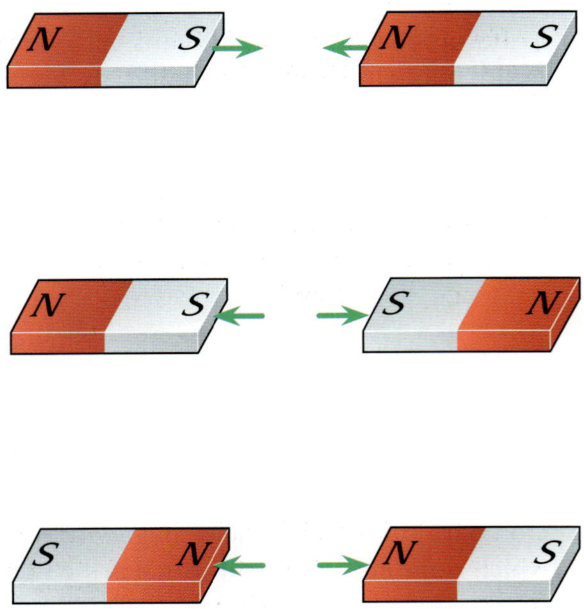

Two magnets can attract or repel each other.

Questions

1 In each of the diagrams are the magnets attracting each other or repelling each other?

2 a Copy and complete the sentence: When a north pole is close to a south pole, the magnets ...

b Write a similar sentence to say what happens when two north poles are close to each other.

Magnet rules

Here are the rules which tell us whether two magnetic poles will attract or repel:

- Like poles repel.
- Unlike poles attract.

In these rules, 'like poles' means both poles are the same (both north poles or both south poles). 'Unlike poles' means one north pole and one south pole. Sometimes people simply remember the phrase 'opposites attract'.

Activity 12.2A
Checking magnetic poles

1 Use two bar magnets and test the rules given on the opposite page. Are they correct?
2 Wrap one magnet in paper so that you cannot tell which pole is which. Exchange your wrapped magnet with another group. Test the wrapped magnet and label its poles. Unwrap it and see if you are correct.

Making a magnet

You can use a permanent magnet to **magnetise** a piece of iron or steel. Here is how:

- Lay the piece of iron or steel on the bench.
- Using one pole of the magnet, stroke it gently from one end to the other.
- Stroke it several times, using the same pole. Make sure you always stroke it in the same direction.

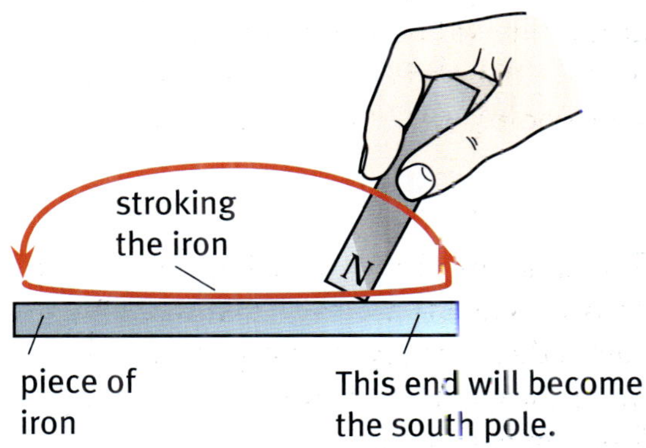

Question

3 Copy the diagram which shows how to magnetise a piece of iron. Label the poles of the iron when it has been magnetised.

Activity 12.2B
Magnetising steel

SE

1 Use a bar magnet to magnetise a piece of iron or steel.
2 Devise a way to show that the metal has been magnetised.
3 Test the new magnet: which end is its north pole?
4 Can you devise a way to produce a magnet with north poles at both ends?

Summary

- The north pole of a magnet will turn to point north.
- Like poles repel, unlike poles attract.
- A piece of unmagnetised iron or steel can be magnetised by stroking with one pole of a permanent magnet.

12.3 Magnetic field patterns

Magnets are surprising. A magnet can attract a piece of magnetic material without touching it.

We say that a magnet is surrounded by a **magnetic field**. Any magnetic material placed in the field will be attracted by the magnet.

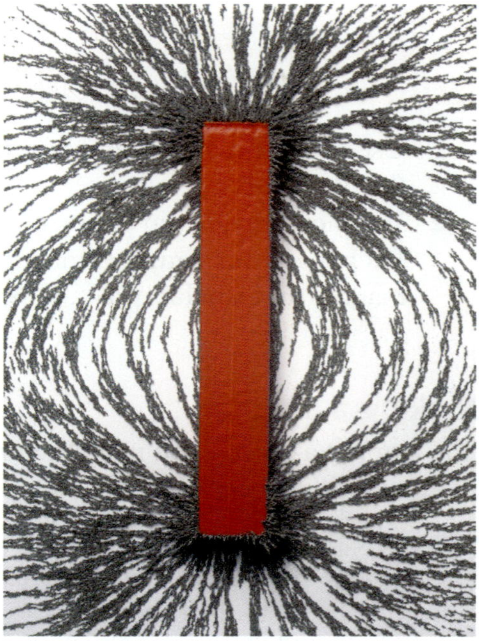

The iron filings show that the field of the magnet is concentrated (stronger) near the poles.

The shape of the field

A magnetic field is invisible. Here are two ways to show up the shape of the magnetic field around a bar magnet:

- Use iron filings. These tiny pieces of iron cluster together and line up to show the pattern of the field.
- Use small compasses called plotting compasses. They show the direction of the field.

Magnetic field lines

We can represent the magnetic field of a magnet by drawing **magnetic field lines**. These are imaginary lines.

Magnetic field lines start from a north pole and end up at a south pole. They show two things about the field:

- The arrows show the direction of the field.
- Where the lines are closest together is where the field is strongest.

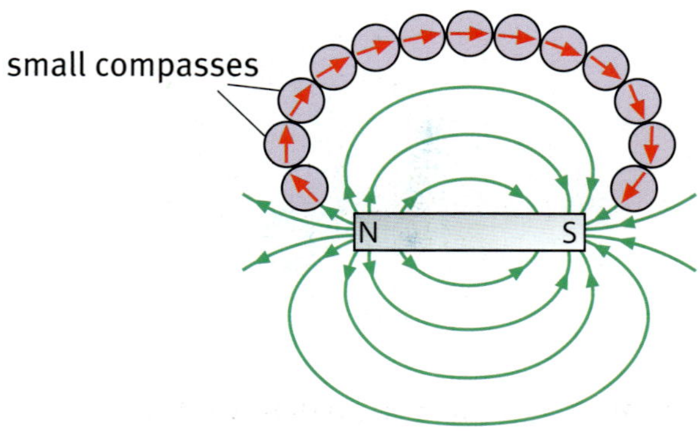

The compasses show the direction of the magnetic field.

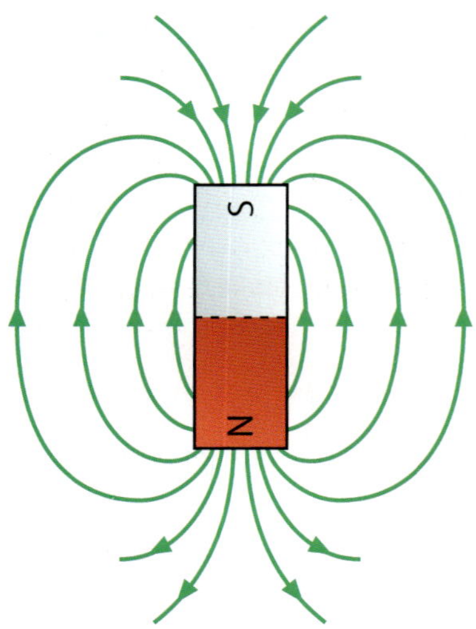

Using magnetic field lines to represent a magnetic field.

Questions

1. Look at the diagram of the field lines around a bar magnet. Where is the field strongest? Explain how you can tell.
2. Compare the diagram of the field lines with the photograph. In what ways are they similar?

Activity 12.3
Investigating magnetic fields

SE

1. Use iron filings to show up the magnetic field of a bar magnet.
   Safety! Take care to avoid getting the filings on your hands as you might rub them into your eyes.
2. Place two bar magnets so that their poles are attracting each other. Investigate the shape of the magnetic field between them.
3. Repeat this with the magnetic poles repelling each other.

The magnetic Earth

People use a compass to help them find their way around. A compass has a needle which is magnetised. The needle can turn round so it always points north–south.

A compass needle points north–south because the Earth has a magnetic field. It is as if there were a giant magnet inside the Earth. A compass points along the lines of the Earth's magnetic field.

The red end of the compass needle points towards the north.

Question

3. Look closely at the diagram of the Earth's magnetic field. Explain why the imaginary magnet inside the Earth is shown with a south pole at the top (the north end).

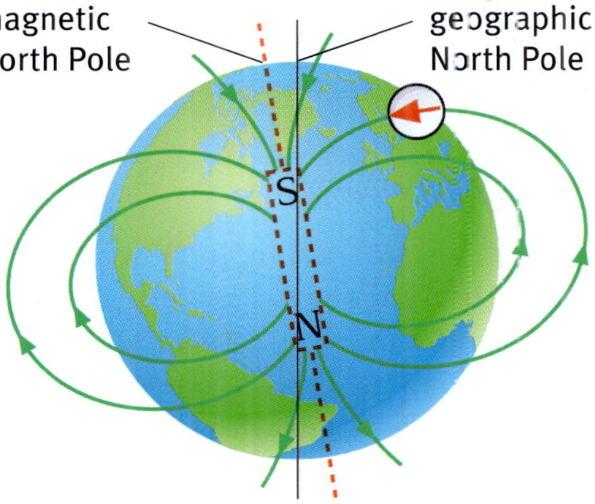

A compass needle will point towards the Earth's magnetic North Pole, which is in the Arctic near to the geographic North Pole.

Summary
- The area around a magnet where it can attract a piece of magnetic material is called a magnetic field.
- Magnetic field lines are drawn to show the direction and strength of the field.

12.4 Making an electromagnet

Permanent magnets are useful because they are always magnetic. There is a second type of magnet, called an **electromagnet**, which is different. It works using electricity and it can be switched on and off.

An electromagnet is simple to construct. All you need is a coil of wire and a battery or low-voltage power supply to make an electric current flow through the coil.

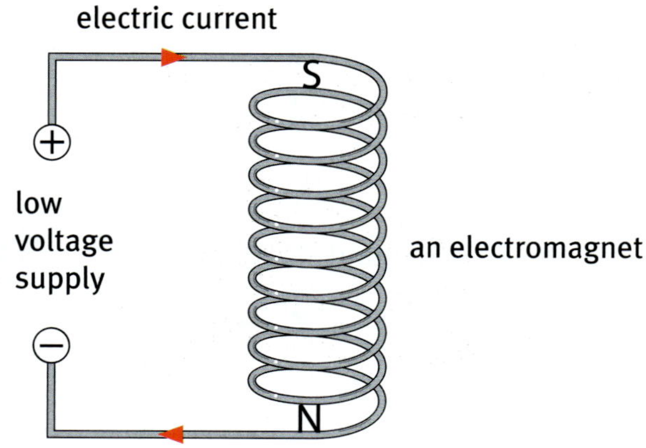

When an electric current flows through the coil of wire, the coil becomes magnetised.

Activity 12.4A
Constructing an electromagnet

1. Make a coil by winding some wire around a pencil or a wooden or metal rod. Remove the pencil or rod.
2. Connect the ends of the wire to a battery or power supply.
3. Bring a compass close to one end of the coil. Can you detect the magnetic field? What happens when you disconnect the coil from the battery or power supply?
4. What happens to the compass if you swap over the connections to the battery or power supply? (This makes the electric current flow through the coil in the opposite direction.)

Questions

1. State **two** differences between an electromagnet and a permanent magnet.
2. Describe how an electromagnet can be switched on and off.

Switching on and off

It is easy to switch electricity on and off. This means that we can switch an electromagnet on and off.

This is made use of in a scrapyard where heavy metal objects are moved around using a crane. On the end of the crane is an electromagnet instead of a hook.

- In the left-hand picture, the crane driver has switched on the electromagnet to lift the old car.
- When the car has been moved into position, the driver switches off the electromagnet. This releases the car and it falls onto the heap.

Using an electromagnet to lift a scrap car.

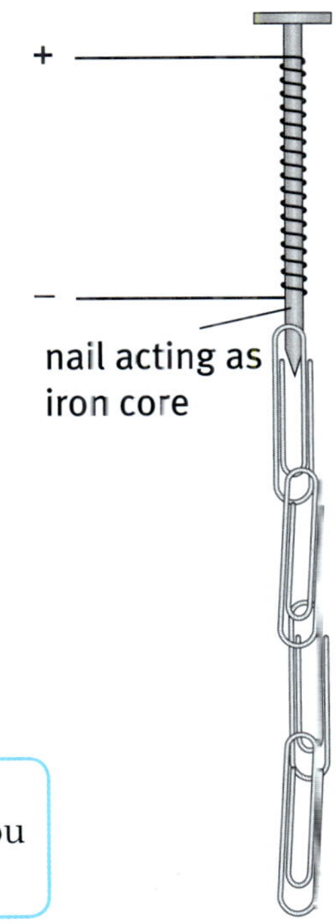

An improved electromagnet.

An improved electromagnet

Here is a way to make a stronger electromagnet. Wrap the wire around a piece of iron, called a **core**.

You should remember that iron is a magnetic material. When a current flows in the coil, the iron becomes magnetised and this makes the magnetic field of the electromagnet much stronger.

Question

3 Adam suggests using a wooden rod as the core of an electromagnet. Do you think this would make the electromagnet stronger? Explain your answer.

Activity 12.4B

Testing an electromagnet

SE

1 The electromagnet you made earlier is not powerful enough to lift a car. Test it: is it powerful enough to lift a steel paperclip? Does the clip fall when you switch off the electric current?

2 Now add an iron core – a thick iron nail will do. Is the electromagnet stronger?

Summary

- An electromagnet is made of a coil of wire in which an electric current flows.
- An electromagnet can be made stronger by adding an iron core.

12.5 A stronger electromagnet

Electromagnets have many different uses.

- They are used in electric motors and generators.
- They are used in doorbells and in electric switches called relays.

An engineer needs to be able to design an electromagnet which has just the right strength for a particular job.

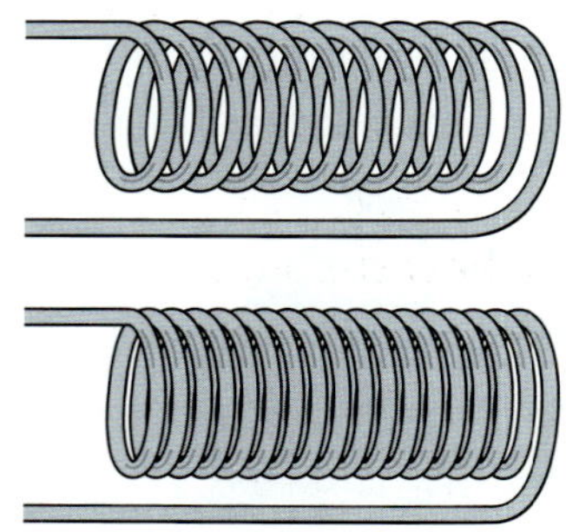

The coil with more turns of wire will be a stronger electromagnet.

Making a stronger electromagnet

We have already seen one important way to make an electromagnet stronger – add an iron core. Here are two other ways:

- Make a coil with more turns of wire. The picture shows a coil with more turns of wire. The wire is longer and so, as the electric current flows through it, it makes a stronger magnetic field.
- Make a bigger electric current flow in the coil of wire.Connect two batteries to the coil, instead of one. This will make a bigger electric current flow so that the magnetic field will be stronger. (The batteries must be connected end-to-end, as shown.)

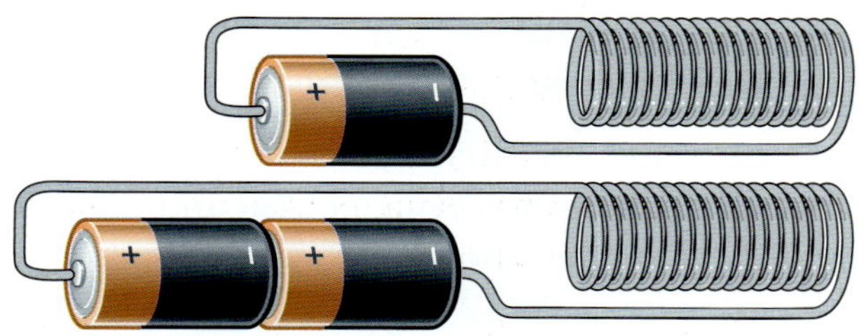

The coil connected to two batteries will be a stronger electromagnet.

Measuring electric current

If you use two batteries instead of one, the current in the electromagnet will be twice as great.

You may be able to use an instrument called an **ammeter** to measure the current flowing in the coil. Electric current is measured in units called **amps**, symbol A.

If you use a low-voltage power supply instead of batteries, you will be able to adjust it to control the value of the current.

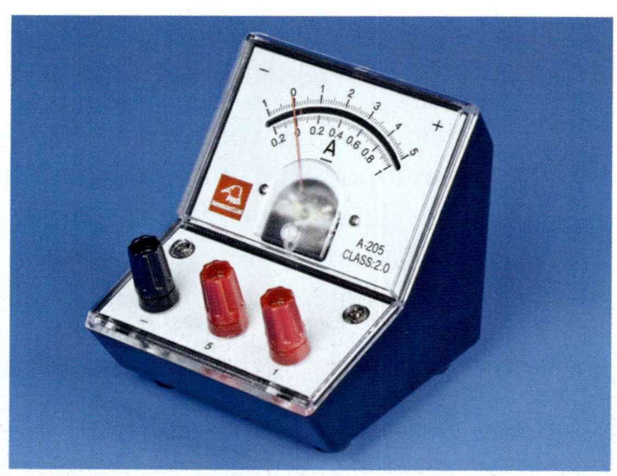

An ammeter measures electric current.

Question

1 Mia makes two electromagnets, one with 10 turns and the other with 20 turns. She connects the first one to a single battery and the second one to two batteries. Mia finds that the second electromagnet is stronger than the first. She says, 'This shows that more turns and more current make a stronger electromagnet.'

a Explain why Mia cannot be sure that her conclusion is correct.

b Describe how she should alter her experiment to make it a fair test.

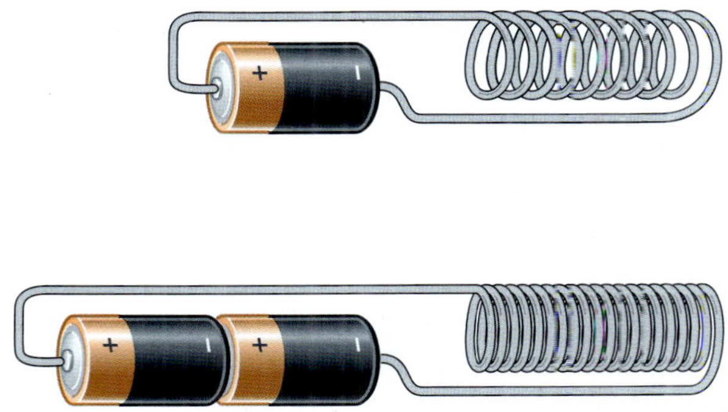

Activity 12.5

Improving an electromagnet

SE

You are going to investigate whether some ideas are correct or not by constructing a fair test.

You have already learnt how to make an electromagnet by winding a coil of wire around a nail and how to test the electromagnet using paperclips.

In this investigation, your task is to test two ideas:

- An electromagnet is stronger if it has more turns of wire.
- An electromagnet is stronger if the electric current flowing through it is greater.

Plan your investigation. Check your ideas with your teacher before you carry them out. Remember – you must only change one factor at a time.

Summary

- An electromagnet can be made stronger by adding more turns of wire.
- An electromagnet can be made stronger by increasing the electric current in the coil.
- An ammeter is used to measure electric current in amps (A).

12.6 Electric currents make magnetic fields

An electric current must flow through an electromagnet if the magnet is to work. The current makes the magnetic field.

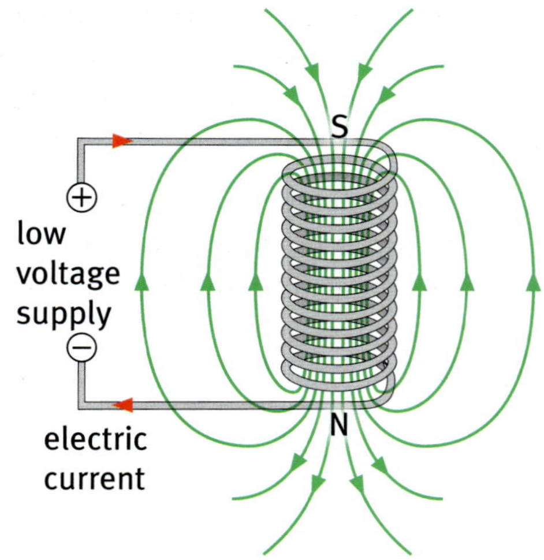

The magnetic field lines of an electromagnet have a similar pattern to the field of a bar magnet.

The field of an electromagnet

The magnetic field of an electromagnet is like the field of a bar magnet.

- The magnetic field lines come out of one end of the electromagnet. This is its north pole.
- The field lines go round and back into the other end of the electromagnet. This is its south pole.

Activity 12.6A
The field of an electromagnet

SE

Use iron filings or small compasses to investigate the magnetic field of an electromagnet.

Safety! Take care to avoid getting iron filings on your hands as you might rub them into your eyes.

Here is a question to investigate: Is the field of an electromagnet different when it has an iron core?

Question

1 Draw a diagram of an electromagnet. Add magnetic field lines. Mark the places where the magnetic field is strongest.

Current and field

Hans Christian Oersted was a Danish scientist. He thought that there might be a connection between electricity and magnetism.

One day, in 1820, he was giving a lecture about electric circuits. A magnetic compass was lying nearby on the bench. When he switched on his circuit, he noticed that the compass needle changed direction.

Hans Christian Oersted carrying out his famous experiment.

Oersted had discovered that whenever an electric current flows in a wire it makes a magnetic field around it. The photograph shows a modern version of his experiment.

When the switch is closed, the battery makes a current flow in the wire. The compass needle moves round, just as in Oersted's experiment.

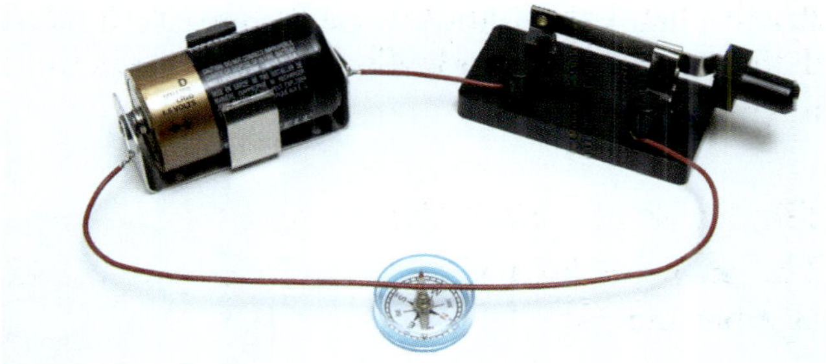

A current in the wire makes a magnetic field.

Activity 12.6B

Oersted's experiment

SE

Set up an electric circuit like the one shown in the photograph. Place a plotting compass under the wire. Does the needle move when you switch the circuit on?

Find out what happens if you swap the connections to the battery, so that the current flows in the opposite direction.

Find out what happens if you place the compass in different positions.

How an electromagnet works

The magnetic field around a wire is quite weak. An electromagnet is a clever idea because, by winding the wire into a coil, you concentrate the magnetic field into a smaller space, making it much stronger.

Question

2 The diagram shows the magnetic field around a wire when a current flows in the wire.

- **a** What shape are the magnetic field lines?
- **b** Where is the magnetic field strongest? Explain how you can tell from the diagram.

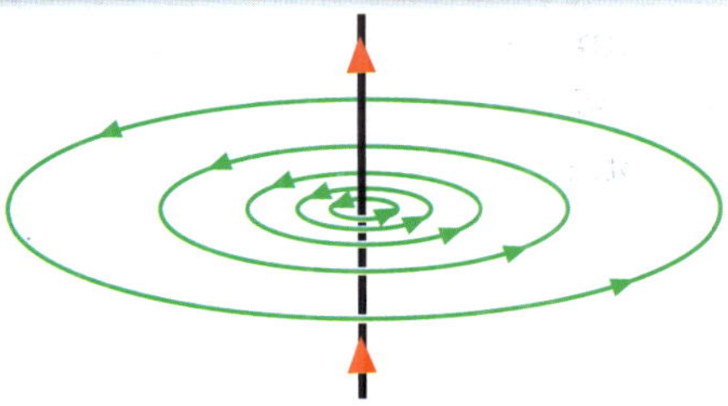

The magnetic field around a wire with an electric current flowing in it.

Summary

- An electromagnet has a north pole at one end and a south pole at the other. Its magnetic field is similar to that of a bar magnet.
- Whenever an electric current flows, there is a magnetic field around it.

Unit 12 End of unit questions

12.1 The picture shows a small compass. The compass needle is free to turn. It turns to point north–south.

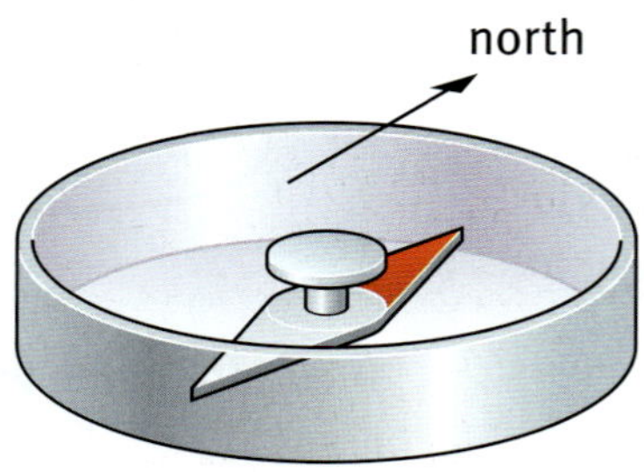

a The compass needle is a small magnet with north and south poles. Which pole points towards the north? [1]

b Why does the compass needle turn? Choose the correct explanation from the list below.

- The ends of the compass needle are painted different colours.
- The case of the compass is made of a magnetic material.
- The Earth has a magnetic field.
- The Earth rotates on its axis once each day. [1]

c Describe what you would expect to observe if you turned the compass needle so that it pointed in the opposite direction, and then released it. [2]

12.2 Each of the diagrams, **A**, **B** and **C** below, shows two magnets lying close to each other.

A

B

C

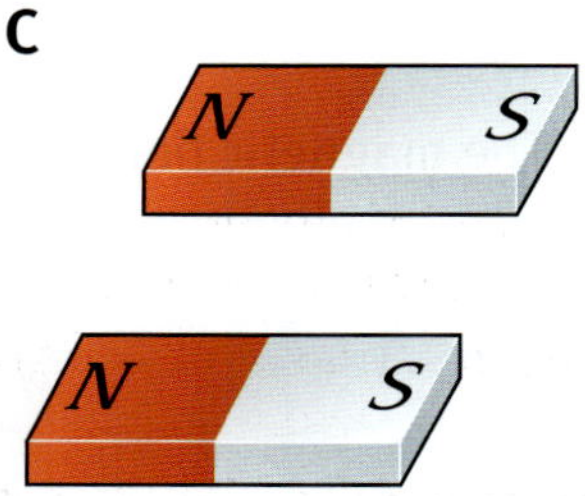

a For each pair, copy the diagram and add force arrows to show the forces of each magnet on the other. [3]

b State whether the magnets will attract or repel each other. [3]

12.3 The diagrams show three electromagnets, **A**, **B** and **C**. Each electromagnet has an electric current of 1 A flowing through it.

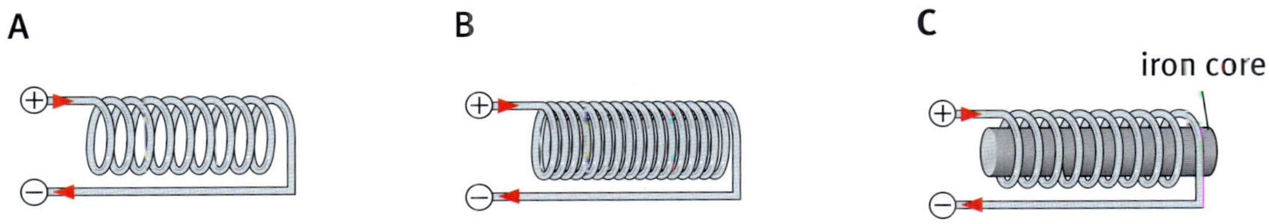

a Explain why **B** has a stronger magnetic field than **A**. [1]
b Explain why **C** has a stronger magnetic field than **A**. [1]
c Describe how you could find out which of the electromagnets, **B** or **C**, has the strongest magnetic field. [2]

12.4 Umar was investigating magnetic forces. He wanted to find out if the magnetic force of a magnet could pass through iron.
The two pictures show how he investigated this.

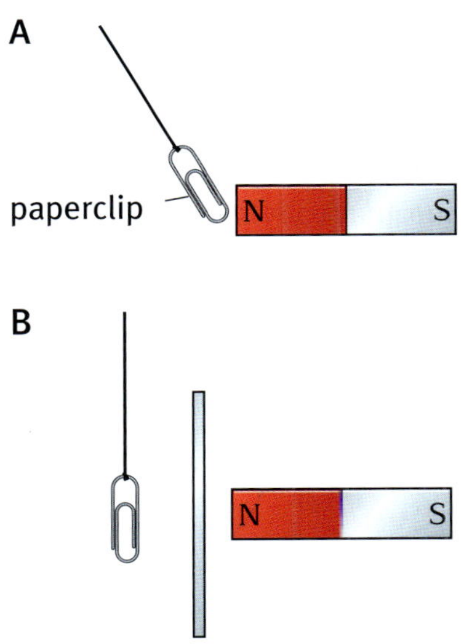

a Describe Umar's first observation, as shown in **A**. [1]
b Describe Umar's second observation, as shown in **B**. [2]
c Write a sentence to state the conclusion Umar would draw from his experiment. [2]
d State how you would change the experiment to find out if the magnetic force of a magnet can pass through cardboard. [1]

Reference

Making better measurements

In Science, we often make measurements. We do this to find out more about something that we are interested in.

Measurements are made using measuring instruments. These include rulers, balances, timers and so on.

We want our measurements to be as **accurate** as possible. In other words, we want them to be as close as possible to the **true answer**. Then we can be more confident that our conclusions are correct.

Measuring instruments

How can we be sure that our measurements are as accurate as possible? We need to think about the instruments we use. Here are two examples:

- You want to measure a 50 cm^3 volume of water. It is better to use a 100 cm^3 measuring cylinder than a 50 cm^3 beaker, even though the beaker may have a line indicating the level which corresponds to 50 cm^3. A 100 cm^3 measuring cylinder is better than one which measures 1000 cm^3 because 50 cm^3 is only a small fraction of 1000 cm^3.
- You want to time a toy car moving a distance of 1.0 m. You could use the clock on the wall – a poor choice. You could use a stopwatch, but it is tricky to start and stop the watch at the exact moments when the car crosses the starting and finishing lines. You would have to take account of your reaction time. It is best to use light gates since these automatically start and stop as the car passes through. The gates are connected to a timer which will show you the time taken to within a fraction of a second.

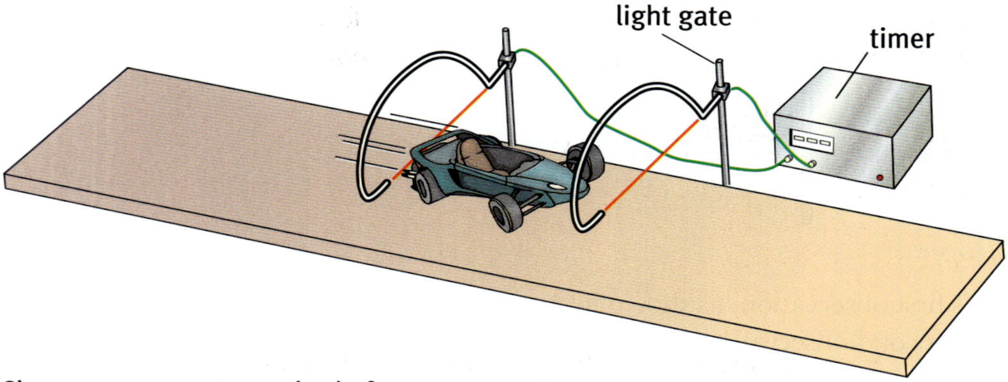

Choose an accurate method of measurement.

We also need to think about how we use measuring instruments. For example:

- When using a ruler to measure the length of an object, the ruler needs to be placed directly alongside the object. Make sure that one end of the object is exactly next to the zero of the ruler's scale.

Don't do it like this. You might think the end of the leaf stalk is at 0 cm but it is actually at 0.2 cm.

- When using a measuring cylinder, look horizontally at the surface of the liquid and read the scale level with the bottom of the meniscus.

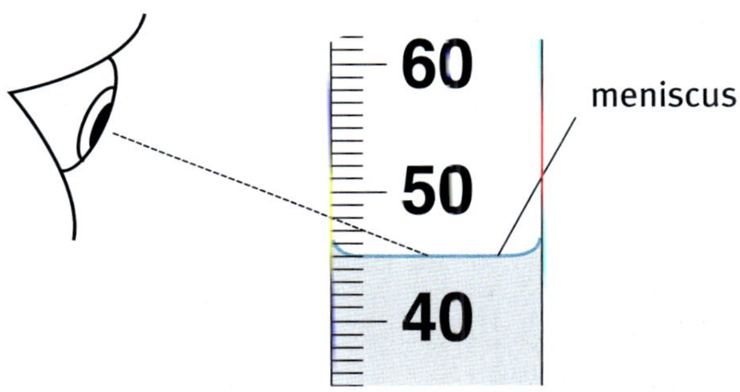

Don't do it like this. You might read this as 48, when it should be read as 45.

- When using a balance to weigh an object, check that it reads zero when there is nothing on it. Similarly, a forcemeter should read zero when no force is pulling on it. It may be possible to reset these instruments if they are not correctly set to zero.

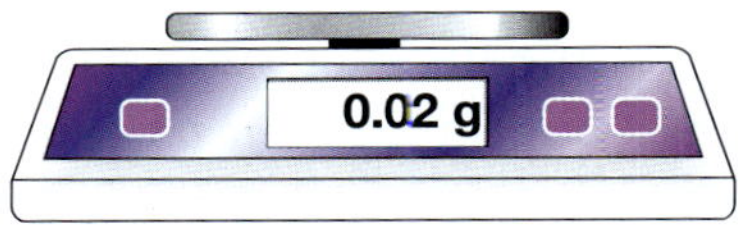

Don't use it like this.

Improving accuracy

You can see that, to make your measurements as accurate as possible, you need to think carefully about the measuring instruments you use and how you use them.

It can help to make repeat measurements; that is, to measure the same quantity several times and then to calculate the average.

With practice, you will find that your measurements become more accurate and so you will be able to trust your findings more.

Anomalous results

Paula did an experiment to find out how light intensity affects the rate of photosynthesis of a water plant. She placed a lamp at different distances from the plant, and counted the number of bubbles it gave off in one minute.

Paula made three counts for each distance of the lamp from the plant. This table shows her results.

Distance of lamp from plant / cm	Number of bubbles per minute			
	1st try	2nd try	3rd try	Mean
20	28	29	27	
40	19	33	18	
60	12	14	13	
80	8	10	10	

Paula thought that one of her results didn't look right. Can you spot which one it is?

A result like this, that does not fit the pattern of all the other results, is called an **anomalous result**.

If you get something that looks like an anomalous result, there are two things that you can do.

1 The best thing to do is to try to measure it again.
2 If you can't do that, then you should ignore the result. So Paula should not use this result when she is calculating the mean. She should use only the other two results for that distance from the lamp, add them up and divide them by two.

Questions

1 Which is the anomalous result in Paula's table?
2 Explain how you picked out the anomalous result.
3 Calculate the mean number of bubbles per minute for each distance of the lamp. Remember – don't include the anomalous result in your calculation!

Spotting an anomalous result in a results table can be quite difficult. It is often much easier if you have drawn a graph.

Ndulu did an experiment to investigate how adding ice to water changed its temperature. He added a cube of ice to 500 cm^3 of water and stirred the water until the ice had completely melted. Then he measured the temperature of the water before adding another ice cube. The graph on the next page shows his results.

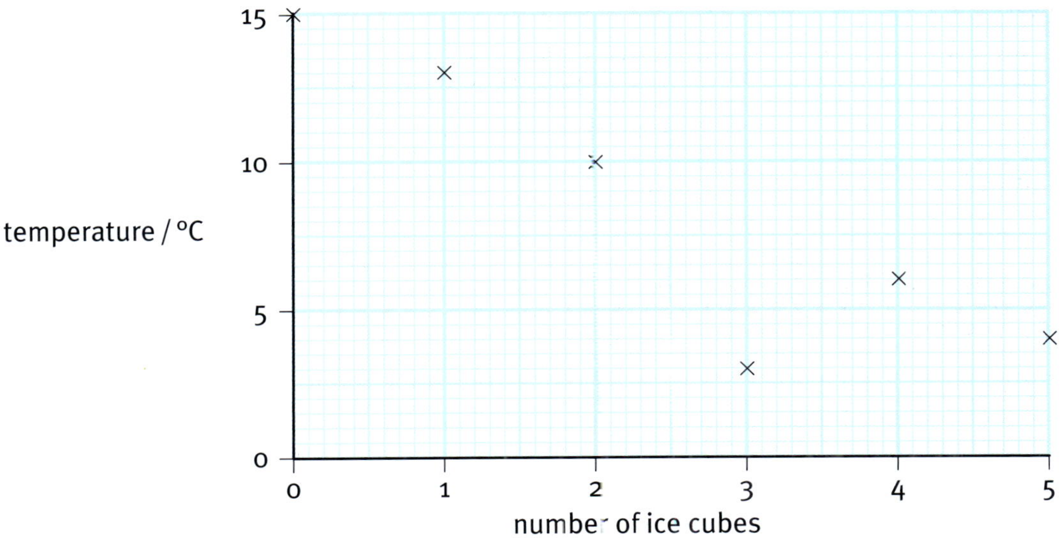

It's easy to see that the point at (3, 3) doesn't fit the pattern of all the other results. Something must have gone wrong when Ndulu was making that measurement.

When Ndulu draws the line on his graph, he should ignore this result. He should also think about why it might have gone wrong. Perhaps he misread the thermometer – was the correct reading 8 °C? Or perhaps he forgot to stir the water and measured the temperature where the cold ice had just melted. If you think about why an anomalous result has occurred, it can help you to improve your technique and avoid such problems in the future.

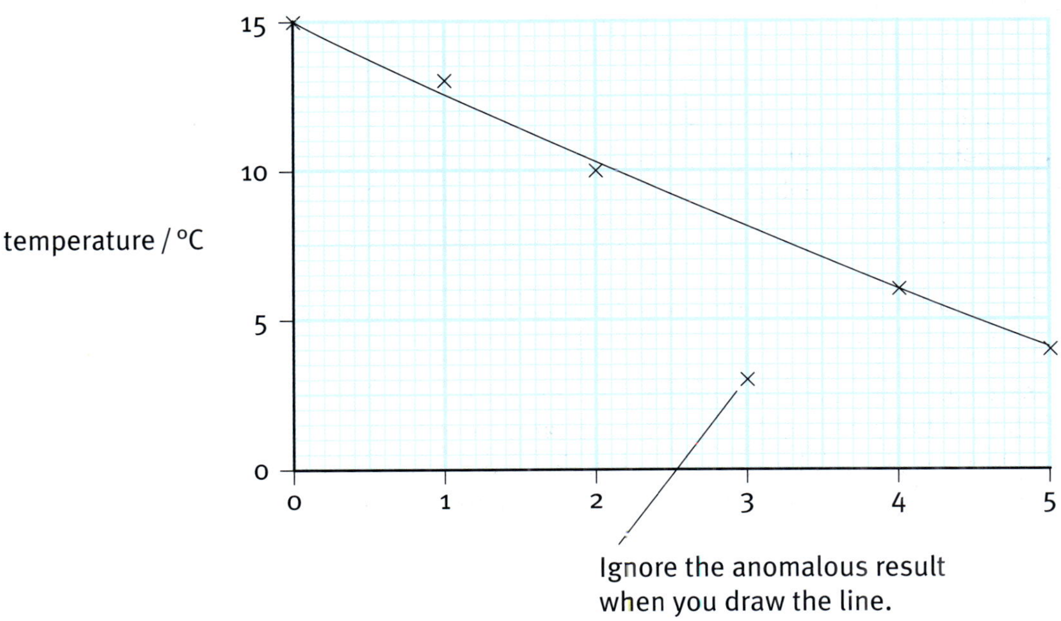

Understanding equations

In **Unit 9 Measuring motion**, you studied three equations which relate speed, distance and time. Here are the three equations:

$$\text{speed} = \frac{\text{distance}}{\text{time}}$$

$$\text{distance} = \text{speed} \times \text{time}$$

$$\text{time} = \frac{\text{distance}}{\text{speed}}$$

How can you remember these three equations? It will help if you think about the *meaning* of each quantity involved. It can also help to think about the *units* of each quantity.

Speed is the distance travelled per second or per hour. The word 'per' means 'in each', and this should remind you that the distance must be divided by the time.

Another way to think of this is to start with the units. Speed is measured in metres per second, so you must take the number of metres (the distance) and divide by the number of seconds (the time).

Distance is how far you travel. The faster you go (the greater your speed), and the longer you go for (the greater the time), the greater the distance travelled. This tells us that the two quantities must be multiplied together.

The train is travelling at 75 m/s.

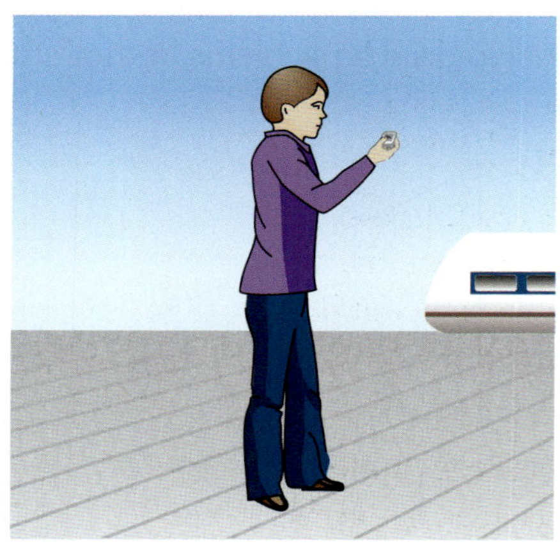

Time to pass observer = 3.6 s.

$$\begin{aligned}\text{length of train} &= \text{speed} \times \text{time}\\ &= 75 \times 3.6\\ &= 270\,\text{m}\end{aligned}$$

Glossary and index

absorption the movement of nutrient molecules from the alimentary canal into the blood 22

aerobic respiration respiration that uses oxygen 46

air sac a tiny, air-filled space inside the lungs; also called an alveolus 44

alimentary canal the tube through which food travels, starting at the mouth and ending at the anus 22

alloy a mixture of two or more metals 80

alveolus a tiny, air-filled space inside the lungs; also called an air sac 44

ammeter a meter used for measuring electric current 156

amp the unit in which electric current is measured; symbol A 156

amplitude the maximum movement of a vibration from its central position 124

anaemia a disease caused by a lack of iron in the diet 20

anomalous result a measurement or reading that does not fit in with the pattern of the other results; such a result is not necessarily wrong, but it should be checked. 164

antibodies substances produced by white blood cells, which can kill micro-organisms 37

artery a blood vessel that carries blood away from the heart 38

atom a tiny particle of matter 66

average speed the average rate at which an object moves;

$$\text{average speed} = \frac{\text{distance travelled}}{\text{time taken}};$$

measured in m/s 111

balanced diet a daily food intake that contains some of all the different types of nutrients, in appropriate quantities and proportions 20

Benedict's solution a blue liquid that is used to test for reducing sugar; if heated with reducing sugar (for example, glucose), it forms a brick-red precipitate 19

biomass material made from living cells and tissues 7

blood vessel a tube that carries blood around the body 32

bonding the way in which atoms join together to form molecules 72

bronchus one of the two tubes that splits off from the trachea and carries air into the lungs 42

Brownian motion random movement of microscopic particles, caused by even tinier particles colliding with them 60

burning (also called combustion) a chemical reaction in which a substance reacts with oxygen and heat energy is released 96

canine one of the pointed teeth near the front of the mouth 26

capillaries tiny blood vessels that deliver blood close to every tissue 38

carbohydrate a nutrient used as a source of energy; starch and sugar are carbohydrates 18

carbonate a compound that contains carbon and oxygen 73

chemical reaction a change in which new substances are produced 94

chemical symbol shorthand way of referring to an element 68

chloride a compound that contains chlorine 72

chlorophyll a green substance found in some of the cells in plant leaves, which absorbs energy from light 8

chromatography a method for separating mixtures of dissolved chemicals 84

cochlea the organ in the ear which converts sound vibrations into electrical signals to the brain 130

compass an instrument with a magnetic needle that can turn freely 152

compound a substance in which atoms of two or more different elements are bonded together 72

compress squash together 54

concentrated solution a solution in which a large amount of solute is dissolved 88

condenser a piece of apparatus used to separate mixtures of liquids; one liquid is evaporated off, then condensed through a cold tube and collected in a different container 82

conservation of mass the principle that there is no loss or gain of mass in a chemical reaction 87

control variable something that is kept the same in an investigation so that the test is fair 90

core a piece of iron inside the coil of an electromagnet to make it stronger 155

dentine a layer of living material beneath the enamel of a tooth 26

deoxygenated blood blood that has been around the body and given up its oxygen to the body cells 33

dependent variable the variable that changes in an investigation as a result of changing the independent variable; this variable is measured 90

diaphragm a sheet of muscle that lies below the lungs, which helps with breathing 42

diffusion the spreading out of particles, in a gas or dissolved substance, as a result of random movement 56

digestion breaking down large molecules of food into small ones, so that they can be absorbed from the alimentary canal into the blood 22

dilute solution a solution in which a small amount of solute is dissolved 88

dispersion the spreading out of the different colours of white light to form a spectrum 142

dissolve when particles of a substance mix completely with a liquid so that a transparent solution is formed 81

distance/time graph a graph showing how the distance moved by an object changes with time 117

drug a substance that affects the way the body works 50

eardrum a membrane at the end of the ear canal which vibrates when a sound wave enters the ear 130

electric current a flow of electricity in a wire 154, 156

electromagnet a coil of wire with an electric current in it; it behaves like a bar magnet 154

element a substance that is made of only one type of atom 66

enamel a very hard covering over the surface of a tooth 26

enzyme a biological catalyst; a substance that speeds up chemical reactions in living organisms, without itself being changed 28

epidermis a layer of cells covering a plant organ, such as a leaf or root 9

fibre material in food that cannot be digested; it helps the digestive system to work efficiently 18

formula uses chemical symbols to show how many atoms of different elements are present in a molecule of an element or compound 70

frequency the number of vibrations each second of a sound wave 124

galvanisation method of protecting iron from rusting by covering it with a layer of zinc 107

gas pressure effect of the forces caused by particles of a gas colliding with the walls of a container 62

glucose a kind of sugar, used as an energy source by living cells 29

group vertical column in the Periodic Table 70

haemoglobin a red pigment found inside red blood cells, that transports oxygen 22

hertz the unit of frequency; symbol Hz; one hertz equals one vibration per second 124

hydroxide a compound that contains hydrogen and oxygen 75

image an object's reflection in a mirror 133

incident ray a ray of light which strikes a surface 133

incisor one of the chisel-shaped teeth at the front of the mouth 26

independent variable the variable that is changed in an investigation 90

insoluble a substance that will not dissolve 98

interval the gap between readings in an investigation; for example for readings taken every 2 minutes the interval is 2 minutes 59

light gate a device used to measure the time taken by an object moving between two points 112

light ray a line drawn to show the path followed by light 136

light source an object which produces light 136

loudness how loud or soft a sound is 122

luminous describes an object which is a source of its own light 135

magnetic field a region where there is a force on a magnet or a piece of magnetic material 152

magnetic field lines lines which show the direction and strength of a magnetic field 152

magnetic force the force of a magnet on another magnet or on a piece of magnetic material 152

magnetic material a material which feels a force when placed in a magnetic field 152

magnetic poles regions of a permanent magnet where the magnetic field is strongest 150

magnetised describes a piece of magnetic material which has become a permanent magnet 148

mixture something that contains two or more substances (elements or compounds) that are not combined chemically 78

molar one of the broad, ridged teeth near the back of the mouth 26

molecule a particle that contains two or more atoms bonded together 67

neutralisation a reaction in which an acid and an alkali form a salt and water 104

nicotine an addictive drug present in cigarette smoke 50

noise unwanted sounds 131

non-luminous describes an object which is not a source of its own light 135

normal a line drawn at right angles (90 °) to a surface at the point where a ray of light strikes it 138

nutrient a type of substance that is required by a living organism – for example, carbohydrates and proteins 18

opaque describes a material which does not transmit light 136

oscilloscope a device which converts varying electrical signals into a trace on a screen 128

oxide a compound that contains oxygen 63

oxygenated blood blood that has been to the lungs and picked up oxygen 33

oxyhaemoglobin haemoglobin that has combined with oxygen 36

palisade layer a tissue inside a leaf in which photosynthesis takes place 9

particle theory the idea that all matter is made up of particles; scientists use particle theory to explain the properties of substances 54

particulates tiny particles of soot and other substances, present in cigarette smoke and polluted air, which can damage the lungs 50

period horizontal row in the Periodic Table 70

Periodic Table arrangement of the elements in order of mass of their atoms 70

permanent magnet a magnet which remains magnetic without the need for an electric current 148

photosynthesis a chemical reaction that takes place in plant leaves, in which carbon dioxide and water are converted to glucose and oxygen, using energy from light 6

physical change a change in which no new substances are produced; changes of state and dissolving are examples of physical changes 94

pitch how high or low a sound is 122

plasma the liquid part of blood 36

platelets tiny fragments of cells, found in the blood, which help with clotting 37

plotting compass a very small compass, used to find the directions of magnetic forces around a magnet 152

precipitate insoluble solid that forms from a reaction in a solution 105

primary colours the three colours of light (red, green, blue) which can be mixed to produce any other colour 144

product a new substance made in a reaction 144

protein a nutrient used for building new cells 18

pulp cavity the material in the centre of a tooth, containing nerves and blood vessels 26

pulse the rhythmic expansion and recoil of arteries, which you can feel near the surface of the skin, caused by the beating of the heart 32

reactant a substance that you start with in a chemical reaction 94

red blood cell the commonest type of cell in the blood, which has no nucleus and transports oxygen 36

reflected ray a ray of light which has been reflected by a mirror or other surface 138

reflection the bouncing back of a ray of light when it strikes the surface of a non-transparent material 136

refraction the bending of a ray of light as it travels from one transparent material into another 140

respiration a chemical reaction that happens inside every living cell, in which energy is released from glucose so that the cell can use it 46

respiratory system the organs that help oxygen to get into the body and carbon dioxide to be removed from it 42

rickets a disease caused by a lack of vitamin D in the diet 20

root hair a cell with a long, thin, extension that grows out of a root and absorbs water and minerals from the soil 12

rusting a chemical reaction in which iron combines with oxygen in the presence of water to form iron oxide 106

saturated solution a solution in which no more of the solute will dissolve 88

scurvy a disease caused by a lack of vitamin C in the diet 20

shadow an area or a space where the light from a source does not reach 136

soluble a substance that will dissolve in a given solvent 88

solute a substance that is dissolved 86

solution a mixture in which particles of a substance (solute) are mixed with particles of a liquid so that the substance can no longer be seen 86

solvent a liquid that other substances will dissolve in 86

sound wave a vibration in the air or other material; how sound travels 126

spectrum the different colours which make up white light, spread out in order 142

speed how fast an object moves; $\text{speed} = \frac{\text{distance}}{\text{time}}$; measured in m / s 110

spongy layer a tissue inside a leaf that contains many air spaces 9

stoma a tiny hole in the surface of a leaf, through which gases can diffuse 9

sulfate a compound that contains sulfur and oxygen 73

tar substances found in cigarette smoke that damage cells and increase the risk of cancer 50

trachea the tube that carries air from the back of the throat to the lungs 42

transmit to let light through 136

transparent describes a material through which light can pass 136

ultrasound sound whose frequency is too high for us to hear 131

vacuum a region which contains no matter 126

valve a structure that allows fluid to flow in only one direction 34

variable something that can be changed in an investigation 14

vein a blood vessel that carries blood towards the heart 32

vibration a backwards and forwards movement 122

Visking tubing a tube with a thin, membrane-like wall made out of a material with molecule-sized holes in it 23

vitamin a type of nutrient needed in only very small quantities 18

white blood cell colourless blood cells that have a nucleus, and help to protect against invading microorganisms 36

word equation shows the chemicals that react and are produced in a chemical reaction 94

xylem vessels tubes made of dead, empty cells, that transport water upwards from the roots of a plant 14

Acknowledgements

The authors and publisher are grateful for the permissions granted to reproduce copyright materials. While every effort has been made, it has not always been possible to identify the sources of all the materials used, or to trace all the copyright holders. If any omissions are brought to our notice, we will be happy to include the appropriate acknowledgements on reprinting.

The publisher would like to thank the language reviewer for reviewing the content:

Ángel Cubero, International School, Santo Tomás de Aquino, Madrid, Spain

Cover image: Steve Bloom/Alamy: pp. 6, 8, 12*b*, 14, 18*t*, 18*mt*, 18*mb*, 18*b*, 56*tl*, 56*tml*, 56*tmr*, 56*tr* Geoff Jones; p. 12*t* Derek Croucher/Alamy; p. 13 Power and Syred/SPL; pp. 15, 50 Biophoto Associates/SPL; p. 20 Maximilian Stock Ltd/SPL; p. 24 Living Art Enterprises, LLC/SPL; p. 33 Kari Niemeläinen/Alamy; p. 36 Michael Ross/SPL; p. 37 Susumu Nishinaga/SPL; pp. 44, 66*t* Eye of Science/SPL; p. 46 Scientifica, Visuals Unlimited/SPL; p. 48 PCN/Corbis; p. 49 Chris Rout/Alamy; pp. 56*bl*, 56*br*, 84*m*, 129 Leslie Garland Picture Library/Alamy; p. 60 Medical-on-line/Alamy; p. 61*t* Natural History Museum, London/ SPL; pp. 61*b*, 68*br*, 72*tl*, 115*b* SPL; p. 66*b* BibleLandPictures.com/Alamy; pp. 68*tl*, 72*tr*, 105*t* Charles D. Winters/SPL; p. 68*tr* Russ Lappa/SPL; pp. 68*bl*, 75, 98, 114*m*, 156 Martyn F. Chillmaid/SPL; p. 71*tl* Les Polders/Alamy; 71*tm* Paul Rapson/Alamy; p. 71*tr* Art Directors & TRIP/Alamy; p. 71*bl*, 78*t*, 78*b*, 104*t* Sciencephotos/Alamy; p.71*bm* Phil Arnold; p. 71*br*, 86*l*, 116*b* Sciencesphotos/Alamy; p. 72*b* Victor De Schwanberg/SPL; p. 73 Shawn Hempel/Alamy; p. 80 Interfoto/Alamy; p. 81 Anne Gilbert/Alamy; pp. 84*t*, 96*mt*, 96*mb*, 96*b*, 99, 104*b*, 108, 123, 130, 140*t*, 140*b* Andrew Lambert Photography/SPL; p. 86*r* Bon Appetite/Alamy; p. 94*t* Woodystock/Alamy; p. 94*m* D. Hurst/Alamy; p. 94*b* Moodboard/ Alamy; p. 96*t* Finnbar Webster/Alamy; p. 97*lt* Steve Teague/Alamy; p.97*tm* amphotos/Alamy; p. 97*rt* Purepix/Alamy; p. 97*rb* JG Photography; p.97*mb* Stephen Giardina; p.97*lb*, *107l* Justin Kase; p.103 Jean-Loup Charmet/SPL; p. 106*t* Prisma Bildagentur AG/Alamy; p. 106*m* David Hancock; p. 106*b* Keith J. Smith/Alamy; p. 107*r* Holmes Garden Photos/Alamy; p. 110*t* Martin Bond/Alamy; p. 110*m* incamerastock/Alamy; 110*b* moodboard/Corbis; p. 112 Marco Secchi/Alamy; p. 112*t* Andre Jenny/ Alamy; p. 112*b* CuboImages srl/Alamy; p. 115 Charles Polidano/Touch The Skies/Alamy; p. 116*t* Allsorts Stock Photo/Alamy; p. 116*m* Photoshot Holdings Ltd/Alamy; p. 122 i4images rm/Alamy; p. 131*t* Asia Images Group Pte Ltd/Alamy; p. 131*b* Paul Parker/Alamy; p. 134*t* Lew Merrim/SPL; p. 134*b* Dan Sams/ SPL; p. 136 Tim Gainey/Alamy; p. 137 Steve Bloom/Alamy; p. 138 GoGo Images Coporation/Alamy; p. 142 TAO Images Limited/Alamy; p. 148*t* Fancy/Alamy; p. 148*b*, 159 GiPhotostock/SPL; p. 152 Cordelia Molloy/SPL; p. 153 Stockimages/Alamy; p. 158 Sheila Terry/SPL.

SPL = Science Photo Library, *l* = left, *r* = right, *t* = top, *b* = bottom, *m* = middle

Typesetting and illustration by Greenhill Wood Studios www.greenhillwoodstudios.com